E
Sleep
Work
Repeat

30 HACKS FOR BRINGING JOY TO YOUR JOB

BRUCE DAISLEY

HarperOne
An Imprint of HarperCollinsPublishers

Photos reproduced by Unsplash: house p. 198 by Luke Stockpoole; bearded man p. 198 by Tanja Heffner; happy face p. 264 by Hian Oliveira. Photo reproduced from Pexels: angry face p. 264 by Pixabay. All tweets reproduced courtesy of Twitter, copyright © respective Twitter accounts.

HarperCollins books may be purchased for educational, business, or sales promotional use. For information, please email the Special Markets Department at SPsales@harpercollins.com.

Originally published as *The Joy of Work* in Great Britain in 2019 by Random House Business Books.

FIRST HARPERCOLLINS PAPERBACK EDITION PUBLISHED IN 2022

Designed by SBI Book Arts, LLC

Library of Congress Cataloging-in-Publication Data is available upon request.

ISBN 978-0-06-294451-1

22 23 24 25 26   LSC   10 9 8 7 6 5 4 3 2 1

To Billy, Coco, and Tula

Contents

Author's Note

A character in Ernest Hemingway's *The Sun Also Rises* was asked how he went bankrupt. He replies, "Two ways. Gradually, then suddenly." And so it is that we saw work change before our eyes in 2020, right after the hardcover edition of this book was published. It is interesting to me to think about how we envisioned the future of work before the COVID-19 pandemic. At every stage of civilization we've speculated about what the future will hold for us, and as technological innovation has exploded over the last decade or so, we've dreamed of how technology could free us from our traditional tethering to the office. Meanwhile, our real jobs were only slowly adapting. We found ourselves in back-to-back meetings, and then doing emails on the commute home. It seemed a long way from our future-facing reverie of dialing into video calls from the side of a lake, connected across continents but still involved in intense creative dialogue within earshot of the shore.

Then everything changed in 2020. Those who still had jobs after cities issued shelter-in-place orders had to adapt to working remotely. This phenomenon was the catalyst for untold reinvention and innovation. Wonderfully, having been forced to work from our homes, many of us found parts of this new way of living to be highly agreeable. While there were certainly very real challenges to this new normal, notably childcare and the challenges of shortages at the supermarket, many of us found space to be ourselves in our later waking times; we found moments to connect over family meals that gave meaning to the rest of our hectic existences. Looking forward, it's clear that lots of these changes will stick. Many workplaces will abandon their archaic demands for workers to be present for five days a week—some shifting to a hybrid model (Tuesday, Wednesday, Thursday for creative workers in the office, or Monday and Friday for salespeople) and some allowing workers to untether themselves and work from wherever they find a broadband connection.

There's an unintended consequence of this change—and it will only become apparent slowly. Users of Glassdoor, the site where employees can post reviews of their employers, cite that the single most important consideration for choosing a new job is the workplace culture.[1] It begs the question: to what extent can culture exist when workers find themselves collaborating with others through their screens?

That's where this book comes in. The disruption to our ways of working opened our eyes to different ways of getting our jobs done—and made some of the suggestions in this book feel like their moment has arrived. This book is filled with fascinating stories that experts shared with me and clear examples of how other organizations have forged cohesive cultures. Hopefully it will be your essential field guide to making sure that colleagues feel part of something special—even if they are thousands of miles apart.

As you're reading through this book, it's an interesting question to ask yourself: What review would I like a colleague to write on Glassdoor? How would I want my team members to describe their workplace experience? I hope you can use this book as a way to construct something intentionally special for your coworkers.

Introduction

Love Where You Work

Is it reasonable to expect to enjoy your job? That's a question many have wrestled with, often as they lie awake with anxious thoughts about an occupation that causes them daily unhappiness. If we're getting paid, then maybe it's unreasonable to additionally expect personal satisfaction as part of the exchange.

It goes further than that. Steve Jobs famously once argued, "You've got to love what you do." For many of us, that's just a step too far. Much easier said than done. It's one of those casual exhortations (most easily made by a billionaire) that can leave people feeling inadequate. If we should expect to love our jobs, then who is to blame if we don't? Is it our fault? Could it even be used against us? "If you really wanted this job, you wouldn't be asking for more pay/saying you've got too much to do/complaining about stress. Maybe we should find someone else who really *wants* to work here."

Today, 83 percent of American workers report that far from making them happy, their jobs are causing them stress.[1] Two-fifths of us have gone further and actually quit our firms to escape a stressful job.[2] And this anxiety isn't just a nuisance frustration of our occupations; a 2015 analysis of over three hundred different surveys concluded that the health toll of workplace stress was comparable to that of secondhand smoke—stress is shortening our lives.[3]

The suspicion that "work used to be way more fun than it is today" really does seem to have a basis in reality. Many of us don't love what we do, and we feel exhausted trying. A national survey of the workforce conducted by the survey company Gallup suggested that only 32 percent of employees were "engaged" in their jobs, meaning that they were highly involved in and enthusiastic about their work and workplace.[4] And this is often because our workplaces seem to treat us as voiceless pawns in the game—another Gallup survey found that only three in ten workers believed that their opinions even counted at work.[5]

For many, the realities of work see us worn down by gnawing feelings of job insecurity and by work environments that seem to be impinging ever more on our free time as we battle to keep up with our email or glance at our smartphone on a Sunday morning in case that ping we've just heard heralds some minor emergency.

Living in a constant state of adrenalized stress can pretty soon leave us feeling depleted. In 2019, Anne Helen Petersen wrote an article that immediately became a viral sensation. In her Buzz-Feed piece, she described "the Burnout Generation," who were experiencing symptoms such as "errand paralysis" in their private lives directly as a consequence of having "internalized the idea that [they] should be working all the time."[6] As we will explore fully in this book, a growing understanding that our cognitive powers are both finite and inhibited by stress means that the way we're working today is the enemy of our aspirations to be the best versions of ourselves.

When this book was first published in my native United Kingdom, it became a *Sunday Times* number one bestseller. Many of my American friends told me that an evidence-based focus on fixing work wouldn't succeed in the United States. I was shocked. "Why?" I asked. "There's just too much focus on profit," one former colleague insisted. "No firm is going to encourage employees to work sustainably if it makes them less money." But in many ways, that's the point of this book. In so many ways, *work is the lie we tell ourselves*—you'll see clear evidence in these pages that working longer doesn't make firms more profit. Longer hours might make us feel like we're doing more, but we're achieving less with every second of extra toil. While we might hear business leaders such as Elon Musk boast that "nobody ever changed the world on 40 hours a week," when we delve beneath the bluster, it seems that evidence gives us a different answer.[7] Zeynep Ton, an inspirational academic, found that retail businesses that set out to provide better working conditions for their employees were strategically hitting upon "the best and most sustainable way to provide superior returns to their investors in the long term."[8] Providing good jobs was more profitable than treating workers badly. Many of us, if we were to use a fresh perspective and look anew at our daily lives, would see our jobs for what they truly are. We'll go on to see that average office workers are spending between two and three days a week in meetings, *where they pretend to be paying attention*. We waste our freshest hours sitting still in meetings, resisting the temptation to look at our phones, and then we have idiot bosses judging us for not clocking in another four or five weary hours per day to keep on top of our actual work. The evidence contained in this book can help you fix these things. In the same way that the evidence on the restorative power of sleep has transformed the argument on proper recovery in the past two or three years, the evidence on working is about to transform the way we work.

Creating a good working culture helps futureproof our workplaces. If we want to foster the creative environments that will be essential in a future world competing with and being assisted by artificial intelligence, then stress is something we need to strive to eliminate, as I'll demonstrate. Overwork isn't a competitive advantage in creative endeavors, and firms that rely on it will be swept away, shown up for their lack of inventiveness.

The path won't be straightforward; discussions of workplace culture in recent years have been distracted by misdirection and marketing. Compelling speakers such as Simon Sinek have told us to seek to answer not *what* we do but *why* we do it. Answering the question *why* is certainly important—as we'll go on to see, when we are driven by a sense of purpose, motivation isn't hard to find. But finding purpose alone doesn't seem to be the answer to making work a happier place. The teaching profession is one of the most clearly purpose-driven occupations—teachers know the answer to *why* they chose their vocation—and yet nearly half a million American teachers move or quit the profession each year.[9] The Alliance for Excellent Education reported that "forty to fifty percent of new teachers leave the profession in their first five years."[10] To some extent, while answering the question *why* can get us up in the morning, we need to answer *how* for us to feel we can work sustainably in (and feel rewarded by) our jobs.

Firms have also used workplace culture as a marketing channel. Photographs of neon-colored slides cascading through offices can make our own workplace seem uninspiringly inert by contrast. In this book, I attempt to separate the aspects of company culture that can help us create meaningful work from the parts that are just hyped-up, caffeinated spin.

My own journey to unearthing the insights afforded us by workplace psychology began when I started my weekend breaks from my day job as a vice president at Twitter with running a podcast on making work better. That podcast, *Eat Sleep Work Repeat*, began as a passion project, and my motivation was more self-education than reaching a large audience, but the show soon became a number one business podcast in the United Kingdom (with regular excursions into the US top ten). An opportunity to pick the brains of experts in organizational psychology—the people who really understand what makes workplaces tick—helped me to start building a manifesto of changes to modern working. The response to my UK publication was extraordinary. Police forces, nurses, lawyers, and bank workers got in touch, saying how they had used the work to help improve their working lives.

I have discovered that there is no shortage of science, research, and investigation regarding what makes work more fulfilling. It's just that none of the evidence ever seems to reach people doing everyday jobs. In this book, I've therefore distilled the wisdom of experts into thirty simple changes that people can try out for themselves or suggest at a team meeting. Some are changes I've long been familiar with and have used successfully myself. Others are useful correctives to bad habits I'd developed and that I'd noticed in others. A few may seem perversely counterintuitive—but they do work.

Our jobs—no matter what they are—can help give meaning to our lives. While we might be reluctant to profess our fondness for them, we should never be ashamed of feeling proud of being made happy by our work.

I hope this book helps you love where you work again.

Under Pressure

For all that he could project a carefree calm, Julian was a man under pressure. Everywhere he looked, there were demands and rising expectations being placed upon him: people phoning him just to "check in," but with a couple of extra notes of insistency in their voice; colleagues anxious to hear what he'd come up with in his latest creative sessions. Most of us probably think our jobs are way too humble to be compared with those of rock stars, but the lessons we can learn from Julian Casablancas are an important step in helping us to enjoy our own jobs again. Let's take a step back and tell his story.

The Strokes' first album, *Is This It*, was a massive critical and commercial hit from the moment of its release in 2001. A score of 91 percent put it in the top forty albums of all time on the Metacritic website. The *Guardian* rated it as one of the top five albums of the decade, and NME (New Musical Express) considered it the fourth best ever and sighed that the band could "save rock." A critic for *Rolling Stone* magazine said it was "more joyful and intense than anything else I've heard this year" and described it as "the stuff of which legends are made." Within a year, the band was playing sold-out shows in the most prestigious concert halls across the world.

As with most debut albums from unknown artists, the creation process was unglamorous. The Strokes—a five-piece group originating in New York—had recorded the album in a raw, stripped-back recording studio in the basement of a lower East Side apartment in Manhattan. Sole songwriting duty on the record fell to lead singer Julian Casablancas, his preoccupation with penning new anthems leaving him the unfortunate owner of only the fourth-best haircut in the ensemble. But the end result, though knowingly informed by musical nods to garage rock and music from the 1960s and 1970s, was also fresh. And as the Strokes toured and promoted the record over the next year, they quickly built a passionate fan base. Soon, talk was turning to what the next album would be like.

If a debut is a way to plant a flag in the sand, a second album is often the foundation of a reputation. Very few artists reach iconic status with their first record, but they may achieve it with their second: *Nevermind* by Nirvana, *Back to Black* by Amy Winehouse, *Late Registration* by Kanye West. So for the Strokes, recording a second album that built on the success of the first was a vital next step. And given that the first had gone platinum, there was a lot to live up to.

The result was pressure: pressure from fans, pressure from critics, pressure from supportive family members, pressure from the band members themselves. Stories emerged of scrapped recording sessions and multiple restarts to the project. Julian Casablancas was certainly preoccupied enough with the stresses he was feeling to unburden himself to a visiting journalist from *Mojo* magazine: "I feel like I will break under the pressure that I put on myself. What if a critic, or the general consensus, says, 'He really let us down this time,' that would fuck with my head and hurt me."[11]

Conscious of the demands on them to deliver a strong follow-up, the band pushed on and delivered the new album, *Room on Fire*, to their record label in time for it to hit the peak sales period of the fourth quarter of 2003. CDs were pressed and dispatched to fanboy journalists. Casablancas's fear of letting people down must have been in his head as he opened the first reviews on the album's October release. I hope he was sitting down.

The write-ups were roundly unfavorable. Reviewers argued that the record sought to repeat the debut's tricks but lacked the freshness of the original. A *Guardian* journalist suggested that "for much of *Room on Fire*, you're confronted with what sounds like a weary band desperately trying to remember how the good bits on their debut album went. . . . Half of *Room on Fire* is uninspired filler."[12] *Entertainment Weekly* nailed what many listeners felt about the new record: "[It] amounts to a less vivid Xerox of *Is This It*."[13]

Could it be that stress killed Casablancas's creative instincts? Was his inventiveness crushed by the pressure to be original? There's compelling scientific evidence that the stresses and expectations heaped on Casablancas—by both himself and others—were directly responsible for destroying his capacity to invent. Possibly, at a certain point, pressure ceased to be an energizing jolt and actually stifled his imagination. His mind became filled with noise and distraction rather than ideas. When we're feeling stressed, ingenuity often goes out the window. Instead, we take refuge in whatever seemed to work last time. We repeat rather than innovate. As the writer from *Entertainment Weekly* went on to say, "It's worrisome that the Strokes are repeating themselves so early in their lifetime."[14]

Modern Work Is Changing

Why is that relevant to your own job? Well, stress is increasingly becoming the normal state in our workplaces. And the same forces that have such a negative impact on the songwriting process are also conspiring to disrupt everyday decision making taking place across the whole world of work. Evolution in the way our daily labor is carried out is adding to these negative forces. Put simply, modern work is getting worse. And the outlook is even bleaker. Essentially, we're caught in the midst of two trends that are profoundly altering both the nature of work and its psychological impact on us. These are epoch-changing, so let's call them *megatrends*. One is constant connectivity. The other is artificial intelligence.

Constant Connectivity

Over the past twenty years, the demands of work have seriously turned the screw on us. Email on our phones has fundamentally transformed our relationship with our jobs. We're connected to work on the train, on the bus, and on the couch. We're working longer hours, though there's no evidence that we're getting more done.

At first, it seemed so great. Taking email on our cell phones snapped the relationship between *work*, the place, and *work*, the verb. We were free to answer messages anywhere—and it genuinely felt liberating. At last we could reply to customers' requests from the comfort of the couch; we could chase suppliers during our bus commute; Steve in sales could send everyone a video that an open-minded friend had shared with him on a Friday night. Little did any of us realize that taking email on our phones would lead to our working more. And certainly no one knew how much more.

But we've got a pretty good idea now.

One study found that 60 percent of professionals were remaining connected to work for 13.5 hours per day every weekday and another 5 hours on weekends—adding up to a workweek of over 70 hours of connectivity.[15] As a contrast to the previous norm of 8 hours of work per day, this represents a transformational change in the mental burden of work. And as we've made ourselves ever more readily available, our employers have come to assume that's how it should be: a workforce survey conducted by Gallup found that where firms had an expectation that employees would stay connected outside office hours, 62 percent of them duly did.[16]

As I'll show later, the benefit of longer working hours isn't remotely proven. In fact, all the evidence suggests that the law of diminishing returns operates as our hours increase and that one of the first consequences is that our creativity suffers. By burning ourselves out, we reach what psychologists refer to as a state of "negative affect" (this is how the phenomenon is spelled; see p. 12). More than anything, this can transform our jobs from something we enjoy into something we hate. Scientists have shown that unless we're in a state of high personal well-being, we start to dislike our jobs.[17] Simultaneously, the connectivity that is burning us out is making us unhappier. Half of all people who check email outside working hours now exhibit high stress levels, according to scientists who measured the cortisol levels secreted in saliva.[18]

Additionally, the other trend—sorry, *megatrend*—is artificial intelligence.

Artificial Intelligence

The Arrival of the Robots is an intimidating prospect—largely because no one really knows where it will lead. It certainly seems that automation will have a profound impact on lots of low-paid jobs. But because artificial intelligence is ideally placed to deal with repeated tasks, it may well have a wider disruptive effect. Kai-Fu Lee, former boss of Google China and author of a bestselling book on artificial intelligence, is convinced that "about 50% of our jobs will, in fact, be taken over by AI and automation within the next 15 years."[19] And this isn't restricted to manual occupations; it extends into all realms of work. One of the professions often discussed as being imperiled is the legal industry. Why? Well, a lot of legal work involves studying documents and trying to spot precedents from previous cases. In other words, it involves pattern recognition of the type that computers are particularly well equipped to carry out swiftly and efficiently.[20] So while the legal profession may seem an attractive prospect at the moment, plenty of forecasts suggest that close to half of all legal jobs will be wiped away in time.[21] Soon it will be computer software determining that "this legal dispute is similar to another case that had this outcome."[22]

If Kai-Fu Lee is right, with half of all jobs being challenged by 2035, we will see society transformed, especially at a time when most of us are contemplating the need to work well into our seventies. We probably need to ask ourselves which jobs have staying power. Relatively speaking, the more routine a task is, the easier it is to swap a human for a machine. What should be clear to us is that the hardest jobs to replace are likely to be those that require brainpower to solve an unpredictable array of problems. Jobs in which the person doing them is in a constant state of asking "How about . . . ?" How about if we tried this? How about if we packaged this in a different way? Creativity, but at an everyday level. Invention, intelligence, thinking: these are the things that artificial intelligence is least likely to replace in the short term.

The unacknowledged consequence of the first megatrend of connectivity is that work is frying our brains. There's a reason why life in general feels more anxiety filled today, and it's that the main part of our lives, work, is more stressful than before. Sure, work has always involved labor, but the previous generation or two were spared the lack of separation between work and home lives, the wearing need to check whether anyone needs us just one more time.

But here's the problem. If we are to survive the consequences of artificial intelligence, we need to nurture more creative lines of work. However, the pressure of constant connectivity is making us so stressed that a creative mind-set is becoming ever harder to achieve. We're in a double bind. As mentioned earlier, scientists sometimes describe this state as negative affect. In this book, I'll show how fifty years' worth of scientific research has revealed the downsides of negative affect and the upsides of positive affect.

The evidence suggests that the capacity to change and improve things rests with us. Most of us aren't the boss in our workplace. Even if we manage a few people, a lot of the decisions about how things are done in the workplace are made by senior leaders. But that doesn't prevent us from having an impact on the way we feel and on how our immediate team interacts. This book is for everyone in that situation. Whether you manage only yourself or your only opportunity for reform is to suggest that the team all watch a TED Talk together about ways to improve things, you can make a difference in your own life and the lives of those around you.

Eat Sleep Work Repeat is divided into three parts. Together they build into a scheme for creating happier work environments, but I've also tried to ensure that each chapter stands on its own.

Recharge—In Part 1, we look at how we can recharge our own energy. How can we get back to a full battery? What are the simple hacks that make work feel more manageable? How can we move from negative affect to positive affect?

Sync—In Part 2, I draw heavily on groundbreaking scientific research to offer suggestions on how to bring trust and connection to your team. I'm working on the assumption that you probably don't call the shots—that you can't just tell the people you work with what to do. But you can't assume that your boss will know how to change things for the better. CEOs don't read books like this; they send themselves to seminars costing thousands of dollars. Yet I've seen dozens of examples of teams that were improved by one teammate motivated with a vision and a couple of good articles.

Buzz—Part 3 outlines the nirvana for teams: a work culture that has a special buzz to it. Some of the most exciting science I'll cover in Parts 2 and 3 comes from the Massachusetts Institute of Technology, where one particular enlightened thinker has led the way in showing that successful teams don't just have a hum to them; they have a measurable buzz. What lessons can we learn that will help us stimulate creativity, energy, and success in the workplace? How can we reach a state where the team has *Buzz*?

The enlightened thinker I'm referring to is Professor Alex "Sandy" Pentland. Before he came on the scene, the principal way researchers looked at different work situations was to simulate approximations of them in the lab. Pentland got rid of the reliance on artificially re-created situations. Instead, he and his team created "people meters"—small sociometric badges that hang around your neck with your work ID integrated into them. Most of us wear similar things as a matter of course, the sort of things that we bleep in and out of the office with, so there was no need for anyone to adapt their behavior. Pentland's souped-up badges enabled him to study what happens in offices in the manner that we might watch a heat map in a televised sports game. He was able to genuinely perceive what people actually did and what impact their actions really had on those around them. By the same token, he was also able to pinpoint what *didn't* work. What he discovered should help us rethink our own behavior in the office, in terms of both what we should do and what we shouldn't. Spoiler alert: email contributes almost nothing to modern levels of productivity.

Through studies such as this, we'll find a way to bring more Buzz back to your office. Choose a chapter. Read it, try it, bring it to a team meeting, loan it to a friend. You'll see that all of us can make work more fun again.

Let's start enjoying our jobs again. It's time to rediscover the joy of work.

Part 1

Recharge

TWELVE PERFORMANCE-ENHANCING ACTIONS TO MAKE WORK LESS AWFUL

Introduction

Why Recharge?

Alexandra Michel, a former banker turned academic, spent nine years studying investment bankers as they worked their way up the magic money tree of banking. Investment banking firms aren't renowned for the love and care they apply to the working practices of their teams. For decades there has been an unwritten agreement that young starters will put in a fifteen-hour workday—that's 8 a.m. till 11 p.m.—in return for the opportunity to ascend to the 0.1 percent of the megawealthy. While precise figures are hard to find, a required public disclosure for Goldman Sachs revealed that in 2015 the average salary in its UK office was $1.3 million—and as this includes lesser-paid support workers such as administrative assistants, the bankers' average wages were even higher than this. For the firm's top earners, the figure can be a significant multiple of that $1.3 million.[1] Workers putting in fifteen-hour days at the start of their careers might begin with only a fraction of the biggest pay packets, but the promise of a future jackpot salary is a big driver for a few years untroubled by sleep or human intimacy.

While few of us are likely to have to endure such remorseless hours, we can learn plenty from observing the toll of relentless work on bankers' bodies. And from this we can discover what the pressure points might be in our own lives.

Michel's study found that extreme working almost always had a physical impact—dramatic weight change, stress-related hair loss, panic attacks, and an inability to sleep. By years three and four, health could be seriously impaired, with workers suffering from diabetes; heart, endocrine, and immune system problem; and even cancer. Often the impact of overwork was evident to others: "She could not keep her eyes open," one client observed when asked about a particular staff member.[2]

The mental consequences were equally stark—addiction (to drugs, to drink, to pornography), a loss of empathy for others, depression, and anxiety. In fact, physical and mental effects were inextricably linked: physical exhaustion created a deficit in people's *body budgets* that addiction then tried to fill. "I am the most disciplined person I know. But sometimes it's like my body is running the show and doing things for which I loathe myself but I just cannot stop it. I am desperate," said one banker. Another who struggled with addiction added, "I sometimes wake up in the morning and remember what I have done the day before and wished that it was just a bad dream and all I want is to keep it together for the day ahead and not allow my body to take over again." Another banker explained that their attempts to get their body to comply often had a physical consequence: "Without thinking about it, I did everything I could to numb my body so that it would not get in the way."

Michel's overall conclusion was that ultimately the bankers she studied became worse versions of themselves. "I stormed toward the taxi," one recalled, "but the door was locked. The driver wanted to unlock it but couldn't because I kept operating the handle. I became so furious that I kept banging against the windows like crazy, swearing at the poor guy." *Uber driver looks to camera. Blinks. Presses one star.* "When you lose the feeling for your body, and compassion and respect for yourself, you do the same to others. Bankers who have been riding themselves become people-eaters," one bank director told Michel. Alarmingly, overwork affected their moral compass, too. And, of course, ultimately the relentless pace started to extinguish any creative spark there might originally have been: "There were times when I just felt alive and ideas came easily. I now have to work much harder and they are often not very original," said one afflicted employee.

Unsurprisingly, the *Hunger Games* of workloads leaves a high body count in banking. *Churn and burn.* For the big firms, bringing in fresh meat is part of the process. There's no room for much compassion because next year's intake is only a few months away. And, after all, it's nothing new: banking has had these practices for decades. For many years these excesses went unchecked—indeed, they were the hazing rituals to earn a place in the legions of mega-earners. In August 2013, a twenty-one-year-old intern at Bank of America Merrill Lynch's investment arm collapsed and died from an epileptic seizure. After Moritz Erhardt's body was discovered, colleagues reported he'd gone three days without sleep.[3]

But something changed after this point. There was a collective scramble within the industry to refine its working cultures. In autumn 2013, Goldman Sachs stepped in and asked its freshest intake of recruits to adopt a different approach: "Please don't work on Saturdays," the company implored with newfound compassion, adding that workers shouldn't put in more than seventy to seventy-five hours' work a week. Goldman's "Saturday Rule" evolved to become a decree that workers should be out of the office from 9 p.m. on Friday until Sunday morning. They weren't alone. Credit Suisse also introduced a Saturday Rule, and Bank of America Merrill Lynch suggested that workers should work no more than twenty-six days out of thirty per month.[4]

Let's take a moment to unpack this. Clearly, there's a lot going on there. Are we meant to feel sorry for these aspiring millionaires? Or applaud the crocodile-teared awakening of the banking bosses? Either way, through the excesses of banking we can see an extreme version of what's happening in our own rather more mundane lives.

Almost certainly your own workweek is shorter than that of bankers, but if the toll of *their* work causes (sometimes irreversible) damage within three or four years, it follows that the stress that accompanies *our* work also has an impact, even if it impacts us at a slower pace. Like the bankers, we try to pretend this harm isn't happening. Most of us haven't yet leveled up to people-eater stage, but we can recognize some of the symptoms.

There's a burnout epidemic sweeping the world. Of course, avoiding employee burnout isn't an expense that unscrupulous employers always want to avoid. As with the banking sector, there are whole industries built on a *churn and burn* workforce model. Bring in young, hungry graduates, work them fifteen hours a day, and then switch them out when they can't cope anymore. Burn them out and then churn them over for new workers.

But if these long working hours have existed in some industries for generations, why is their toll so severe right now? The answer is that these days we are constantly connected to our phones.[5] Bankers have always spent excessive hours at their desks, but before mobile phones, those miserly seven hours a day out of work were *off work*. Now even that respite has gone. Increasingly, there is no escape. In the face of that change, a generations-long practice is leading to collapse. Industries built on churn and burn are now finding that they are churning and burning too many of their future stars.

Such is the state of modern work that in survey after survey, over half of all the workforce report feeling burned out or exhausted.[6]

Another rising trend that has been observed over recent years is the growth of workplace loneliness. Researchers have found that in parallel with the rise of exhaustion, a sense of isolation has also massively increased.[7] People are coming to their workplaces, often sitting in the middle of vast seas of seats—and then feeling alone. One recent survey suggested that 46 percent of Americans say they sometimes or always feel alone.[8] This is an extraordinary state of affairs. Historically, people who worked were happier and more fulfilled than those without a job. Our jobs, no matter what we did, used to give us meaning and companionship in our lives.

Through some delightful twist of timeliness, we've all been born in an era of dazzling technological advance. If you missed that show on TV last night, you can watch it on your phone on the bus to work. From the device in your pocket you now have the capability to speak to every other person on the planet. When we dreamed of this future, we didn't imagine ourselves as zombie life-forms stumbling to bleep ourselves electronically into the office; we envisaged robot butlers bringing us ice cream sundaes as we lounged in the sun.

Something has gone wrong. How can we expect to fix it unless we examine the evidence?

This part of the book will start you on a process of recovery. *Recharge* is a set of reforms designed to make you happier at work—and to help you make your whole workplace happier. It's filled with the latest scientific research for you to share with your boss and your fellow team members to help make suggestions to improve your working life. Consider it a set of proven performance enhancers. All of these changes have been tested and shown to increase productivity, creativity, and enjoyment of work.

The past fifteen years have seen incredible advances in our understanding of work. Thanks to neuroscience, behavioral economics, and the arrival of "people analytics," we know more than ever before about what work is doing to us—and the actions we can take to make it better. You'll find lots of impactful suggestions here. Ideas that will truly transform your attitude toward your job—and consequently make you happier.

Work used to be a lot more fun than it is today. But we can fix this. We need to accept that the demands on us have changed and to adapt to them.

Recharge 1

Have a Monk Mode Morning

What does your office look like? The chances are it's an open-plan space. Increasingly, the only debate about offices is what *sort* of open plan you're going to end up with, and this in turn generally boils down to a discussion of whether your boss has an office or whether they have a desk outside a "meeting room" that they end up working in.

The boss of Google—has an office.[1] The boss of Facebook—sits outside a meeting room. Netflix—no office.[2] Boss of Gap—office (but no desk; just keeping you guessing here).

What our bosses do is a reflection of the two conflicting factors at play here—a desire to appear connected with their teams and the struggle to get anything done in open-plan offices.

Offices started to disappear as work became less formal, as fewer firms asked us to wear ties all day, as we were allowed to be something a touch closer to our real selves. For many, offices seemed a relic of hierarchy. A lack of corridors and delineated spaces implied the company was keen to promote a flatter structure and was not concerned with layers of management.

Of course, the other reason why open plan became popular was that it is very, very cheap. When property rentals are high, one of the most economically sound things a business can do is to take walls down. One columnist for London's *Financial Times* cited evidence that the cost of workspaces for desks in London in 2017 were around $20,000 per year for open plan—and personal offices clearly cost even more.[3] So down tumbled the walls. Big open-plan spaces came to every workplace. Many ended up looking beautiful and stylish. The extra space permits wall art or better decoration. It allows in more natural light.

And, its adherents argue, it creates a better work environment—one of serendipitous encounters, colleagues coming together and reaching delightful epiphanies across their desks. Jony Ive, Apple's design chief, described the vision for the company's new 13,000-employee office in California as a "statement of openness, of free movement." He told *Wired* magazine, "The achievement is to make a building where so many people can connect and collaborate and walk and talk."[4]

The only problem with this utopian view is that it's not true. Open-plan offices have been studied time and time again, and the conclusion is always the same: in terms of productivity, they're a disaster. Take the findings of a survey of one particular oil and gas firm. "The psychologists assessed the employees' satisfaction with their surroundings, as well as their stress level, job performance, and interpersonal relationships before the transition, four weeks after the transition, and, finally, six months afterward," the preamble to the report stated. And what they discovered was not encouraging: "The employees suffered according to every measure: the new space was disruptive, stressful, and cumbersome, and, instead of feeling closer, coworkers felt distant, dissatisfied, and resentful. Productivity fell."[5] A survey of a different company suggested that when workers switched to an open-plan office, the number of email messages people sent to each other increased by 67 percent and face-to-face time dropped by 70 percent.[6]

One New Zealand survey found that open-plan offices not only increased the demands on workers but also made colleagues less friendly to one another—perhaps because they felt frustrated that they weren't able to do their jobs properly.[7]

When presenting the dream of the new space at Apple, Jony Ive painted it with beautifully empowering words. But as it turned out, many of the employees disagreed. Indeed, according to the *Silicon Valley Business Journal*, some of the most senior engineers chose to work in separate buildings.[8] By some accounts, the response was far from polite. The blogger John Gruber gave an account that one lead creator exclaimed, "Fuck that, fuck you, fuck this, this is bullshit." Quite simply, it said, the noise and distraction of open plan wasn't consistent with the way Apple teams had created their world-famous products.[9]

The evidence in favor of open plan is singularly lacking. People in open offices take significantly more sick days than those who work in offices where only a handful of colleagues (fewer than six) are nearby.[10] When they *are* at work, according to one report, constant distractions mean that the average worker is being interrupted every three minutes: by colleagues with quick questions, by overheard fragments of conversation, not to mention all the other distractions of modern office life.[11] Given that experts argue that it can take up to eight minutes to get back into a concentrated state again after an interruption, the amount of time wasted is considerable (others have even suggested that the time to get back fully into deep concentration could be as much as twenty minutes).[12] The fact is that humans are not good at attention switching. One study of software engineers suggested that among engineers who were working on five projects concurrently, 75 percent of their time was lost to switching mentally between them—leaving only 5 percent work attention per project.[13]

Number of Simultaneous Projects	Loss to Context Switching	Time Subsequently Available per Project
1	0%	100%
2	20%	40%
3	40%	20%
4	60%	10%
5	75%	5%

Business school professor Sophie Leroy described what's going on here. "People need to stop thinking about one task in order to fully transition their attention and perform well on another," she explained. "Yet results indicate it is difficult for people to transition their attention away from an unfinished task and their subsequent task performance suffers."[14] Leroy says when we switch from one job—answering an email, say—to another, like writing a presentation, there is an "attention residue." We are still half thinking about whether the email response was right or when our boss will get back to us. The end result is that we spend longer doing a less thorough job. Some scientists have gone so far as to suggest that when we mentally multitask, our IQ is reduced by as much as ten points—for all intents and purposes we may even seem stoned.[15]

Constant interruptions and distractions also make us *feel* that we're getting less done. And this has a significant impact on our sense of personal worth. Psychologist Teresa Amabile, who has done extensive research in this area, has established that people feel satisfied at work when they are confident that *they have made progress on something*: not powering through a mountain of email but focusing on a single task.[16] It's something that Hungarian American psychologist Mihály Csíkszentmihályi describes as "flow." In Csíkszentmihályi's words, flow is "being completely involved in an activity for its own sake. The ego falls away. Time flies. Every action, movement, and thought follows inevitably from the previous one, like playing jazz. Your whole being is involved, and you're using your skills to the utmost."[17]

Amabile observes that these moments of flow don't need to be prolonged in nature. Often the benefits can result from short periods of concentration. Having delved into more than nine thousand daily work diaries that she had asked volunteers to keep, she and her team discovered that a fulfilling day for participants in her study was invariably one in which they reported making meaningful progress on something they had been trying to accomplish. It was a day when there was a moment of—normally solitary— headspace when ideas seemed finally to come together. As one of the participants recounted, "The event of the day was that. . . . I was able to concentrate on the project at hand without interruptions. [Earlier] there were so many interruptions for chit-chat that I couldn't get any decent work accomplished. I eventually had to go work very quietly in another room to get some of it done."[18] Absence of distraction leads to quiet, quiet leads to flow, flow leads to progress, progress leads to satisfaction.

This may seem counter to what we're often told about creativity these days: that it's a collective effort, that it's about teams. At a certain point, of course, it is, and group discussion can happen productively in open workspaces designed for it. Nevertheless, our meaningful work is more likely to be done in solitude. If you've ever found yourself saying, "I can't get anything done at work," or "I go into the office before everyone gets in, because I can power through my work," then you're quietly recognizing this, too.

Writer and academic Cal Newport has his own term for the flow this involves: "Deep Work," defined by him as "professional activities performed in a state of distraction-free concentration that push your cognitive capacities to the limit." And he has a practical suggestion for how to achieve it. "I'm starting to see more entrepreneurs," he told me, "especially CEOs of small startups—doing what I call the Monk Mode Morning, where they say, 'As far as anyone is concerned I'm reachable starting at 11 a.m. or noon and I never am available for meetings, I'm never going to answer an email and never going to answer the phone before then.' Their whole organization adapts to this idea that the first part of the day is *depth time*. The second part of the day is for other things." It's an approach that resonates with Amabile's recommendation that we adopt a mixed model of work—a blend of quiet time and comingling. To Amabile, getting meaningful work done "means ruthlessly guarding protected blocks of the work week, shielding staff from the distractions and interruptions that are the normal condition of organizational life."

How about trying this out? Why not tell your team that on—say—Wednesday and Friday, you won't be getting into the office until 11 a.m. and you'll be working on things at home until then. One of my colleagues at Twitter has tried a version of Monk Mode Morning. David Wilding has a fiendish two-hour commute each way to work. He decided that getting on a train during rush hour was wasted time: you don't get a table; you are squeezed against strangers. So he chooses to get a slightly later train—when he can sit at a table and (thanks to the rail operators' lack of Wi-Fi) concentrate on deeper work projects rather than email and work chat. He may not be in the office at 9:30 a.m. on days when he has a scheduled "late train," but by the time he arrives, his Monk Mode Morning has given him an hour or more of valuable Deep Work.

Renowned adman and executive creative director of OgilvyOne Rory Sutherland goes even further. His view is that we shouldn't even come into the office to do email. We should come to work only to have conversations and meet people. He says in the former life of the office "you had to come into work to make a photocopy, you had to come into work to produce a document, to produce a presentation, even to make an international phone call—you basically came into the office to do it because it cost a fortune and you didn't want that on your unitemized phone bill. And so the office fulfilled a lot of functions. And once you left the office there was a limit—other than working with pencil and paper and just generally thinking—to how much work you could do." Now, however, "90 percent of what an office used to be for is just as available at home, assuming you have reasonable broadband. So you have to ask the question: 'What's the office now for?'" His take is that if you want to be your most productive and engaged, then it's a mistake to come into work simply to sit at your computer and deal with email. You should be meeting people by prearrangement, or meeting people by accident. "And the problem I always notice," he says, "is that when you're doing email you're not meeting people by accident because it's a fundamentally antisocial behavior."[19]

If part of the secret of being happier and more fulfilled at work is to feel that you're getting genuine work done, then perhaps a Monk Mode Morning twice a week could work for you and your colleagues. Why not suggest it to your team?

What You Can Do Next:

» Think about the last time you got a satisfying block of work done. Are there ways you could create the same conditions for the next assignment? What would you need to decline, cancel, or move to give yourself three hours of uninterrupted work twice a week?

» Most people find that Monk Mode works best in the morning, but it may be that in your case, an afternoon slot works better.

» While you're in your Monk Mode, try to avoid all distractions or interruptions. That means silence your phone, log out of email.

» Keep a record of what you have accomplished while in Monk Mode. It may prove helpful in converting naysayers to the wisdom of trying it.

» If you find this new approach isn't working, experiment with different times and days of the week.

Recharge 2

Go for a Walking Meeting

When you're sitting at a desk or locked in a meeting scrambling for ideas, getting up and going for a walk might seem like a distraction. After all, if you're swamped with work, taking a break is only going to make things worse. You'll end up with just as much to do, but less time to do it.

But something magical seems to happen when we get blood pumping through our bodies. And for many, going for a walk offers one of the best ways to liberate their thinking and get their creative synapses pinging. As J. K. Rowling said, "There's nothing like a nighttime stroll to give you ideas." Fellow writer Charles Dickens—by any account a heroically prolific author, who wrote fifteen novels and hundreds of short stories and edited a weekly magazine—worked in intense five-hour blocks of concentration from 9 a.m. until 2 p.m. each day, and then, with his own version of Deep Work finished, Dickens would take a ten- to twelve-mile walk. "I could not keep my health otherwise," he argued. Perhaps the philosopher Søren Kierkegaard put it best: "I have walked myself into my best thoughts," he wrote, "and I know of no thought so burdensome that one cannot walk away from it."[1]

Is there any hard scientific evidence for this, though? This is something that Marily Oppezzo and Daniel Schwartz from Stanford University have studied. In the course of their experiments they used a series of recognized tests for creativity—such as the "alternative uses" test whereby an item is suggested to a subject and they're asked to propose imaginative, but appropriate, ways in which it can be used. (One volunteer was shown a key and, prompted by its vaguely eye-shaped form, suggested it could be used as a new eye; this *didn't* count as an "appropriate novelty," whereas the idea put forward by another that a key could be used by a dying victim to carve the name of their murderer in the ground *did* count, even if it did elicit some wary looks from her fellow test subjects.)[2] These tests were then tried in various different ways: on people who were sitting, then walking; walking, then sitting; solely walking; or solely sitting.[3]

And what Oppezzo and Schwartz discovered was that walking led to a very significant uplift in creative thinking: in fact, 81 percent of participants saw their scores for giving creative suggestions go up when they were walking rather than sitting (the average increase was 60 percent). Their explanation was that aerobic exercise during (or prior to) creative thinking had the effect of energizing those thoughts. Walking proved highly effective when it came to liberating ideas, even if it wasn't the most effective way to resolve complex logical puzzles. As the scientists put it, walking may not be good for *convergent thinking* (i.e., homing in on the "correct," standard answer to a question), but it is a powerful tool for *divergent thinking* (coming up with fresh, imaginative ideas). Better still, that power lingered. Those volunteers who went for a walk *before* they needed to be creative scored higher in the tests that followed than those who just stayed seated.

Where we walk can also have a beneficial impact. Another

research paper, published in 2012, suggested that a fifty-minute walk out in the open can aid concentration: the experience of wandering in natural surroundings has the effect of "cleansing our palate" and allows us to sit down with a clean mental sheet of paper afterward.[4]

But it's not just about coming up with productive ideas. Walks are a way of having meetings, too. Chris Barez-Brown, who runs a leadership training company called Upping Your Elvis, which has built a reputation for inspiring leaders to have more creative ideas, strongly believes that the creative brainpower unleashed by walking also has a dramatic impact when we use it alongside colleagues. His company employs a process called "Walk It Out" to help people unblock subconscious mental obstacles.

Barez-Brown's approach is to send pairs of people away for short walks—sometimes thirty minutes, often a fraction of that. During the walk one of them is instructed to talk (or "rant and rave," as he puts it) about a dilemma they are facing. People, he says, tend to be skeptical beforehand: "I'll give it a go, but I can't imagine it will have a benefit." But, "half an hour later they come back saying, 'Wow, revelation! I'm so much clearer.'" Barez-Brown believes the power of this approach comes from the fresh perspective we gain from unjumbling our unprepared thoughts as we start ranting and raving through them. "We often don't get a chance to talk about our life without being edited," Barez-Brown says; however, when we're walking side by side with someone, we feel as though we're able to reorganize our thoughts and present them afresh. In some situations, half an hour is about right, but when Barez-Brown is running corporate offsite sessions his preferred technique is actually to send people outside for seven and a half minutes: one person to listen, the other to talk. "Often when people come back they have a lot more clarity—about things they haven't been paying attention to, things that were bothering them."[5] Talking in this way allows them to trigger the idea-generating divergent thinking that walking stimulates and also combines it with the *narrowing things down* style of convergent thinking.

Some might object that wandering around in the open discussing matters that might well be highly confidential is fraught with danger. What happens if you're overheard? Isn't it safer to stick to the secrecy of the meeting room? Not according to the Mafia. Joseph C. Massino, the only New York mafia boss ever to cooperate with the authorities, once told a courtroom that, among the golden rules for a discreet conversation, "You never talk in a club, you never talk in a car, you never talk on a cellphone, you never talk on a phone, you never talk in your house."[6] (I like this; it reads like the missing Doctor Seuss Mafia book.) Massino testified in court that *walk-talks*, where conversations would take place as the participants roved the streets, were in fact the safest. If the Mafia—suspicious that there are FBI agents actively trying to listen to them—feels that walking is safe, then I suspect you're probably going to be okay talking about next year's marketing plan out in the open, too.

So when you're looking for a way to make today's work feel less overwhelming—or you want to unblock your thoughts—it might be an idea to get up from your desk and go for a few strides in the open air. In the words of the German philosopher Friedrich Nietzsche, "All truly great thoughts are conceived by walking."

What You Can Do Next:

» Suggest a walking meeting with a colleague in place of your normal get-together.

» Factor in an expectation that the first couple of attempts are likely to be awkward—stick with it.

» Bear in mind that there will probably be some people who are more likely to go along with your suggestion. It's also likely that some will prove hostile partners who will dampen the experience. Don't waste good science on bad subjects.

» Try different time lengths. The "Walk It Out" sessions of Chris Barez-Brown at seven and a half minutes are just long enough to get our divergent thinking going, before we sit down again to harness convergent thought.

Recharge 3

Celebrate Headphones

The issue of headphones really divides offices, doesn't it?

Have there "been words" about headphones in your office? Do you find that older workers—those who perhaps had their ideas of work established in the days before there was a computer on every desk—scoff at them, or complain, or reminisce about the days when people worked properly?

Human resources forums display a furious generational divide about the perceived toxicity or otherwise of headphones.[1] Younger people tend to support them; older people are suspicious. In an article in the *Harvard Business Review*, a former boss at Nickelodeon, Anne Kreamer, spoke for many at the conservative end of the debate when she expressed her firm disapproval.[2] Had she worn headphones earlier in her career, she argued, she would—among other things—have missed out on the "collective high" when a good piece of news rippled through the office.

Now, I don't want to challenge Kreamer's track record of success, but I do wonder if she might be romanticizing the past a little. Like Kreamer, I'm not exactly young, but I can't remember waves of euphoria sweeping across any office that I worked in. Maybe they clapped in every new episode of *Rugrats* at Nickelodeon? But then, during the period Kreamer is writing about—the 1990s—surely one-third to one-half of people would have been on the phone at any given moment? We'd all agree that the sight of colleagues gleefully jumping around wouldn't be regarded as sufficient reason to end a phone call—even when they have just watched an awesome episode of *Kenan & Kel*.

The truth is that because power in workplaces is unequally distributed generationally, it's become popular to blame millennials and Gen-Z workers for most of the things bosses don't like. Headphones are one of the things that get blamed on younger workers. There's a mistaken belief that in no-headphones workplaces there are intense Socratic conversations going on, with colleagues scribbling at whiteboards as they capture incisive thoughts on the plan for next year. In reality, offices that allow headphones and ones that don't have very similar atmospheres.

Headphones are essentially a coping mechanism: they help their wearers avoid distractions in an office where otherwise they'd be constantly interrupted. Just as Apple's senior engineers wanted to avoid open plan (see Recharge 1), headphone wearers like to zone themselves off. As it happens, in some of the biggest open-plan offices it's not uncommon to have white noise pumped into the space (either directly or via headphones) to try to block out unwanted stimuli.

In my view, headphones should not be banned. Instead they should be celebrated—in exactly the same way that we celebrate Christmas. Celebration doesn't mean we do it all the time; it means we mark an occasion. And the best way for us to work with headphones is to have periods when they're allowed and others when teams agree not to use them. If your office isn't willing to have Monk Mode Mornings or doesn't provide a space for you to go and work in quiet, then the optimum time for headphones is the morning. Being able to power through work during the first few hours of the day fits best with most people's circadian rhythms.

The hours before and after lunch, by contrast, are better suited to a no-headphones zone. These are the moments in a day when colleagues can connect, share, and discuss. As the former boss of Campbell's Soup said, "These thousands of little interruptions aren't keeping you from the work, they *are* the work."[3] Of course, it's easier to say this if you're in a soundproofed corner office: the past ten years have probably pushed the interruptions of work beyond what even the Soup Baron could handle.

I've tended to focus so far on the advantages of *not* being interrupted. But it's worth pausing for a moment to register the advantages, because although interruptions have been proven to be very bad for cognition and complex problem solving, they can actually be quite helpful when it comes to creative thought. And here again, the correct headphone regime can play an important role.

Many people are now familiar with right-brain and left-brain thinking. Or they may have heard about what behavioral economist Daniel Kahneman has styled "System 1" (fast, instinctive, visceral decision making) and "System 2" (slower, considered, reflective thinking). It's worth noting that while many scientists are comfortable with using these simplified terms to help illustrate different types of behavior, there are neither right and left hemispheres dedicated to specific tasks nor discrete fast and slow sections of the brain. As one of the leading thinkers on the understanding of the brain, Lisa Feldman Barrett, reminds us, "Kahneman is *very careful* to say it's a metaphor, but many people seem to be ignoring him and essentializing Systems 1 and 2 as blobs in the brain."[4] As frustrating as it might be for us, the brain's processes are much more messy than we would like.

One view of the brain is that it contains specific neurons for incredibly precise jobs (one study suggested there was a brain cell that seemed universally to be triggered by Jennifer Aniston, for example,[5] and the newly created field of neuroeconomics has been intent on finding which brain neurons might make us make specific decisions). Feldman Barrett, by contrast, argued that while the brain may indeed allocate a cell to the concept of, say, a sitcom actress, that cell will be located in a different place in each individual brain. Our brains contain overlapping networks responsible for the performance of different functions. If, for example, we want to get concentrated work done, requiring "convergent thinking" (see Recharge 2), scholars suggest that we will be triggering the executive attention network. This is a system in the brain that allows us to push away distractions and to focus, serving us if we want to—say—power through email. If, on the other hand, we want to think more imaginatively—to engage in divergent thinking—we need to reduce our focused executive attention network and allow our default and salience networks to fill the space.[6] The salience network observes stimuli around us and predicts their implications for our actions. The default network appears to be disengaged when we're doing things but becomes active when we're remembering the past or thinking of others; it's the home of daydreaming in the brain. One way to trigger both these parts of the brain, as I pointed out in Recharge 2, is to go for a walk; researcher Marily Oppezzo and her colleagues have demonstrated that this can be very beneficial. Essentially, to be creative we need to let our mind wander and imagine, something that is very hard to do when our executive attention network is fully fired up.[7] We more readily achieve divergent thinking by doing something disruptive.

Here's ad executive Rory Sutherland talking about how ideas appear: "I notice that Archimedes had his idea [of displacement] stepping into the bath, not while he was sitting in the bath. Because when you are on the line between one state of action and another one tends to be when you're making that flick. Getting off a train too, for some reason. We have these strange little moments which seem to be hugely productive and enjoyable. It is almost that you're training your brain into letting go of the usual straitjacket of assumptions that it's brought to bear. When that jacket briefly falls off that's when you suddenly have some sort of creative insight or magical leap."[8] In other words, when the salience and default networks are busy running lots of routine management, the mind can wander into unexpected places. In a similar vein, when scientists looked at creativity, people who were more easily distracted by irrelevant stimuli were found to produce more and better ideas. When you want ideas, distraction is a good thing.[9]

Further evidence for this viewpoint comes from three researchers at Columbia University, who have demonstrated that when we're trying to be inventive in our problem solving, a shift in attention can prove more productive than sustained concentration on a single thing. The researchers gave three groups of people two problems each to solve. One group had to attempt the first challenge and then move on to the second. The second group was asked to switch back and forth between the two challenges at predetermined intervals. The third group was allowed to allocate their time as they chose.

Most people would assume that the group that had the freedom to split the time as they saw fit would come up with the best answers to the problems. In fact, the best results were achieved by those who switched between the two tasks at fixed intervals. Why should this be the case? The team at Columbia explained it in the following terms: "Because when attempting problems that require creativity, we often reach a dead end without realizing it.

We find ourselves circling around the same ineffective ideas and don't recognize when it's time to move on."[10] Their conclusion was that the group that had to switch between the two challenges at set intervals found themselves resetting their thought processes, discovering fresh angles and options in the process. This discovery wasn't an isolated experiment. Researchers Steven Smith, David Gerkens, and Genna Angello asked subjects to produce lists of words, each time giving them two different categories for their lists (like "cold things and heavy things" or "items you take camping and fattening foods"). They found that people who switched between the two lists produced more responses—and more original responses—than those who just made uninterrupted lists of each category in turn.[11]

In 1939, James Webb Young, an esteemed advertising exec, wrote humanity's definitive guide to the process of creativity, *A Technique for Producing Ideas*. For the price of a cup of coffee you should be able to download or purchase a copy of this enlightening pamphlet. In his text, Webb Young reminded us of what we all already know, "namely, that an idea is nothing more nor less than a new combination of old elements."[12] He said that ideas are created when we spot the opportunities to combine two thoughts: "The second important principle involved is that the capacity to bring old elements into new combinations depends largely on the ability to see relationships." In spotting this, the adman was over fifty years ahead of our favorite inventor, Steve Jobs. Jobs said something remarkably similar: "Creativity is just connecting things. When you ask creative people how they did something, they feel a little guilty because they didn't really do it, they just saw something. It seemed obvious to them after a while. That's because they were able to connect experiences they've had and synthesize new things."[13]

So what is James Webb Young's famous technique? There are three simple stages:

1. **Gathering raw materials**—ideally as diverse and interesting provocations as possible. Webb Young cautioned that this process can be laborious and unrewarding. He said it is often so dull that we try to avoid it: "Instead of working systematically at the job of gathering raw material we sit around hoping for inspiration to strike us."

2. **Digesting the material.** Webb Young's favored method was to fill in small index cards. "What you do is to take the different bits of material which you have gathered and feel them all over, as it were, with the tentacles of the mind. You take one fact, turn it this way and that, look at it in different lights, and feel for the meaning of it. You bring two facts together and see how they fit." Pretty soon your mind will become frustrated: "You will get very tired of trying to fit your puzzle together."

3. **Unconscious processing.** "In this third stage, you make absolutely no effort of a direct nature. You drop the whole subject and put the problem out of your mind as completely as you can." Webb Young even testified to the power of sleep in helping us evolve new ideas. After you've put aside the problem, "turn to whatever stimulates your imagination and emotions." Maybe go for a walk, listen to music, watch a film.

Webb Young said that having done the (often frustrating) preparatory work, "out of nowhere the Idea will appear." Often the idea will find you when you're not fully thinking of the challenge at hand. "It will come to you when you are least expecting it—while shaving, or bathing, or most often when you are half awake in the morning."

Whether it is this considered assessment of creating ideas, or the scientific explorations above, there is a common thread. Creative ideas are formed by the collision of two or more ideas—and those collisions tend to become more likely when we have challenges at hand and are distractible. And this is where headphones come in again: having done some seriously productive work with headphones on, we can step into a creative zone precisely through the action of taking them off.

If you want to try the experiment, you'll probably need to have a team discussion first. Bring some of the evidence and research I've just outlined to the table. Explain what Deep Work is and how ideas are formed. And then ask the team to create its own rules of engagement. Maybe there should be a trigger: perhaps you all put a radio show on as background noise at noon to act as the prompt? Maybe you aim to have the first ninety minutes after lunch as the chat time? As the scientific experiments above have shown, a disciplined scheduling of time (to a schedule previously agreed on by the team) can often prompt better outcomes than allowing a casual drift each day.

Ben Waber, boss of workplace analytics company Humanyze, points out that some of these daily phases already exist in embryonic form in most offices. "Focused work time increases for most of the day, with the exception of times around lunch and right before people leave the office." He says that the times he sees conversation in offices is already clustered: "From 12 p.m. to 1 p.m. and after 4 p.m. interaction more than triples [in open-plan offices] but there are significant reductions in conversations at other times in the day."[14] A separate study of office interactions has suggested that 2:30 to 4 p.m. is the noisiest time.[15] Afternoons seem to be most prone to chat and conversation. This is something you can build on to create a day that both manages workflow and produces ideas.

And headphones could be your secret weapon.

What You Can Do Next:

» Remember that people tend to have strong views about headphones: they love them or hate them. So before you do anything, discuss your ideas with colleagues. Make sure you know what time they would feel most comfortable allowing headphones in the office.

» If you use laptops at work, utilize the flexibility they give you to create headphones areas and conversation areas. Some teams choose to put in anchor times when their teams try to gather together to work alongside each other.

» If you're one of those people who is unhappy about headphones, make sure you're not simply being nostalgic about returning to a way of working that is now in the past. Instead, figure out how to make today's office work.

Recharge 4

Eliminate Hurry Sickness

Next time you use an elevator, I want you to choose your destination floor and then do nothing. Don't press "Close Door." Don't reach for your phone. Just wait. Wait for the doors to close. I suspect even the thought of doing nothing probably makes you feel uncomfortable. After all, it's so different from what you normally do. The elevator arrives, and if the doors don't immediately swoosh open you hit the button again, just so everyone understands how busy you are right now. Maybe you jiggle the button a little, like playing a PlayStation game, seeing if you can get the whole thing to happen faster.

Someone told me recently about their dad's strange behavior when they were a child. He would come home from work and sit in a chair. That was it. No TV, no radio, no book. No attempt to chat to anyone. He just sat. And quietly pondered. I suspect if you'd have asked him what he was thinking about he would have calmly replied "nothing much." This wasn't active cognition. This was just calm reflection.

Today, such inactivity would seem ludicrously unproductive.

We need to get stuff done, and we accept that in an era of hyper-stimulation and intense activity sitting and doing nothing seems like a barbarous waste of time. We've all got hurry sickness. And it's not always the end of the world. It means we can get lots of stuff done. There's a management truism that "if you want something done, give it to a busy person." We believe that action breeds productivity.

Back to the elevator. Depending on where you live in the world, the Close Door button might actually be legally mandated not to work or be triggered to play an audio message but still to close after a preset delay. In many countries the minimum amount of time a door stays open is legally controlled to permit those using wheelchairs and canes to make their way into the elevator, and so the door doesn't respond to insistent demands.[1] In 2004, the *New York Times* reported that pedestrian request buttons to cross busy roads in the city weren't even set up to do anything in peak hours: walkers would see the panels in front of them light up, but this was merely a placebo reward. The finely tuned traffic systems were set up to optimize mass traffic movement, not to respond to hurried pedestrian commuters.[2] We're surrounded with devices lying to us, trying to appease our gnawing need to *get something done*.

This is hurry sickness in action. One consequence of systemic overstimulation in our lives is an uneasy state of restlessness, a continual feeling that we can't complete everything that we need to. Increased connectivity has created more expectations from us at work. According to the California-based Radicati Group, the average person sends and receives almost 130 email messages per day.[3] Since this figure was derived from the email habits of 2.8 billion email users worldwide, it is more than likely that the number for Western office workers is close to 200 messages sent and received every day. Then there are meetings. Most firms don't keep accurate records of the amount of time we surrender to meetings—perhaps out of a sense of embarrassment—but one recent study suggested that managers were spending twenty-three hours a week sitting around meeting tables.[4]

And it's not just email and meetings. The volume of information that each of us now processes is dizzyingly vast. Daniel Levitin, author of *The Organized Mind*, has argued, "In 2011, Americans took in five times as much information every day as they did in 1986—the equivalent of 175 newspapers. During our leisure time, not counting work, each of us processes 34 gigabytes or 100,000 words every day."[5]

The end result is that most of us find ourselves in a constant state of worry, never feeling that we've got everything done. Our parents' generation might have felt uneasy if they had a few things on their handwritten to-do list. Now even the fleeting joy of Inbox Zero is stolen from us by the sense that we have unfulfilled responsibilities elsewhere that we forgot to get back to.

Hurry sickness is a genuine condition, and it's why those whose job it is to study workplace stress have observed a rise in anxiety among those who feel the need to be connected all the time. A 2017 survey by the American Psychological Association found that 61 percent of respondents chose work as a top source of stress.[6]

So what can any of us do to push back against this burning sense of urgency? In my view, the first thing is to recognize that constant busyness doesn't equate with achieving more. "We used to have a single weekly meeting," a group of highly successful London architects told me. "One meeting. It did everything. Then we'd get on with work. Now we have meetings about meetings." Their conclusion? "As a firm we're still building the same number of buildings. It's just a lot more painful to get it done."

Once you've recognized that busyness is not everything, the

next step is to calibrate urgency. That familiar acronym ASAP can create an unnecessary level of anxiety in an office. As the founders of software company Basecamp said, "ASAP is inflationary. . . . Before you know it, the only way to get anything done is by putting the ASAP sticker on it."[7] On the next occasion you find yourself asking for something urgently, ask yourself whether you really do need it ASAP. If you can make some things less urgent, you're being more honest with yourself and helping to create a better working environment for everyone else.

And on top of that, you need to take time to reflect and to do nothing. A moment's peace and quiet will reduce your stress levels. Moreover, it will boost your creativity. Dr Sandi Mann from the University of Central Lancashire, who has become something of an expert on boredom, championed the notion that we should harness the power of the default network that I discussed in Recharge 3. "Once you start daydreaming and allow your mind to really wander," she said, "you start thinking a little bit beyond the conscious, a little bit into the subconscious. This allows different connections to take place. It's really awesome, actually."[8] In other words, when our brain goes into the default mode, it starts to connect disparate ideas. It diverts energy from switching between competing urgent demands to wandering in a state of pleasurable dreaminess. For this to happen, though, you genuinely have to surrender to boredom. You can't play with your phone or listen to audiobooks—free your mind from stimulation.

If you succumb to hurry sickness, on the other hand, you may find yourself caught in something of a vicious cycle. "We find that when people are stressed, they tend to shift their attention more rapidly," said Dr. Gloria Mark, who has carried out research in this area. And, of course, the more you restlessly shift your attention, the more stressed you become. The long-term effects can be dramatic. Scientists who looked at teenagers who filled evenings with continuous switching between social interactions and stimuli on their phones found that it had a silent toll on their thinking: "Two years down the road, they are less creative and imaginative about their own personal futures and about solving societal problems."[9]

So the next time you're in an elevator, press the button and then wait. Those extra few seconds might be your path to a brilliant new idea. The dad sitting in a chair wasn't doing nothing. He was allowing his mind space to think.

What You Can Do Next:

» Don't see gaps in your schedule (and other people's schedules) as time when you're not working. Our best ideas often come when we're sitting around and our mind is wandering.

» Try driving with no music on. Showering with no radio. Exercising with no Spotify. See what thoughts fill the space.

» Allow yourself time to do nothing. Check how you feel afterward. Do you feel less anxious and stressed?

» You may find meditation helps you—for some people it pushes away pressing concerns and creates mental space.

Recharge 5

Shorten Your Workweek

His name might not be the first one that springs to mind, but it is essential that you pay heed to the words of Andy Murray. A three-time Grand Slam winner and former number one tennis player, Murray stumbled upon something that will help you think about your work in a different way.

I'll explain why in a moment, but first it's worth considering how our workweek has mushroomed in recent times. Once upon a time, we finished at the office and went home. Now email has extended the working day to the commute, to the sofa, even to the bathroom. Even when we're at work, our day is being stretched by the burdens placed on us by what Microsoft researcher Linda Stone has termed "continuous partial attention."[1] As we're presented with such a vast constellation of demands upon our thought, we're constantly dividing our attention between fresh floods of email or trying to conduct meetings while keeping an eye on our handheld devices, preoccupied with something other than what is happening in the moment.

And we blame ourselves for not being able to keep up. The modern way of working has piled unprecedented expectations on us, yet we've told ourselves that a failure to cope is our fault. We don't tap out responses to email on the bus home out of a sense of bookish overachievement but out of burning guilt that we'll be seen as slacking. To make matters worse, experts have sprung up who argue that the secret of success is a series of life hacks that enable us to get more done in much less time. Books and podcasts suggest it's possible to deliver on the requirements of success with a four-hour workweek. It reminds me of the hitchhiker in *There's Something About Mary*, whose genius insurgent idea is to outdo the bestselling fitness video *Six-Minute Abs* by marketing his own, undercutting them by a minute. I should have channeled him and called this book *The Three-Hour Workweek*. Implicit in these books and podcasts is a clear message that there's not a problem with work; there's a problem with you. *You need to change your approach to catch up, you dinosaur* is the covert meaning.

As Daniel Levitin asserts in *The Organized Mind*, there's a limit to what we can do. "Our brains are configured to make a certain number of decisions per day," he writes, "and once we reach that limit, we can't make any more, regardless of how important they are." Read that sentence again and think about what it means for your job. Human cognition is a zero-sum game. We can't keep working and working and expect that the output will be of high quality.

And if you want proof of Levitin's assertion, it's worth considering the findings of Kathleen Vohs and her colleagues in a paper they published in the *Journal of Personality and Social Psychology* in 2008. They observed that when student volunteers were asked to make a lot of mundane choices (for example, "What video would you prefer to watch in class?") and decisions ("Solve this [unsolvable] puzzle"), they tended to start demonstrating mental fatigue or "ego depletion." That fatigue led them in turn to choose to do low-energy activities like watching TV and playing video games rather than activities that required concentration (like studying or reading), even when a meaningful academic reward for success was on offer.[2] Because they wasted finite attention on trivial things, their brains stopped being able to access inventiveness at the times they needed it.

This is where Andy Murray's wisdom comes in. In 2013, in answer to a question why longer matches were more difficult, he explained it wasn't so much the physical demands that proved so challenging—after all, players train hard to develop herculean stamina. It was the mental tiredness that resulted from having to make thousands upon thousands of decisions. At a certain point, the quality of decision making started to suffer.[3]

I realize this runs counter to what we're used to hearing. We've been brainwashed into believing that long hours are essential to success. We assume that if we really want to get ahead we need to be a bit more like tech executive Marissa Mayer, the youngest person—at thirty-three—to appear on *Fortune* magazine's Fifty Most Powerful Women list and subsequently the first woman to top the magazine's 40 Under 40. Asked to describe the formula for success that she helped create in the early days of Google— where she was employee number twenty—she declared it was the collective resolution of early Googlers to work 130 hours a week.[4] And she described how she achieved this by minimizing bathroom breaks, sleeping under desks, and pulling "at least one all-nighter a week, except when I was on vacation—and the vacations were few and far between."

Good grief. And the worst thing is that there's no science to prove this paycheck martyrdom works. Sure, most of us can remember when we worked long hours to get an academic assignment done or to meet a tight deadline. But these were bursts of activity with commensurate payoffs. Blowouts and sleeping in acted as rewards for depleting our energy.

Historical evidence confirms what science suggests: that shorter hours tend to be more productive. Back in 1810, progressive industrialist Robert Owen campaigned for a ten-hour working day, and within a decade he had evolved it to the slogan "Eight hours' labor, eight hours' recreation, eight hours' sleep" in the belief that productivity would be increased by adopting this cycle. And so it proved. At the end of the century, in 1893, weekly hours at the Salford Iron Works (near Manchester, England) were controversially cut from fifty-three to forty-eight, and the result was a reported increase in total output. And when in the following century the Ford Motor Company reduced the working day to eight hours while simultaneously doubling pay to a minimum of $5 per day—in a move seen by many as radically provocative—the company's profits doubled the following year.[5] Ford's annual report released in January 1914 reads like an enlightened text compared with what we're familiar with from contemporary firms: "It is our belief that social justice begins at home. . . . Believing as we do, that a division of our earnings between capital and labor is unequal, we have sought a plan of relief suitable for our business." Arguably it was something of a smokescreen; the union-hating Ford was very far from being an enlightened pioneer in the treatment of labor. Economics was what determined the decision: the company rightly predicted it could increase profits if it changed the employees' work patterns. (It was assisted in this by the mathematics of the twenty-four-hour day—the move to an eight-hour workday allowed for three eight-hour shifts rather than two nine-hour runs.)

When trying to work out how many hours the optimum workweek might contain, it's worth considering the research carried out by John Pencavel from Stanford University, who in 2014 undertook a comprehensive exploration of long working hours.[6] His data were drawn from logs of workers in a munitions factory in the First World War, in part because meticulous records of their working hours survived and in part because Pencavel felt that, since they were operating in a vital sector at a time of war, the munitions factory hands would have had a serious purpose to drive them on. After all, no one wants to lose a war.

His findings were unequivocal. The ideal *maximum* working week was fifty hours. As he put it, "The marginal product of hours is a constant until the knot at [about fifty] hours after which it declines."[7] After fifty-five or fifty-six hours, as exhaustion began to kick in, output actually started to decrease. According to Pencavel's data, workers who clocked in seventy hours a week (ten hours a day, seven days a week) achieved no more than those who worked fifty-five hours.

A weekend break also had a positive impact. Total output was higher in a forty-eight-hour week with a Sunday break than in a fifty-six-hour week (with no day off). Think about that. Having a day off work made every working day so much more productive that the work-free Sunday was more than paid for.

If an example drawn from a First World War factory seems too remote, there are plenty of more recent ones to draw on. Take the management consultancy firm McKinsey. Scott Maxwell, who was an exec there (he later went on to a successful career in venture capital), recalled how an early mentor tipped him off about a glitch in the firm's working practices. McKinsey celebrated its machine-like seven-day-a-week working style. If you didn't work all week, colleagues would be scornful; they'd be dismissive of your indolence. But Maxwell's mentor, Jon Katzenbach, quietly mentioned to him that his religious beliefs required him to work for only six days (though he never told anyone), and yet he seemed to get more done than his seven-day colleagues.[8] Katzenbach's conclusion was that the norm of overworking was performative rather than productive—it was all for show, like sleeping under a desk or always looking as though you've been holding a pee in for an hour. And Katzenbach went further: he felt a four-day week would probably be his own sweet spot.

Maxwell went on to observe the trade-off between the hours people worked and their output when he formed his own VC fund. And he didn't just observe it; he tracked it. His findings were unambiguous: "For every hour [the team] worked over forty hours a week, productivity dropped. In fact, productivity peaked just *under* forty hours a week." Maxwell therefore set out a new policy: no more working nights and weekends, and no more working on holidays.[9] He was instructing his employees to work less to ensure they got more done.[10] He took pride in sending workers home on time.

Stewart Butterworth, the CEO of office communication start-up Slack, has adopted a similar approach in his company. Slack believes strongly in a tightly delineated day. The company's value of "work hard and go home" is reflected in its decision to remove Ping-Pong and foosball tables from offices and to encourage workers to have lively side hustles (from kiteboarding to running small businesses) in their personal lives. We've seen that, whether it is the manual factory work of the Pencavel study or white-collar work like management consultants', if we want to be our most productive the answer is not to work longer hours.

What applies to individual companies applies to countries, too. Long average working hours do not lead to greater productivity or prosperity. Indeed, an *Economist* magazine analysis in 2013 showed that countries that worked least had the highest productivity.[11] Countries with high capital investment per capita turn out more productive workers—these countries (Germany, for example) reward that productivity with shorter working shifts, which in turn helps protect staff from burnout.

What's the answer? In my view, we need to change the way we think about work. We need to approach it with more firmness. If we treat work as forty hours of output, then that forces us to make decisions. It invites us to question whether we think three-hour meetings are a good use of time. It makes us question how we use our commuting time. It makes us think more carefully about when we are feeling energized to do our best work.

A useful thought exercise is to treat work as forty one-hour blocks spread across a week. You might choose to use up a couple of those blocks on a Saturday morning working on something that's been hanging over you for a while. The quid pro quo for that might be to leave the office early on Wednesday to see the early showing of a movie.

Or consider adopting the technique advocated by Tony Schwartz. Schwartz, a successful author, used his own experience of exhaustion as motivation to create an organization intent on creating a revolution in the workplace. His Energy Project suggests that we should shift from a focus on longer working hours to an understanding of how to manage our bursts of energy. Most people work best in ninety-minute energy cycles.[12] Getting ourselves ready to maximize the output of each cycle is the best way to get the most from our work.

You may have heard of the vast social experiment in Sweden in which the working day for a large number of public sector workers was reduced to six hours—with no pay cut. (Those colleagues who were left on an eight-hour day as a control group must have felt that they had been professionally trolled—imagine the daily infuriation of a colleague packing up and heading home two hours early "for the experiment.") For those fortunate enough to be included in the experimental group, there was a fall in absenteeism, improved health, and increased productivity. One participant described the experience to the *New York Times* as "a life changer." Another summarized what happens when you are asked to do a job in less time: "Simply put, we work more efficiently."[13]

For most of us, a six-hour day is well beyond our grasp. But at the very least we should all aim to do forty (or fewer) energized, focused hours of work per week. And no more.

What You Can Do Next:

» Stop celebrating overwork. Working in concentrated bursts allows you to achieve just as much but leaves you plenty of scope to relax, think, and be creative.

» Discipline yourself to leave work on time unless there's something so pressing that you can't leave it until the next day—and encourage your colleagues to do the same.

» Split work into one-hour chunks. If you take on something extra, ask yourself what you are prepared to stop doing as a trade-off.

» Remember that, at best, working longer dilutes energy, creativity, and imagination. At worst, it leads to exhaustion and burnout.

Recharge 6

Overthrow the Evil Mill Owner Who Lives Inside You

Our model of life goes something like this. First we go to school, where there are rules for everything: get in on time; show up for lessons; get your work done. Then, if we choose to go to college, we move briefly into a parallel universe where the previous rules don't apply: it would be good if you could be here by 11 a.m., but don't sweat it; your essay's two days late, but don't worry about it. And then, as we move into the world of work, we're back to the old rules: get in by 9 a.m.; deal with your email; get to meetings on time.

The problem is that we so quickly buy into this. Have you ever found yourself looking across your office and wondering, "Where is everyone?" Even though we know that people are probably getting their work done, we all revert to the norms of school and discipline. People need to be in front of us to convince us they are working.

For me, the best description of this mind-set came from the inspiring Dan Kieran. Kieran is a successful author and the founder of a crowdfunded publishing platform, Unbound. He's created a brilliant, creative culture infused with audacious ideas and a preparedness to take risks. Yet, as he confessed to me, he struggles to free himself of a deep-rooted prejudice: "I hate myself for it," he confided, "but there's no doubt I have an 'inner eighteenth-century mill owner.'" If the office seems quiet and empty, he rears his head and asks, "Where is everyone?" And yet, as he is the first to admit, "to run a company people actually want to work for you have to fight off the mill owner instinct and focus on what they deliver instead."

The mill owner wants us to clock in and out. The mill owner wants us working at our desk, not chatting about last night's TV. Kieran is completely right. Not only is the mill owner real, but he's deep inside us and very hard to get rid of. He's like a sour-tongued figure in the back of a movie scene, just sliding out of view with a catty barb.

The Results-Only Work Environment (ROWE) offers a different way of doing things. Pioneered by Cali Ressler and Jody Thompson, and swiftly adopted by big companies such as Gap and Best Buy, ROWE involves setting clear short-term goals for teams—and then leaving them to get on with their jobs in any way they want. ROWE people don't have to keep any particular office hours. In fact, they don't need to come to the office at all. Meetings are held only if people want to come to them. In many ways ROWE is to work what college education is to school: get your work done and no one will really care how you did it. It's the end of "presenteeism"—the way we assess whether someone is working by whether or not they are at their desk.

The ROWE creators explain that before a company can achieve the enlightened state of being focused on results rather than employee presence, it needs to perform a workplace cleansing. This is where the office is purged of "sludge," which they describe as "the negative commentary that occurs naturally in a workplace and is based on outdated beliefs about time and work." In other words, it's much like the toxic opinions of our inner mill owner.

Obviously, such an approach isn't right for every employment sector. Ultimately, it's best suited to highly individualized work, in which the need for collaboration or physical presence (as, for example, on a shop floor) isn't a constant. But if people do work alone, or if some aspects of their job are wholly within their own control, then it's a perfect way to maximize autonomy. A former international correspondent of a respected newspaper described to me how when she was based alone in a European capital she would wander the city, consuming the place, understanding what was going on by flitting into cafés, chatting with people, and interviewing influencers, before quietly filing a piece of informed copy several times a week. Then she returned home. She was given a desk in the corner of the office next to the bathroom. If she wasn't in by 9 a.m. her boss asked her to explain what she was going to do to turn her performance around. She'd gone from a college style of working back to a school approach, and the result was less job satisfaction—and lower-quality journalism, too. Within six months, she'd quit the newspaper she loved. It's worth bearing in mind, though, that the main home for ROWE, Best Buy, abolished the system in 2013 because it didn't think it was getting the best out of its teams. "This [system] was based on the premise that the right leadership style is always delegation," the CEO of Best Buy told an interviewer, hinting that because all work had been devolved to empowered individuals, teams were working less closely together.[1]

Clearly, there's a balance to be struck here. ROWE might or might not work for you, or you may decide that some sort of halfway measure is best. But the basic principle behind it is a powerful one, if only because it's an essential counterbalance to our inner eighteenth-century mill owner. If you find yourself piping up "Half day?" to someone wandering in at 9:30, that's a warning sign. If you know that Phil needs to pick up his kids on Wednesday afternoon, but find yourself thinking "Phil's taking advantage again" as the poor guy furtively tries to slide out of the office unnoticed at 4 p.m., you need to do something about it.

It's not just that mill owners are bad for morale or that they can get in the way of people doing their best work. They also make us focus on the wrong end of the productivity equation. The author Daniel Pink told me of an instance of this involving a former governor of New Jersey, Chris Christie. Christie is a product of the global political movement that has allowed plain-looking figures volubly espousing "common sense" to seize positions of power. Back in 2016, a bipartisan state bill had been drawn up—after considerable research—that mandated a daily twenty-minute break for New Jersey schoolchildren under the age of eleven. The evidence was clear: children's attention (and therefore their capacity to learn) was measurably enhanced by the opportunity to refresh themselves in a break. Then Christie waded in, giving his best mill owner swagger. "That was a stupid bill," he declared and vetoed it.[2]

The trouble is that despite all the evidence and science in the world, we often find ourselves in front of the Chris Christies of this world. They blurt out something about speaking common sense, something about being against "trendy ideas." It's normally at this stage that they look for boorish laughter from the men in the room.

We'll make work better only if we prevail over the mill owners. And that includes the one inside all of us.[3]

What You Can Do Next:

» Focus on what you (and your colleagues) have committed to achieving rather than on how you are doing it.

» If you think what you or your colleagues are achieving isn't enough, address that concern rather than simply suggesting more work.

» Ban jokes about people taking half days or sleeping in. I have found a simple statement of intent helps: "We never, ever say 'Half day!' or joke about someone sleeping in." It takes the pressure off people.

» Try a "de-sludging session" in which team members can discuss times they've felt the burden of colleagues' catty comments.

Recharge 7

Turn Off Your Notifications

Cortisol sometimes gets bad press. While the hormone is certainly associated with stress—both psychological and physical stress—its main job is simply to help inject more energy to the body. Cortisol is like the accelerator pedal in a car.[1] In small doses it makes us more attentive, more focused. The danger comes when we have our foot flat on the accelerator pedal. It's been suggested by a German team led by Clemens Kirschbaum, for example, that a flood of cortisol to the brain hinders our powers of recall.[2] Why this should be the case is still not fully understood, but it would appear to have something to do with the effect stress hormones have on the hippocampus. Scientists understand that the hippocampus and the amygdala act together to store stressful experiences but that they seem to register them rather than to record them in vivid detail. The brain wants to know that you were scared that time you saw a snake—but it doesn't want you to relive the anxiety of the moment.

Of course, there are times when the pressure of the moment leads to extraordinary feats of human achievement. The psychologist Teresa Amabile cites the example of the Apollo 13 space mission, during which, following an onboard explosion, a team at

Mission Control in Florida had to work around the clock to come up with a way for the astronauts to repair the damaged air filtration system using only the limited materials they had on hand in the space vessel.[3] Ultimately their ingenious solutions—including repurposing the cover of an instruction manual—saved the mission and the astronauts' lives. But Amabile's overall findings are that such episodes are the exception rather than the norm. Certainly, after crunching data from the diary reflections of people in rather less unusual situations than astronauts—office workers—her conclusion was that in most circumstances creativity and stress are enemies of each other. They cannot comfortably coexist. In her words, "When creativity is under the gun, it usually ends up getting killed."

Evidence for this is both consistent and widespread. Take the performance of home teams in ice hockey games or soccer ties.

How can it be that a game played at home has a "home advantage"—in which the host side of a tie is more likely to win? If the only factor determining the result in a game were the capability of the players, home and away records would be much the same. But that's not the case: home teams consistently win 60 percent of their games.[4] Why? Because a large, supportive crowd reduces the stress levels of team members and enhances their ability to play well and creatively. A close study in ice hockey revealed that the key ingredient is home supporter crowd density—a tightly packed, noisy home crowd effectively acts as an additional team member.[5]

It's the same story in the arts. I've already touched on the challenges faced by Julian Casablancas of the Strokes as his band made its second album (see p. 6). This "difficult second album" syndrome is sometimes styled the "sophomore slump." Second albums by

Sam Smith, Duffy, and MGMT in recent years have followed critical acclaim with creative disappointment.

And it isn't exclusive to music. Authors who received international acclaim for their first novels have often struggled to live up to their own high standards—and found themselves in endless prevarication about releasing their work. It took Donna Tartt ten years between her first novel, *The Secret History*, and her second, *The Little Friend*. Joseph Heller went thirteen years from the publication of *Catch-22* until his second attempt, *Something Happened*. J. D. Salinger was never able to muster the courage to publish a second novel, despite reports suggesting he completed at least five between the 1951 publication of *The Catcher in the Rye* and his death in 2010.[6]

When asked to be creative, we can find stress debilitating—our brain struggles to differentiate between different sorts of mental anxiety. "The most concrete thing that neuroscience tells us is that when the fear system of the brain is active, exploratory activity and risk-taking are turned off," says neuroscientist Gregory Berns.[7]

Stress can also cause us to make false judgments about what we're really achieving. "Although time pressure may drive people to work more and get more done, and may even make them *feel* more creative," Teresa Amabile says, "it actually causes them, in general, to think less creatively."[8] In the course of her research on office workers, she discovered that once people felt pressure, a growing gap opened up between how they thought they were performing and what their observable performance was: "In their assessments of their own creativity each day, the participants in our study generally perceived themselves as having been *more* creative when time pressure was high. Sadly, their diaries gave the lie to those self-assessments. There was clearly less and less creative thinking in evidence as time pressure increased."[9]

Thanks to the work of Jaak Panksepp, we also now have some understanding of the longer-term effects of stress on creativity. Panksepp, who was a scientist at Washington State University, dedicated his life's work to understanding the brains of rats and proving that his beloved rodents exhibited many of the thought patterns—and emotions—to be found in other mammals, including humans. (He noted, for example, that rats can laugh when you tickle them.)[10] In the course of his research he categorized the functioning of the mammalian brain into seven emotional command systems, each relating to a particular function in human cognition. His conviction was that each of these—seeking, rage, fear, lust, care, panic/grief, and play—was derived not from the cerebral cortex, the area of the brain associated with complex thought, as was previously believed, but from the amygdala and the hypothalamus. In other words, these emotions are hardwired into our instinctive behavior and so we have little conscious control over them.

In the case of rats, Panksepp found that the thrill of searching was often more potent than the satisfaction of achieving something. They'd stop feeding when they were full, but they never seemed to tire of exploring. In Panksepp's opinion, each rat's brain was "an exploratory system; it was about generating expectancies, seeking rewards."[11] It fulfilled the neuroscientist Sophie Scott's view of the brain as "a novelty-seeking machine."[12] Panksepp's rats displayed an innate desire to explore new places, to try new things, to test openings—what Panksepp characterized as seeking and play systems. In human terms, those seeking and play systems are what you or I might call creativity.

Or that's the case until fear is triggered. When Panksepp

placed cat hair among his rat subjects, they were immediately terrified, even though they had never previously encountered real-life cats: it was a primal response (and one that has been observed in rats as young as eighteen days of age). And once the rats were scared, they stopped creative play and exploration completely.[13] What's more, they didn't return to their creative play for three to five days after the cat hair had been removed; even though the cage had been thoroughly cleaned, the trauma of stress persisted in their bodies. With humans, this delay is what Teresa Amabile has described as "pressure hangover." With only the memory of their former anxiety, the rats were experiencing their own pressure hangover.

And this brings me to the real subject of this Recharge: smartphones. According to Professor Tom Jackson at Loughborough University in Leicestershire, England, each of us experiences an average of ninety-six email interruptions in an eight-hour day. Many of those messages will prompt an injection of stress-inducing cortisol into our bloodstreams.[14] Scientists tell us that almost half of all people who check their work email outside of work hours exhibit signs of high stress levels.[15]

And, in turn, stress hampers creativity. "Each email you receive adds another task and at the end of the day you're very fatigued. We see the creativity and productivity of staff depleted by the end of the day," Professor Jackson told the *Guardian*.[16]

It goes without saying that smartphones are not the only source of stress in today's workplace and that we can't ignore them altogether. But how about if we lessened their impact just a little bit? How about if we turned off all alerts on our phones?

It might seem pretty silly to suggest that taking the email number icon off your home screen can make you happier, but it's one of the single best (and easiest) things that any of us can do.[17]

The problem is that the number tugs at your sleeve, begging you to have a quick peek at what fresh hell is awaiting your attention. It's not just an irritant. Some researchers have gone so far as to say that phone notifications cause us to demonstrate the symptoms of attention deficit hyperactivity disorder (ADHD).[18] They also point out that the more we switch our attention from the task at hand to the latest notification, the less mental processing we apply to each. It's an instance of the "switching costs" I mentioned earlier (see Recharge 1). As one expert put it, "The main working memory tasks require attention and . . . memory traces decay as soon as attention is switched away."[19]

Contrary to what any of us might claim (or even believe), our working memory can properly process only one thing at a time. Multitasking is a bit of myth, particularly among those people who believe they're very good at it: in one experiment that involved getting people to talk while they were driving, it was precisely the people who were most confident about their ability to do both who were most wrong (showing the biggest difference between their perceived skill and their actual performance).[20] If we want to get more done, we need to focus on one thing at a time. I mentioned the power of interruptions to spark creative thought, but focus is almost a superpower that takes us to deeper levels of thinking and to developing ideas into something more fully formed.

A while back, Telefonica Research and Carnegie Mellon University collaborated on a project to see what the impact on people's well-being would be if they turned off all their phone notifications for a week.[21] Dubbed the "*Do Not Disturb* Challenge," it hit a brick wall almost immediately. Martin Pielot from Telefonica explained, "We couldn't recruit anybody to take part. We just got empty, horrified stares. And so eventually we backed down to 24 hours."[22]

Interestingly, the twenty-four-hour challenge proved much more fruitful. We're constantly reminded that it takes us sixty days to form a habit, yet the researchers involved in the project found that half of the volunteers who made this change *for a single day* still hadn't gone back to their stress-inducing old ways two years later.[23] Many reported an improvement in productivity: it was "easier to concentrate, especially when working on the desktop [computer]," said one.

For Anna Cox, a professor of human-computer interaction at University College London, such a comparatively small shift in the way we operate is an example of a "microboundary" at work.[24] Microboundaries are strategies people can put in place to make technology work better for them—to make them feel they have control again. "People check social media all the time without even thinking just because it's right there on your phone," Cox told *New Scientist* magazine. "Anything that makes that just a little bit harder can help you avoid the bad habit."[25] Other microboundaries might be deleting an email app when we go on holiday or enabling Do not disturb mode while eating.

We should all consider removing all the notifications from our email. Off desktop, off mobile. Set up your email specifically so that you can see how many messages you have only when you open the application. People who have done it tell me about the sense of space it gives them. "I got all the way to work before I thought about email," said one. "I just got into my document and didn't think to check email till much later," another confessed with surprise. Let people know they can always reach you immediately by phone if they need to. But otherwise, get to things only when you're ready to.

We should remind ourselves that turning off notifications allows us to be more energized and creative when we are working.

Conversely, while opting to clear our email the moment messages arrive may cause a momentary sense of achievement, if they cause a sense of stress they may reduce our effectiveness rather than increase it.

===

What You Can Do Next:

» Reduce stress by giving yourself restorative breaks from the demands work imposes on your mind and your body. As in sports games, as with musicians, as with novelists, as with rats smelling cat hair—we cannot be creative when we are stressed.

» Turn off notifications on your phone. Keep a before-and-after log so you can assess how things have changed.

===

Recharge 8

Go to Lunch

Laura Archer, an events manager at a renowned museum, had a lot on her plate. Responsible for all the institution's fund-raising events, she was under constant pressure to come up with new ways to attract partnerships with other arts organizations or with metropolitan businesses. At the same time, she needed to devise schemes to boost museum membership to help cover the running costs of a major institution.

So, like most of us when the heat is turned up, and when we're worried that we're not quite coping, she started working a little more. It seemed the logical thing to do if she was to deliver projects on tight deadlines and show her colleagues that she was pulling her weight. And it was her lunch break that, bit by bit, yielded her the extra time she felt she needed.

The effect was disastrous, as Archer recalled in her blog (and book) *Gone for Lunch* and in a subsequent conversation with me. "I don't think I noticed the positives of taking a lunch break other than the fact that I really enjoyed them," she told me. "It was when the lunch break was then denied, due to a heavy workload, that I noticed how much of an effect it had on me. I basically just crashed. My mood crashed. My energy crashed. My attitude towards my job crashed. My diet crashed. If I didn't leave my desk all day I would really crave a takeout or a ready meal at night. Something that was easy or comfort food-y. Something that probably wasn't very good for me. With that I'd probably want a glass of wine, whether at home or going to meet friends straight away—you just seek that perk that gets you going again. Also caffeine. I never normally drink coffee, but I was drinking one to two coffees a day—which was a lot for me. And with that you crave sugar."

The effects multiplied: "It all just got really bad. I just felt really heavy. By the time it got to the weekend I'd had such an unhealthy week in terms of energy and diet I just wanted a really long lie-in on the Saturday morning. And then you want to feel excited and energetic so you go out and get drunk on the Saturday night. Then you have a long lie-in on the Sunday. Then you're exhausted by the end of the weekend, and not ready for the week that's about to begin. You know it's going to be a whole other cycle of the same thing."[1]

Archer is hardly unique. Office workers across the United States have become increasingly familiar with the practice of eating *al desko*, pecking their way through their email with a sandwich in the other hand. Surveys suggest that only one-fifth of workers report feeling able to regularly take a lunch break, many of them citing pressure from their managers as their reason to skip the rest.[2]

All the evidence shows, though, that this is a terrible way to work and live. The symptoms that Archer experienced—fatigue and exhaustion, not to mention a craving for unhealthy food and drink—are common to many people who resort to skipping lunch. And there's more to it than the general feeling of tiredness that comes with overwork. Researchers have found that people find what the experts term "self-regulation" wearing. Given free rein to do what we want, we'll lie on the sofa, having donned those disgusting tracksuit bottoms that we find so comfortable—and we'll feel rested at the end of it all. Asked to spend a long weekend with our partner's parents, however, where we have to moderate our words and body language, and feign interest, our mojo rapidly dwindles. This is self-regulation. Self-regulation also has an impact with lunch breaks. If we feel compelled to forgo lunch, researchers have found, we invariably suffer mental and physical exhaustion because we're doing something we don't really want to do.[3]

The lingering tiredness that Laura Archer talked about deserves closer inspection. All of us have something of a *mental* energy tank, which even an hour's physical activity (say, working out at the gym) can help refill. Without that necessary boost, tiredness multiplies. The psychologists Emily Hunter and Cindy Wu have recently established a correlation between lunch-skipping and weekend exhaustion (much in the way Archer felt that working through lunch was ruining her Saturday night).[4] Theo Meijman and Gijsbertus Mulder have suggested that it even leads to sleep disturbance.[5] Maybe your justification for taking a lunch break should be that you won't ruin your weekend with your family and friends.

And, of course, it's our output in the period that immediately follows lunch break that suffers if we skip it. The record of afternoon performance is already poor. Whether or not we take a break, our judgments are noticeably less charitable and our decisions measurably worse than they are in the mornings. So, as Daniel Pink noted in his 2018 book *When*, judges tend to hand down harsher sentences after lunch and doctors tend to make less accurate diagnoses.[6] At Duke University Medical Center in North Carolina, a survey found that the probability of something going medically awry was four times higher at 4 p.m. (when it was 4.2 percent) than at 9 a.m. And that's regardless of whether people were taking lunch breaks or not. Once no lunch break is factored in, the general picture will be much worse.

This is where the restorative power of breaks comes in: we can mitigate the problem of afternoon tiredness, and rebalance ourselves, if we have a pause. Daniel Pink shares countless examples of the advantages of adapting our demand to the "chronobiology" of our bodies. In Denmark, for instance, it was found that children given a break before an afternoon exam were able to more than compensate for the deterioration normally noted in their afternoon performance. Harvard's Francesca Gino has shown that while scores in school tests typically decline over the course of the day (tragically, this is particularly pronounced for the least able kids), adding in a break stops the decline. In fact, Gino says, "If there were a break after every hour, test scores would actually improve over the course of the day."[7]

Two necessary changes to our working habits flow from this. First, we should carry out important activities before lunch. Our minds are freshest then and most able to power through complex cognitive challenges. Second, we should stop thinking that we're going to get more done by not taking a break. I suspect it's something that we all instinctively know, but we hope the rule doesn't apply to us. Faced with the choice of dealing with all our email over a working lunch or going for a walk and returning to all our messages plus another thirty new ones, the decision seems irrational in the extreme. Why would any of us elect to not nail the email? Even if we do pay for it in lost productivity in the afternoon.

But before you shrug and say, "Maybe, but it's not for me," consider Laura's description of the transformative power of a lunch break. "You get a second wind," she told me. "You return to your desk as fresh as you are in the morning because you've given your mind a break; you've given your body a break. By the time you get to the weekend you look back at your week and think, 'Wow, this is the week that I spent three days in art galleries, seeing these exhibitions that I wanted to see.'" "The nicest thing," she concluded, "is that I look back and my year is dotted with color and creativity. I've added all of the time that your lunch break adds up to; it's the equivalent of thirty days of annual leave."

Interestingly, what we actually *do* during our lunch breaks can also contribute to our happiness. This might make introverts squirm, but scientists at Oxford University have found that always eating alone rather than with others is the single biggest contributing factor to an overall sense of unhappiness (only having pre-existing mental illness scored worse in their research).[8] The lead researcher, Professor Robin Dunbar, explained why: "The kinds of things that you do around the table with other people are very good at triggering the endorphin system, which is part of the brain's pain-management system. Endorphins are opioids; they are chemically related to morphine—they are produced by the brain and give you an opiate high. That's what you get when you do all this social stuff." Spending a couple of lunch breaks a week sitting with colleagues can boost your happiness.

And how many colleagues you end up sitting with can be significant, too. As Ben Waber from Humanyze—whose sociometric badges help measure the interactions that take place in offices—explains, the size of the lunch tables in an office can have a direct impact on the levels of communication in that office. "In one company," he says, "we saw that by far the most productive people there were eating lunch with eleven other people and sometimes it was ten, or nine other people [these people's performance was a "double digit percentage higher"]. By far the least productive people there were always eating lunch in groups of three other people. Sometimes it was two." Intrigued, Waber and his colleagues took a closer look at the layout of the cafeteria. "By one set of doors all the tables had twelve seats. By the other set of doors all the tables had four seats. What would happen is, you wouldn't go to lunch with eleven other people. You would sit down at the table. Other people would sit next to you and you'd start talking to them. And later in the week you were significantly more likely to speak with someone if you had lunch with them." The people who used this particular cafeteria were software developers. The fact that they were now chatting with one another directly improved the quality of their work.[9] It's a case history that clearly has wide implications for all types of businesses.

There is, however, a caveat that needs to be made. Yes, chatting with other people at lunch can help lubricate the channels of communication in your office, but this is not something that can be enforced. It has to happen naturally. A team of researchers led by John Trougakos from the University of Toronto found that the moment workers felt they had to socialize in a particular way at lunch, they ended up stressed. Even a team lunch can sap our energy if it's something we have to do. An hour of listening to our boss tell us about his new car can be more exhausting than sitting at our desk doing email. Or, as John Trougakos put it, enforced lunch-break social activities "result in more fatigue as these activities would likely require employees to regulate their behavior."[10]

Laura Archer found that the best way to bring autonomy to her lunch breaks was to plan them. After all, few colleagues will attempt to schedule a lunchtime meeting on a Tuesday if they see that you're already booked for your weekly yoga class. By bringing autonomy and planning to your lunch, you'll help refresh yourself to do your best work in your afternoons.

It's time to reclaim your lunch!

What You Can Do Next:

» Schedule breaks. Planning something to do during a lunch
   break takes a moment but can force a change of scene. Laura
   Archer found that even when she accomplished only one or
   two breaks a week, it helped mitigate the sense of stress that
   hung over her.

» Bring variety to your breaks. Go to lunch (with people you
   like), sit in the park, go for a walk, book yourself into an
   exercise class. Try scheduling time for something that's been
   sitting on your personal to-do list for a while (writing a letter,
   phoning your grandparents).

» Decline meeting requests that impinge on your lunch break.
   Politely ask the organizer to find another time. Even a gentle
   decline a few times can make the worst-offending meeting
   schedulers think again about when they should hold their
   meetings.

Recharge 9

Define
Your Norms

What if someone told you the way to love your job again was to do it a bit less? To go on a break from it? To push it away—just a little— from your life? That's what I'm going to suggest here. But first, let's go to Scandinavia.

Very few people outside Sweden have heard of Birgitta Lundblad, Elisabeth Oldgren, Kristin Ehnmark, and Sven Säfström. They were four bank workers who in 1973 were taken hostage in their Kreditbanken office. Most of us, however, are familiar with happened to them during their six days in captivity. Much to the surprise of hostage negotiators, they developed a bond with their captors. They might have been expected to exhibit rage or fear. Instead, when offered small acts of kindness (as trivial as permission to use the bathroom or being given food) they expressed gratitude to the people threatening their lives (people who terrified them with nooses and dynamite), and by the end of the ordeal they felt sympathetic to them, even to the extent of refusing to testify in court against them. Their unexpected response has become known as the "Stockholm syndrome."[1]

Many of us find ourselves experiencing a kind of Stockholm

syndrome at work, albeit one without an obvious hostage taker. Demands flood in from all quarters—not just from our manager or the boss of the company but also from other colleagues and from clients or customers outside the business—and our response is not frustration or rage but quiet resignation. The psychologist Martin Seligman has labeled this condition "learned helplessness."[2] We become so used to what is being thrown at us that we end up accepting it.

Seligman discovered the condition wholly by accident back in 1965 while pursuing research on depression. His initial experiment, a version of the "classical conditioning" experiment made famous by Pavlov (dog/bell/food), involved ringing a bell and then giving dogs an electric shock. Sure enough, the dogs soon associated the ringing of the bell with the shock that followed. But it was a subsequent refinement of the experiment that led to the theory of learned helplessness. Now dogs were put into a crate that was split into two, one half containing a floor that transmitted an electric shock, the other half with a normal floor. The dogs could, if they wished, jump from one half to the other, and indeed that is exactly what some dogs did when they found themselves in the half that generated a shock. However, dogs that had already experienced the earlier experiment, in which the shocks had come randomly, chose to lie down when they heard the bell. They had come to assume that nothing they did could improve things. They opted, quite simply, to give up.

Learned helplessness pervades the modern workplace. We're overwhelmed with demands and expectations placed on us by others, but we have come to accept it all because we assume that's the way it is and has to be. There is no escape from the electrified floor.

Harvard ethnographer Leslie Perlow discovered this for herself in the course of her research on the nature of productive work. Her instincts told her that constant connectivity outside the workplace—email at the dinner table, for example—harms personal relationships and is far less genuinely productive than we tend or like to think. Yet whenever she talked to the engineers or management consultants involved in her study, she was almost invariably told that she didn't understand the nuances of their situation and that things were as they were because that was how they had to be. "Each of these groups was convinced their way was the only way if they were going to be competitive," she said.[3]

Intrigued by this passive acceptance of constant connectivity, Perlow decided to study a group whose work had "completely infiltrated life"—her reasoning being the Sinatra-esque "if you could change it there, you could change it anywhere."[4] The group she chose were executives at the Boston Consulting Group. These were people who were emphatic that their clients expected care and attention 24/7 and that queries and demands could come in at any hour of the day or night. They believed it was essential to put in long and exhausting hours at work and that it was similarly essential to spend hours on email even when away from the office. Perlow estimated that each individual was spending around twenty to twenty-five hours per week working on email on their phones outside office hours, and that there was an expectation they would respond to an incoming email within an hour.

Perlow's first step was a modest one. She wanted to see if each member of the group could be persuaded to spend one night a week away from email. She made it clear, however, that the whole team had to respect this. If someone were to work on email on their designated night off, the whole test would fail. This was a difficult challenge for the people of BCG, who were used to an all-hands approach whenever an emergency arose.

Sure enough, an emergency did arise. Perlow was pleased to see, though, that the team responded to this with resolve and commitment to their pledges. They assured the designated night-off person that she was excused. "It's your night off—don't worry: we can cover for you!" they told her.

But it was the more general effect of such moments that delivered the real surprise. Once people had to take turns, the team as a whole started to collaborate more effectively in all sorts of ways. They began asking permission from the group for certain important nights off. They shared more about their personal circumstances and home lives. What's more, taking a total break (and let's remember this was just a single evening, albeit among exhausted workers) had a remarkably reenergizing effect. One participant in the study told Perlow, "My project manager pushed me out of the office to make sure I took the time off even though it was a busy week. I came back really refreshed."[5] According to Perlow, "Time-off teams reported higher job satisfaction, greater likelihood that they could imagine a long-term career at the firm, and higher satisfaction with work/life balance." It's almost as if we start to think bad things about the jobs we love when we're at our lowest. Our most worn-out selves have thoughts that we wouldn't agree with when we're at our freshest best.

With this under her belt, Perlow went on to an even more ambitious experiment with the Boston Consulting Group: she suggested that the consultants try introducing a scheme whereby they took turns unplugging from the Matrix and being completely uncontactable for an entire day. No phone, text, email, instant chat, nothing. Not surprisingly, her proposal was met with considerable alarm. "At first, the team resisted the experiment," she recalled. "The partner in charge, who had been very supportive of the basic idea, was suddenly nervous about having to tell her client that each member of her team would be off one day a week."[6]

But strangely, the outcome of the unconnected day was that the consultants all fell in love with their work again. Communication between team members became more "intentional"; colleagues felt more deeply connected rather than less. Perlow said that the biggest revelation of the experiment was that the team ended up convinced they had "a better product delivered to the client."

What is intentional communication? To find out, I spoke with Deborah Rippol, who at the time was responsible for finding new talent for the software company Buffer. Buffer is a fascinating organization to look at when thinking about the way we'll work in the future. I'm not sure it has all the answers, but it's trying its best to ask all the right questions. Way back when, faced with visa challenges for one of their founders, Buffer abandoned its San Francisco office and the team started working remotely around the world. The founders would hop from place to place, their laptop and a Wi-Fi connection their only essentials. That fleet-footed response to the company's first challenge became rooted in the staff's psyches—and its legacy stayed with them even when they had resolved the challenges that had faced them and reopened a California base.

Rippol told me what the seventy-strong workforce at Buffer looked like: "We have people in forty cities, in sixteen different countries and eleven time zones." And she explained how they worked together: "What we want is for teammates to be happy wherever they are. This means everyone needs to feel they have the ability to reach decisions and the opportunity to collaborate effectively with others. And for that, synchronous communication doesn't quite work well. If you have a cluster of people who are in the New York time zone, you'd have the ability to communicate on Slack. A real-time back-and-forth. And then a decision is made. But then France and Singapore wake up and they've not had their say in what's going on."

Synchronous communication is coordinated by time: the constant exchange of instant messages. The result is that we feel as though we have to stay up to speed on a dialogue being conducted via lots of different mediums at once. Asynchronous communication may not work if a quick answer is required, but if there is an agreed deadline it can lead to more thoughtful and considered decision making. People take turns responding at a time that suits them. It pushes them away from urgency and immediacy and toward reflective consideration. "One of Buffer's values is 'take time to reflect,'" Deborah Rippol told me. "Split across so many time zones it makes it hard for the company to develop norms of communication that are more effective and efficient. We try to avoid emails like 'What are your thoughts on this?' Open-ended questions like that, if you have an eight-hour or twelve-hour time difference, don't work. You have to be more specific about your question in order for them to answer it."

Taking turns, then, rather than everyone constantly piling in, offers huge potential benefits. If you're not commenting all the time, your interventions, when they do come, will have more impact. If you're relying on other members of the team to pick up the slack when you're not there, you'll grow to trust them more and collaborate with them better. And you'll feel happier and more rested, too.

What You Can Do Next:

» Don't assume that your work culture is inevitable.

» Agree with your team on when people can go off-grid, and stick to what you've agreed.

Recharge 10

Have a Digital Sabbath

We've all seen how memes sweep the world, taking hold and embedding themselves in popular culture within days. The Ice Bucket Challenge seemed, almost overnight, to reach right into the Facebook world and beyond. The Mannequin Challenge (people standing as though frozen in ice as a camera passes among them) even reached your aunt. These are viral ideas that spread themselves with urgency and excitement.

I'll accept that working hard isn't a *viral* idea, but I want you to show you that it's at least a little bit *fungal*.[1] It spreads not through excitement but via contagion. When researchers from Microsoft looked at the impact the out-of-hours working habits of bosses had on their colleagues, they found that for every hour the bosses put in doing visible work outside normal hours (emailing on a Sunday or weekday evening), their direct reports would each clock up twenty minutes. And if a boss chose to start clearing her inbox on a Sunday, there was clear evidence that a fungal spore landed in employees' laps and they, too, got to work. The bosses' off-hours work, in other words, became a fungal infection.[2]

This contagion spreads in other ways, too. If, for instance, your boss pulls out his laptop and starts emailing during a meeting, you are twice as likely to become a meeting multitasker yourself. We ape what our bosses do.

As I argued in Recharge 9, taking a pause from the conveyor belt of meetings, email, and connectivity can have the effect of mentally renewing us. The ethnographer Leslie Perlow rightly observed that when we're in a constantly connected environment we often feel helpless when it comes to disconnecting ourselves from the incoming traffic of messages. Yet disconnecting can have the effect of making the expectations on us feel less claustrophobic. It also reduces our anxiety: as I mentioned before, half of all workers who check their email outside work hours show signs of being highly stressed. The cortisol that washes through our bloodstreams (see Recharge 7) to give us an energy surge also creates a mental state similar to that of animals on the savanna when they see a predator. We may think that we're checking our email to *avoid being stressed* about work, but our body doesn't know that. It thinks we're triggering an injection of cortisol because there's a danger lurking.

The medium-term effect of cortisol surging through the body is tiredness and exhaustion. It's like the low ebb that follows a hit of caffeine. A break, however, allows us to recover our energy, attention, memory span, and creativity.

And that's why weekends are so important. John Pencavel's research on productivity that I explored in Recharge 5 found that workers produced more in a forty-eight-hour week with Sunday off than they did in a fifty-six-hour week working on the Sabbath. By taking a break, workers truly were more productive.

It's perhaps worth dwelling on productivity for a moment because it's become something of an obsession—and a concern—in this modern high-tech age. One of the great enigmas of the past couple of decades is that we've made unprecedented technological advances and yet we don't seem to be measurably achieving more. It's something the economic historian Paul David has explored in some depth. His view, which I find very compelling, is that, quite simply, we haven't quite worked out what to do with what is now available to us. He offers an analogy between the arrival of high-tech and the arrival of the electric motor. Electric motors represented a huge advance over the steam engines they supplanted. They were smaller and more precise, and they could be operated by lone individuals. Yet it took a while for industrial practices to adapt to what they were capable of; there was a time and a learning lag.

The challenge for us is that we haven't yet learned how to use the tools that modern innovation has given us. We think we're being immensely productive when we reduce our vast inbox down to twenty or thirty email messages. Yet in fact all we've done is catch up with responding to conversational requests from colleagues. We're not using our time productively, even though we think we're devoting more of it to our work. If, on the other hand, we were to stop worrying about busyness, recharge our brains, and focus on what really matters—the Deep Work that I described in Recharge 1—we'd actually achieve much more. As the Deep Work champion Cal Newport put it to me, "The modern work environment is actively hostile to Deep Work. I want to add the caveat that I think this is going to be in the long term a sort of footnote in the evolution of knowledge work. In other words I think the way that we're approaching knowledge work we're going to look back at in maybe fifteen years from now and say that was disastrously unproductive."[3]

Twenty years ago, Erik Brynjolfsson and Lorin Hitt observed

that businesses that were benefiting most from computerization hadn't simply harnessed bytes to an existing work machine—they'd reinvented themselves: they'd taken themselves apart and put themselves back together again.[4] In the process, they'd changed their structures and become more decentralized. In fact, they'd mirrored what management thinker Peter Drucker had outlined in 1988 when he talked about the "coming of the new organization." The winners of the future, Drucker said, would be technology-rich firms that shift toward "flatter, less hierarchical organizations where highly skilled workers take on increasing levels of decision-making responsibility."[5] He didn't say anything about answering more email or working on weekends.

And this is where today's company leaders come in. Instead of patting themselves on the back for being so visibly busy, they should be encouraging a culture in which productive Deep Work, not email sending, is promoted. They should be establishing the norm of a "no-fly zone" for email over the weekend on the grounds that this is when the organization recharges its collective energy and creativity. Few things are as passively destructive as colleagues emailing on a Sunday morning—not only do they harm the creativity and energy of sender and recipient; they also fungally spread the Sunday email culture. Firms can paint corporate values on a wall, they can espouse positive cultures . . . but if they permit weekend emailing, they are undermining their fridge magnet philosophy.

Of course, I completely understand why people feel the need to email outside office hours. It allows them to avoid the guilt that an unanswered email so easily causes. It gives them a brief sense of relief that they're not falling behind. And because I believe that we should all have the autonomy to work in the way that we believe best suits us, I certainly wouldn't advocate—as some people have suggested and some countries have introduced—a regime in which inboxes are unavailable to people outside working hours. But what people do need to bear in mind is that if they choose to send an email on the weekend, they are destroying someone else's autonomy. They therefore need to think very carefully before they push the Send button.

The best balance to arrive at is a norm in which routine weekend email traffic is discouraged, but with a well-understood way to deal with the emergencies that will inevitably crop up. This might take the form of a group text, or possibly a phone call. There will be situations for all of us where we need to be alerted to something of importance that has happened, perhaps something that involves the welfare of one of our colleagues. But for the rest of us, a good working environment has a simple rule: no weekend email. And if people breach that guiding principle, we need to nudge them gently with an "Easy on the weekend email" comment or a brief, friendly reminder in team meetings that will get even the most self-absorbed colleagues to reflect on their working practices. Normally, you'll find, their response will be "I didn't realize."

I once had a boss who aggressively asserted in his "user guide" that he'd penned to give to new people reporting to him, "You might choose not to work weekends, but I do." His weekend email would cease only for the duration of his long morning run. He was fired soon afterward. His "user guide" remains unpublished. It's one of the unlamented lost works of our generation.

What You Can Do Next:

» Don't email on the weekend. That's it. After 6 p.m. Friday, kick back. Have a glass of wine, some cheese or takeout, whatever.

» If you want to get a nonurgent email done, save it as a draft and then send it first thing on Monday. Some email applications, like Boomerang, allow you to delay sending.

Recharge 11

Get a Good Night's Sleep

Almost nothing is as good for us as a good night's sleep. It's better than any other performance-enhancing intervention. It makes us live longer; improves our creativity; enhances our memory; protects us from heart disease, dementia, and cancer; helps prevent colds; makes us considerably happier; and makes us more attractive. And it's free.

My own exploration of happiness at work was challenged from the outset when I realized that the two ways to achieve it have a limited direct connection with our jobs. To be happier, at work and everywhere, we need more sleep. And we need to spend more time with (happier) friends. We'll talk about forging closer and friendlier connections later in the book.

Sleep is powerfully restorative. It not only feels deeply satisfying but also improves our ability to perform every task subsequently presented to us. If we get our full eight hours, it also reduces our reliance on caffeine and sugary foods. The health benefits aside—and those are a pretty big aside—more than anything sleep has the power to make us *feel* better.[1] Scientists have found that people who go to bed earlier and sleep for a regular number of hours have fewer negative thoughts.

Of course, there are people who say they don't need seven and a half hours or so of sleep per night. You'll have met some of them. They scoff at the slothful behavior of the rest of us and argue that what they're doing is normal. It isn't. Scientists have found that the vast majority of these "short sleepers" have to take extreme measures to stimulate themselves to stay alert. Often, it actually transpires that they're kidding themselves about their powers of wakefulness. When scientists set about trying to scan the brains of people who claimed not to need much sleep, they found that an astonishingly high number of them nodded off simply when they were placed in an R-fMRI brain scanner.[2] The conclusion was that the claims of 95 percent of those who agreed to take part in the study were exaggerated. How strange it is that we try to assert status by going without something so vital.

What, then, does sleep actually do for us? Even now, we don't know all the answers, but science has managed to unlock some. First of all, it would appear that sleep is the time when the brain does most of its development and repair work. Back in the 1990s it was discovered that if rapid eye movement (REM) sleep (sometimes called dream sleep) is blocked in baby rats, their cerebral cortexes show no signs of development. Indeed, even if the sleep-deprived young pups are eventually given a reprieve, their development still lags behind and they end up as withdrawn adults—unable fully to engage with their group.[3]

Sleep also helps us sort and make sense of our waking experiences. Indeed, dream sleep often involves something of a playback of our memories. This was demonstrated conclusively in 2001 in a breakthrough experiment conducted by Matthew A. Wilson from MIT's Picower Institute for Learning and Memory. He and his team placed rats in a maze puzzle—something close to a running track with rewards—and then captured the signature patterns of the rats' brain cells firing as they encountered different features on the track. When the rats then went to sleep, the scientists found that those same brain patterns were repeatedly played back. "We found," said Wilson, "that brief memory sequences corresponding to running single laps on the track were replayed in short bursts at high speed. A four-second lap on the track replayed in 100–200 milliseconds." It was almost as though the highlights were being encoded in the rats' memories through constant replay. Interestingly, the scientists found that the rats never returned to stretches of memory that involved inattentive behavior or resting. It was almost as if sleep were encoding the important, memory-worthy highlights of the day and discarding the noise.[4] It was helping the rats make sense of significant wakeful experiences.

This goes some way to explain why there is much truth in the old adage that you should sleep on a problem. In Recharge 3, I described how James Webb Young's "technique for producing ideas" included the suggestion that resting is key to producing fresh thoughts. In fact, his intuition is borne out by solid scientific research. Researchers Robert Stickgold and Matthew Walker, for example, proved this conclusively in a study that involved getting students to undertake a math challenge.[5] Those who were allowed a night's sleep between rounds one and two of a number-decoding test solved the second round 16.5 percent faster than those who were retested before they were allowed to sleep. They proved to be more mentally adroit in another way, too. Hidden in the puzzle was a cheat "hack" solution that enabled the problems to be solved in a fraction of the time that would otherwise be involved. Twenty-five percent of those who weren't given an intervening night's sleep spotted the hack. Fifty-nine percent of those who slept for eight hours did so.

For those two-thirds of adults around the world who don't get sufficient sleep, the prognosis is not a happy one.[6] Not only will their health be affected adversely, but they won't be able to do their jobs as well as they could. Tired doctors, drivers, and military personnel have all been empirically shown to make avoidable errors. A multinational study of nurses found that their power to make good decisions was disrupted and their stress levels went up if they didn't get enough sleep.[7] Like rats speeding on a nocturnal dream journey through a maze, we need to give our brains time to sort, organize, and interpret the day that's just gone if we are to bring some order to our thinking.

So if work seems overwhelming and you reckon you need to burn the midnight oil to get more done, pause for thought. You're more likely to get where you need to be after eight hours of sleep.

What You Can Do Next:

» Set a regular bedtime and try to stick to it.

» Try to ensure that you're getting a good balance of sober sleeps every week. Drinking alcohol before you go to bed can result in lower sleep quality.

Recharge 12

Focus on One Thing at a Time

Let's address that thought you've been having—the one you only dare mention to yourself as a half-formed notion or to friends when tipsy. You have a strong suspicion that you'd be happier doing something else, don't you? Perhaps you could travel the world. Possibly you'd enjoy being a farmer—an organic farmer, perhaps, growing zucchini or purple-sprouting broccoli. Our relationship with work has always been complicated. If we don't have a job, we're unhappy. (Unemployed people, it has been shown, experience more negative emotions, and fewer positive ones, than those who are employed, worrying about not only income but also social status, daily routine, and life goals.)[1] Yet when we do have a job, we invariably rate work as our least favorite activity. We also say that the single thing we most dislike at work is being with our bosses. No wonder that running away to grow squash seems so attractive.

Survey statistics certainly aren't encouraging on this front. Office workers asked to evaluate their lives using a scale of 1 to 10 tend to give it around a 6. When researchers used a smartphone app to record over 1 million observations from tens of thousands of individuals, they found that being at work earned the second-lowest happiness score. Only "being sick in bed" was regarded as worse. Commuting was also regarded as a thoroughly unenjoyable activity. It's worth noting, though, that if being an office worker gets you to only a 6, being a farmworker scores even lower: 4.5. Even if you have a nice porch to sit on in the evenings with your lovely little dog, Rex, for company, you'd probably still achieve only a 5.5. Zucchini cultivation, then, is probably not the answer.[2] What is?

It's been known for some time that money doesn't lead to happiness—or, at least, that while a certain amount of money is key to a sense of security and well-being, it doesn't follow that the more you have, the happier you become. The inverse of that equation, however, is probably much less familiar. Researchers Andrew Oswald and Jan-Emmanuel De Neve looked at the comparative performance of siblings to see whether happier teenagers went on to perform better financially in adulthood. They found that young people who reported being more content with their lives went on to earn significantly more money later in their lives. How much more? Using accepted measures of trying to calibrate happiness into a score, their data suggested that for every 1 percent more life satisfaction that individuals showed at the age of twenty-two, they earned $2,000 more at the age of twenty-nine.[3] (Of course, this is not the case with that tiny number of jobs that involve high pay and huge stress—such as investment banking.)

There's a depressing social sidenote to this: you're less likely to experience an essential baseline of happiness if you come from a poor family. The stress of being poor, with poverty's undermining effect, tends to make people more negative, and that spills over from one generation to the next. Betty Hart and Todd Risley at the University of Kansas found that by the age of four, children in the low-income families that they studied had in total heard 125,000 more words of discouragement than of praise. Those in affluent households, by contrast, had heard 560,000 more words of praise than of discouragement. If, as is surely the case, the words we hear affect how we view ourselves and how we shape our ambitions, then this is cruel news.[4]

However, if you are able to achieve happiness at work, not only are you likely to end up earning more, but you're also more likely to stay in work. Scientists call this "reverse causality." In essence, the relationship runs both ways—a win-win (or lose-lose) type of situation. At the same time, as researchers at Warwick University have found, productivity of happy workers is likely to increase by 12 percent. Any unhappy employees, on the other hand, are shown to experience a 10 percent reduction—meaning a 22 percent total difference in output from their contented colleagues.[5]

So, how do you make yourself happier at work? Well, my recommendation would be to adopt all the other Recharges I've suggested so far—from taking a break from email to getting a better night's sleep—for all the reasons I've outlined. But also adopt them because the greater focus they give you is in itself a source of greater happiness. Time and time again, scientists have found that constant distraction is a sure path to a sense of discontent. Psychologists at Harvard University, using another smartphone prompt to check on what people at work were thinking and doing, discovered that for 46.9 percent of the day they weren't thinking about very much. They were in a fog of blurry mind-wandering. (No doubt this lack of concentration had much to do with the attention switching I mentioned in Recharge 1, though the researchers didn't specifically look at this.) And while mind-wandering can take you down pleasant paths, it seems to be one's darker thoughts that stick: those in the survey who were particularly prone to self-distraction were 17.7 percent less happy than their more focused colleagues.[6] As the researchers put it, "A wandering mind is an unhappy mind."

If you want to be happier in your job, then, doing one thing at a time is a route to happiness as well as productivity. As I've tried to demonstrate throughout Part 1, there are different work modes that we find ourselves needing in different circumstances. There are times when we need to be unstressed and expansive in our thinking—when we need divergent ideas coming to us. But no idea is of any value unless we have the undistracted concentration to bring it to life. In an age when many of us have dozens of internet tabs open in our browsers, when we quickly skip from one activity to another to try to make progress, it can feel that haste means getting more done. In fact, the opposite is true: your mind will most readily serve you with creative thoughts if you've completed more of the jobs expected of you. And to get things done, you need to focus.

=====

What You Can Do Next:

» Find ways to focus (close down notifications, go to a quiet space in the office, put on headphones). It will make you better at your job and happier as well.

» If you can focus your way into greater happiness at work, you will place yourself in the win-win position of being more successful, too.

=====

Part 2

Sync

EIGHT FIXES TO MAKE TEAMS CLOSER

Introduction

What a Brutal Roman Emperor Taught Us About Our Jobs

It might seem surprising to suggest we can learn much about work from a thirteenth-century Holy Roman emperor. Frederick II was a rather complicated guy, and I don't think his antics would make him an office favorite today. Although at one level he was highly successful, forging an empire that brought together much of modern Italy, Germany, Austria, and the Czech Republic, his aggressive ambitions involved constant warfare and political strife that would make weekly status meetings unnecessarily anxious. Pope Honorius III crowned him Emperor of the Romans. Things soon soured, however, and Honorius's successor, Pope Gregory IX, in a medieval precursor to what today would be an international Twitter spat, ended up describing him as the Antichrist.

But it was Frederick's scientific curiosity that makes him worthy of note in a book on modern work. Very unusually—uniquely, perhaps—for the period in which he lived, he was a ruler who had a genuine desire to understand the world around him in general, and humans in particular, even if he brought to his study the ethics of a toddler pulling the legs off insects. In one experiment, for example, a man was taken from his family and sealed in a wooden barrel with no food or water, the object being to find out whether his spirit would be visible leaving a small hole in the barrel at the moment of death. No, it turned out. In what might now be described as a murderous A/B test, two men were given an identical evening meal. On finishing it, the first man was invited to go out on a vigorous nighttime hunting expedition, and the other was encouraged to get a restful night's sleep. When the hunter returned, both men were killed and disemboweled so that Frederick could compare the relative impacts of a good workout and a prolonged rest period on the digestive system.[1] You can imagine that people started to avoid catching Frederick's eye too readily when it looked as though he might be looking for a fresh volunteer.

His experiments on children were particularly inhumane. Intent on unearthing the raw, native language of humankind—the language we'd speak if we weren't taught one—he took some infants into his care, giving the express instruction to their nurses that they were not to touch or interact with the babies in any way: showing them love or talking to them was prohibited. The outcome must have come as a surprise and a disappointment to Frederick. Subjected to social neglect, the children did not discover some true atavistic language. Instead, starved of all affection and human engagement, the infants simply died. Because they had no sense that they mattered to others, there was no reason for them to continue living. Frederick had unearthed a fundamental truth: if we don't feel we are loved or belong, we give up.

It's a fundamental truth that even today is sometimes forgotten. Consider Abraham Maslow's hierarchy of needs, that famous mid-twentieth-century model that seeks to show how some needs and requirements are contingent on others first being satisfied—certain prerequisites needing to be fulfilled before the next ones can be considered. (Some internet wit has suggested that at the base of the hierarchy should be the even more fundamental needs "battery" and "Wi-Fi.")

According to Maslow, the most essential elements of human existence are such physiological requirements as air, water, food, shelter, and sleep. Then, following personal safety, come love and belonging, followed by esteem (for ourselves and by others) and, finally, the overarching, most elevated need—the need for self-actualization.

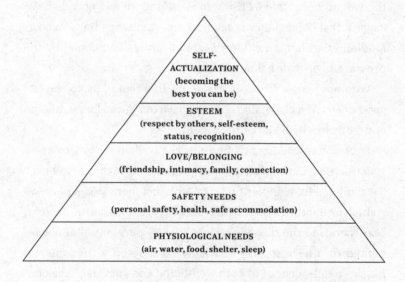

It's a compelling model and is almost universally acclaimed and accepted as a robust guide to human motivation. But it's almost certainly wrong. Think about the babies at Frederick II's court. The Maslow model clearly doesn't explain why infants who were fed and looked after would perish simply because they were deprived of love and affection.

Thirty years after Maslow, Roy Baumeister and Mark Leary

published a widely cited paper that addressed this issue.[2] In their view, Maslow was incorrect to suggest that belonging was not much more than a "nice to have," something that became important only after more fundamental essentials were acquired. Rather, Baumeister and Leary argued, a sense of belonging runs parallel to physiological needs. Humans have always wanted their achievements to be validated, recognized, and valued by others. We are not naturally drawn to acting alone. "Even a quick glance at research on social behavior raises the possibility that much of what human beings do is done in the service of belongingness," the researchers stated. "If we don't belong we feel no value. We suggest that belongingness can be almost as compelling a need as food and that human culture is significantly conditioned by the pressure to provide belongingness."

We want people to acknowledge us, to warm to us, to see our good deeds. If a charitable donation is given in the forest, and no one witnesses it, did it really happen?

Baumeister and Leary's findings are backed up by Professor Julianne Holt-Lunstad's vast study of the medical history of over 3.4 million adults. In her findings, isolation increased a person's risk of premature death by 50 percent (to put that in context, obesity raised the risk of death by just 30 percent). "Being connected to others socially is widely considered a fundamental human need—crucial to both well-being and survival," she concluded.[3] In other words, loneliness is far worse for us than an unhealthy diet.

Any sense that we don't belong damages us every moment of our lives. Frederick II showed that babies cannot survive without attention. Today, teenagers and adults deprived of stable relationships have been shown to suffer higher levels of mental and physical illness. They are more likely to display a range of behavioral problems, from committing more crime to having more car accidents. They are also more prone to suicide.

And if that's true of our lives in general, it's also true of that part of our lives that we spend at work. Of course, we need to feel we belong when we're at home. But we also need to feel the same way when we're at work. It's essential that we *belong* among the people with whom we spend five days of the week.

What does a sense of belonging at work look like? Most people would flinch from applying to our colleagues the words we use about those close to us—words such as "family" or "love." But the truth is that time and time again, members of teams report feeling friendship and something close to familial love for one another. In the course of a conversation with a London firefighter, I was struck by his comment that firefighters feel most motivated when they have a shared sense of enjoyment and experience an emotional connection with each other.[4] His outlook was clearly shared by Bailey McDade, a twenty-five-year-old Virginian about her job as a firefighter in Phoenix, Arizona. She told a journalist that along with a strong work ethic, a good sense of humor was vital. "It's kind of funny that all of these grown adults are sleeping in sleeping bags together, eating sack lunches on a log in the woods, and showering in creek water. Humor goes a long way. . . . Everyone who is here really loves it and all of the ridiculous things that go with it."[5]

Wharton professor Sigal Barsade has championed the notion that we should talk more about friendship, belonging—and love—at work. Most firms may flinch from such words, she says, and of course they don't possess precisely the same meaning that they have when we're talking about partners and families. Nevertheless, we can experience what Barsade describes as "companionate love" in the workplace. "Employees do not leave their humanity at the door when they walk into an organization," she argues.

Employees "do not leave their emotion at the door ... not only does it have a place but companionate love helps employees and the organization's bottom line."[6]

Her own research (involving 3,200 employees across seven different industrial sectors) suggests that companionate love is accompanied by greater job satisfaction, greater commitment to the organization, and also greater accountability. That latter virtue may come as something of a surprise. We normally associate accountability with strict, directive cultures in which a sense of fear drives us to work to the highest standards. But Barsade found the opposite to be the case. Our standards are at their highest, she suggests, when we feel a sense of close affiliation with our group.

According to Barsade, this kind of love is contagious. Consequently, leaders have to lead by example. They need to show an empathetic connection—yes, a *love*—to others if that love is to spread more widely. If that sounds implausible, it's worth remembering that the concept of emotional contagion is well established and acknowledged. When we were babies in our mothers' arms, we experienced an uncontrollable urge to mirror the adult face before us. The same is true of us in our adult state: think how contagious someone else's good mood or display of good manners can be. Former FBI hostage negotiator Chris Voss maintained that his greatest successes came when he was genuinely cheerful and able to project that cheerfulness into a life-or-death negotiation. He would affect a vocal tone something like a late-night FM radio presenter, and that tone would be picked up by those with whom he was negotiating, nudging them into a different emotional state. "The key here is to relax and smile while you're talking," he says. "A smile, even while talking on the phone, has an impact tonally that the other person will pick up on."[7]

The more connected we feel, the more invested in a relationship we become—whether professional or emotional. The number one factor that keeps nonmarried couples together (according to a study of nearly forty thousand of them) is "positive illusion"—the desire to stay with someone because they think we're amazing.[8] In the same way, we will feel we belong at work if we feel special there. To keep a team motivated, one role of a boss (as with a loved one) could be to become "hypeman in chief" (with the absolutely essential qualifier that this works only when it is genuine: the boss who emptily directs her team to acclaim one another's awesomeness is worse than useless).

A sense of belonging, then, is as vital at work as it is at home. The next section looks at how we can achieve it.

The Problem of Company Culture

Are people engaged at your workplace? "Engagement" has become something of a buzzword in recent years. Human resources departments across the world devote endless sessions to it. International conferences convene every week to discuss it. Bosses worry and obsess about it.

The obsession with engagement is bound up with the idea of "discretionary effort"—the belief that there is an amount of work that we all need to do to keep our jobs, but there is also an additional, discretionary contribution that we could offer but might not choose to. We all recognize times—whether it's at work or when exercising, say—when we don't give it everything we've got. Those firms that can tap into discretionary effort, the theory goes, will be markedly more productive than their run-of-the-mill rivals.

As they should be—because ever since data companies started measuring employee engagement in the 1990s, they have invariably found it be astonishingly low. In the United States, according to Gallup, 53 percent of the workforce claims to lack any real commitment to their job, with 13 percent indicating that they are "actively disengaged."[9] Gallup defines disengaged works as having "no meaningful attachment to their job or company. They are unclear about what they need to do to shine and generally feel restricted from doing their best work—all at a cost to their productivity." These figures—as low as they are—are at record highs. We've established a norm in which we accept that workers are disconnected from their jobs.

Gallup's view of the uncommitted majority is that "it probably wouldn't take a great deal to get them engaged; retraining or replacing their current manager would probably do the trick." And it's certainly the case that organizations that do seem to have cracked the employee engagement conundrum achieve better results. The workplace commentator Jacob Morgan found that the companies that invested more in a positive "employee experience" improved engagement and were included twenty-eight times as often in the Most Innovative Companies list compiled by Fast Company, eleven times as much in Glassdoor's Best Places to Work, and four times as much in the Most In-Demand Employers list.[10] Such companies also achieved four times the average profit (per employee) and twice the average revenue (per employee). Interestingly, smaller companies tended to crop up in the list more frequently than the biggest corporations.[11]

That's fine as far as it goes, but, of course, it begs the question: How do you create that sense of employee engagement? How do you actually build an environment that improves the way people interact to the point that morale surges and employees feel happier and more motivated? It's something that the students of work culture have become understandably obsessed with. If you search "culture documents," you'll discover hundreds of beautifully designed PDFs that extol the delights of working at X or Y firm.[12] If engagement is the goal, then building a better culture is seen as the way to achieve it.

Ultimately, much of the modern Western obsession with clearly defined "work cultures" was spawned by the envy of the Japanese world of business that took root in the 1980s as businesspeople in the West woke up to the maglev train–like speed and energy of so many of Japan's big companies. When the question "Why are Japanese firms so special?" was asked, the answer often came back that it was because they had created high-functioning, dynamic, consistent cultures. News programs would show footage of Japanese workers singing company songs or doing morning exercise classes together and would contrast Japanese culture's focus on the importance of the group with the West's championship of the individual. "[They] tend to have a Confucian hierarchy, where the group is sacred," said Richard Lewis, a linguist who studied the differences between the two worlds.[13]

The result was a new philosophy of work and a growing belief by the end of the 1990s that anyone who couldn't beat their chest and roar about their own turbocharged culture should feel ashamed of their anemic efforts. It became popular to parrot the rallying call of business guru Peter Drucker: "Culture eats strategy for lunch!" The work culture movement that grew up was keen to suggest that when you crack the culture formula, the impact is something close to mainlining adrenaline into the brain. The flip side, of course, was the implication that companies that didn't have world-class, fast-moving cultures were destined to become roadkill for what was zooming up behind them.

You can still find relics of the mind-set of this era in the form of a particular kind of motivational self-help book. *Fish!*, for instance, implores firms to channel the excitably frenetic pace of Seattle's Pike Place Fish Market, where (as an accompanying film shows) exhaustingly extroverted salespeople toss salmon around or try to charm potential customers by miming a Whitney Houston song with the aid of a wet halibut.[14] As it turns out, this pescatarian backdrop proves the inspiration for a series of pretty simple values: choose your attitude, be present, play, and make someone's day. But it has to be said that it's quite difficult to transfer the theatrics of a tourist destination to the average office. Karl in accounting is unlikely to win many friends if he starts hurling piles of printouts across reception. Similarly, it's not easy to see how exhortations from other writers to make teams more "gung ho!" or to turn customers into "raving fans!" translate into the kind of environment where most of us would feel comfortable.[15] I can't think of people working in a quiet village law firm taking kindly to their boss informing them that the company has just made the decision to be more gung ho with the final will and testament of Mrs. Burns.

The work culture movement is still going strong, and new invocations, like "Build your tribe," are appearing all the time. But there's also been a discernible shift in focus from culture as a way to drive performance to culture as a means of marketing an organization to the outside world. Adam Grant—the leading expert in the field—explored the realities of most work cultures in comparison with what was claimed. He found that despite all the declared differences between firms, most cultures were largely the same.[16] Over recent years, problems that were always inherent in the culture movement have become more apparent. One is that cultural exhortations tend to make a very selective use of data and evidence. Another is that the colorful examples that are so often paraded to support an argument for cultural change don't apply in all situations and, more crucially, often are not scalable. Sports teams, movie production companies, and restaurants may well have created extraordinary energizing cultures, but they're a particular type of compact unit. How the lessons learned from them can be applied to organizations of several hundreds or thousands of people is not always clear as the cup-winning icon leaves the conference stage to boisterous applause.

Is it really possible to unite a whole company in a single, meaningful culture? On that subject, it's worth considering the anthropologist Robin Dunbar's research on group dynamics. His view is that cohesive groups are restricted in size to around 150 people. Once that number is exceeded, he argues, our cerebral neocortexes struggle to cope, and the result is an erosion of trust and cooperation. And even 150 people is at the high end of what constitutes a sustainable group. Dunbar's research also suggests that when that many people are involved, 42 percent of the group's time is consumed by "social grooming."[17] It's fascinating to consider that 42 percent as you plow through an inbox of internal messages before trotting off to an internal meeting. It's intriguing, too, that the figure should be so remarkably close to the 40 percent of the time that the consulting firm McKinsey believes we spend answering email. Could it be that a bulging inbox is the unproductive trade-off for being part of a large company?

Given how difficult we find it to form large groups, it should come as no surprise that it's not easy to impose a company culture. I would certainly accept that it's helpful to have something that explains "this is how we do things around here," but the problem with the average statement of values is that either it's so vague that it could apply to any company or it's so absolute—in terms of, say, the personality type that the organization thinks fits best—that it's actually impossible to implement in a way that has genuine value. It's very unwise to force people into a particular set of attitudes or way of working. If you do, you'll simply end up either with teams that are cynical and disengaged or with ones that feel compelled to wear a "work mask."

Some companies have gone so far as to employ a "chief happiness officer," an interesting move that makes workers' happiness (which most of us would accept as a complex, autonomous state of mind) the responsibility of their bosses. The former Zappos CEO Tony Hsieh, who was something of a flag-waver for this approach, became so fixated with the notion of getting workers to fit in with a happy, positive culture that he said he was quite prepared to fire the 10 percent who didn't make a clear commitment to the "happiness agenda."[18] That must have come as quite a challenge for those who happened at that moment to be experiencing problems in their personal life, or to the more nervous or introverted people who worried that they might not appear happy enough.

In *Disrupted*, Dan Lyons, a sometime journalist, sometime comedy writer, wrote a darkly funny description of his time at an East Coast tech firm that was obsessed with its culture. Among the various dystopian scenes he evoked was one in which *bro-grammer* colleagues had daily lunchtime gatherings at which they performed competitive push-ups. The company's much-vaunted culture, in his opinion, was simply a barely disguised way to push young workers to drive themselves to near burnout (with the understanding that they could be cheaply replaced).[19] "It was just a bro culture," he recalled, before going on to make a point of fundamental importance. "I realized that idea of culture fit is not a good thing. In fact if you stop for a second, you don't want to hire people who are just like you. You want to hire people who are very different from you—and you bring in a wider range of talent and wider range of world views."

Such are the drawbacks of the average company's declared culture or engagement philosophy. It comes as no surprise, then, that management thinker Dr. Richard Claydon should reckon that the only sustainable company-wide culture in large organizations is actually one of ironic detachment: "You have to mock the culture to survive it."[20] You go along with what you're told to do, while exchanging knowing, sarcastic asides with like-minded people. It's an application of what the philosopher Søren Kierkegaard called "mastered irony," as Claydon notes.

It's unlikely, then, that a homogenous work culture can be achieved across a large organization. Engagement is never likely to be achieved by proclamations from leaders alone. What is required is something far more tribal. Rather than tackle everyone at company level, you need to encourage small teams of individuals to trust one another. You need to give workers the autonomy to focus on their own individual responsibilities, and you also need to provide clear guidelines as to how they should cooperate within their team and in turn with other teams. There needs to be recognition that a team is not toxic (or uncompliant) if it happens to have developed a strong individual character that reflects the diversity of its members, provided that it knows how it sits within the wider organization.

That's why in the Syncs that follow, I focus on improving *team* culture. Because a powerful sense of motivation starts with teams working well together, not with an email from the CEO.

Finding a Sense of Purpose

If you ask people why they work, their obvious immediate response will be that they do so because they need the money. It's what's known as *extrinsic* motivation—something we do not for the joy of it but because it leads to something else. When we make the mistake of assessing how our friends are doing in the game of life, it's invariably the extrinsic factors we look at. Have they had a fantastic pay rise? Are they able to afford an amazing house or a lavish holiday? Similarly, we know that when we, say, watch an Uber driver accept another job on their phone, they're doing this for an extrinsic reason: not because they (necessarily) love driving but because they need to earn a few more dollars to pay their rent.

Intrinsic motivation, by contrast, is what drives us to do something for its own sake. It can be an immensely powerful force. Why otherwise would nurses or teachers do a job they know to be less well paid than so many others? They do it because they believe it to have an innate value, just as those who are prepared to do some jobs for free are happy to see that job as its own reward: volunteers in charity shops, for example, or open-source code writers. Without intrinsic motivation, a vast range of difficult, challenging, and essential jobs would never get done.

The relationship between extrinsic and intrinsic motivation is a delicate one. It's tempting to assume that everybody works harder when extrinsically motivated with extra pay or a performance bonus. In fact, the evidence suggests that the opposite can be true. So much depends on the nature of the work being done. Tasks that are, as author Daniel Pink puts it, *algorithmic*—where you "follow a set of established instructions down a single pathway to one conclusion"—may well be performed more quickly and efficiently if a simple extrinsic bonus is on offer: "Clean more cars and you'll make more money," "Bake more cakes and you'll get a bonus." But when the task in question is *heuristic*—that is, when "you have to experiment with possibilities and devise a novel solution"—an extrinsic reward can backfire.[21] As Professor Teresa Amabile points out, heuristic tasks are the elements of our jobs from which we derive the most pleasure. They get our brain synapses popping, requiring us to think, to create, to reimagine. Incentivize them in the wrong way and, far from working at them with increased vigor, we actually retreat from them.

Amabile demonstrated the truth of this apparent conundrum in a creative challenge—an art test—she staged with two volunteer groups of children.[22] (Rest assured she was no Frederick II; these kids even had a chance of winning a reward.) One group was told that whoever came up with the best pictures would receive unspecified prizes. The other group was informed that they'd be spending some time on an art activity and that at the end of the day there would be a raffle to determine who got a prize. Once both groups had handed in their artistic creations, Amabile got a team of assessors to judge them. The judges unanimously decided that the art created by the group not expecting a reward was significantly more creative. The extrinsic motivation created by the offer of a prize did not lead to better, more innovative work.

That this wasn't an isolated result was shown by Mark Lepper and David Greene, whose not dissimilar experiment has become something of a textbook case. The two researchers took preschool children who had shown an interest in drawing and gave them some free time. One-third of the children were told they would receive an award if they spent their free time drawing. Another third were left to their own devices but received a surprise award at the end if they happened to decide to draw. The final third were effectively a control group, allowed to do what they liked and not awarded anything at the end if they chose to draw.

When the various groups' activities were compared, it was found that the surprise award and no award groups had behaved in precisely the same way: they'd spent about 20 percent of their six minutes drawing. But those drawers who had been incentivized with the offer of an award had drawn for only half as long (and, just to remind you, all these children were chosen because they liked drawing). Two weeks later, when the children were observed again, the researchers noticed that those who had been incentivized on the previous occasion continued to show less interest and to devote much less time to drawing.

So what was going on there? Clearly, what had been a happy intrinsic pleasure had been turned into work by the introduction of an extrinsic motivation. I can almost imagine a group of children with downturned mouths looking miserably at a bunch of crayons. What's more, those of the incentivized group who did decide to draw were judged to have created less interesting work than those who had done it for fun.[23] It was almost as if someone had concreted over a favorite playground. This should perhaps serve as a warning to think very carefully before you decide to turn a hobby into a job. At the very least, we should all bear in mind Amabile's view that "intrinsic motivation is conducive to creativity; extrinsic motivation is detrimental to creativity."

There's even evidence that doing a job purely for an extrinsic reward not only crushes creativity but also can be a route to unhappiness and depression. As London Business School professor Daniel Cable told me, research suggests that "employees who receive lots of extrinsic rewards doing work that feels boring and meaningless to them are making themselves sick."[24] There you have it—the Smoothie Delusion. You can't make people love their jobs by giving them rewards (of smoothies, money, or whatever). An empty job remains an empty job whatever the incentive.

If we're going to get the most out of our jobs, then, we should be trying to find ways to stimulate intrinsic motivation—making those nerve cells tingle rather than throwing unhelpful and destructive rewards into our motivation systems. The problem, though, is that modern work is a constant round of annoyances and distractions that destroy precisely the sort of motivation we should be encouraging. People want to feel that they are making progress. They're ambitious for a sense of achievement. But workplace interruptions (open-plan seating, meetings, email, instant message pings) stifle any sense of satisfying flow. We'd like to enjoy work for its own sake, but everything conspires against it. (And, as I have just shown, throwing extrinsic incentives at people who are flagging not only isn't the answer but may well be counterproductive.)

For writer Daniel Pink, the essential inner intrinsic motivation—the motivation that really drives us, that makes us feel energized and that adds to our sense of self-worth—comes from a combination of three factors: *autonomy*, *mastery*, and *purpose*. Autonomy is our desire to have an impact on the job that we are doing. Mastery is the sense of accomplishment that comes with a realization that we're getting better at what we do. Purpose is what makes us feel that we're making a contribution—to society, to our families—through the work we do.

"I think there are two kinds of purpose," Pink told me. "One of them is what I call capital P *Purpose*. That is: 'Am I doing something big and transcendent?' When I go to work today I'm helping to solve the climate crisis, I'm helping to feed the hungry, put shoes on the shoeless, etc. And there's evidence that's a pretty good performance enhancer. It's important at both the individual level and the corporate level. The truth of the matter is that many of us in our day-to-day job can't access that kind of Purpose every single day. I can't come into my office here in the garage behind my house and say, 'Today I'm playing a role in ending dependence on fossil fuels.' I'm doing something more mundane. I'm going to write a book. The other kind of purpose that's important is what you can think of as lowercase P *purpose*. That's simply this: 'Am I making a contribution?' That's it. In a corporate setting, if I didn't show up to work today would anybody care? Would anybody notice? Would something not get done? Did I help someone out because he was in a pinch and I helped him? I made a contribution. By doing that I didn't end world hunger. But I made a contribution."[25]

The sense of purpose—of making a contribution—has been proven to be a significant driver of workers' engagement with, and commitment to, their jobs. Most cooks, for example, would probably struggle to buy into the idea that their work involves alleviating global hunger; their job does not embody what Pink would style "capital P *Purpose*." Nevertheless, they do have a sense of purpose, and that purpose (with a small *p*) can be immensely rewarding. Researchers from Harvard Business School and University College London who studied a restaurant for a week found that when the cooks could see their customers, the quality of the food they served improved (it was judged to be 10 percent better). And when the cooks could see the customers and the customers could see the cooks, the improvement was even more marked (17 percent better). Quite simply, when the cooks could see that they were making a real contribution, they did a better job. As the lead researcher, Ryan Buell, said, "Being appreciated makes work meaningful."[26]

For Professor Adam Grant, *pride*—which perhaps represents the intersection of purpose and belonging—is a key element of engagement. If we feel that people respect the job we do, that they think it is worthwhile, we'll be boosted by a sense of pride in it. If you're a nurse or a firefighter, you know that society places a value on what you do.[27] (That may not make your job any less stressful or exhausting, but it will probably help keep you going in a way that a job you weren't proud of wouldn't.)

The first of the motivating factors that Daniel Pink identifies— *autonomy*—is clearly key. We need to feel that we are in control, that not every moment of our working day is controlled by someone else. But—coming full circle back to Emperor Frederick II—autonomy needs to be in careful balance with that relationship with others that is so key to our hierarchy of needs—not the Maslow model but the one that places love and belonging alongside physiological needs as a fundamental requirement.

In work terms, that means we need not only autonomy, mastery, and purpose. We need *Sync*.

Sync

What is Sync? It's what holds couples together. It's what can help us withstand more pain and can make schoolkids giggle with delight. It's what gets colleagues to work faster and pensioners to feel closer to each other, and it has the same health benefits as for a smoker giving up cigarettes. While we can't measure it, we can quantify the impact of it. Perhaps the easiest way to define it is to say that it's a connection at a human, empathetic level that brings a team together in trusted alignment.

All the evidence suggests that humans derive joy from being in synchrony with those around us. Sometimes this synchrony can take the form of highly choreographed actions—dancing with others, singing in a choir, sharing a crowd's delight in sporting success. When we're in harmony with others, we tend to sense a moment of euphoria.

Aside from those moments of highly elevated synchronization, there are far more gentle everyday moments that have a measurable impact on our sense of well-being, happiness, and belonging. In 1920 a Harvard psychologist, Floyd Allport, observed that the simple fact of working alongside someone—even if they're working independently—increases productivity, with the slower worker speeding up to be in sync with the faster worker.[28] Anyone who has exercised with a partner will have observed that when you're in sync with someone, you can push your training tolerance to higher limits. I've just glanced out the window and witnessed two children playing a clapping game together, both deriving more and more energized delight as they managed to coordinate ever more complex patterns.

The reason for this, according to the anthropologist Robin Dunbar, is that "synchrony alone seems to ramp up the production of endorphins so as to heighten the effect when we do these activities in groups." When we're in sync with those around us, we achieve greater feats.[29]

Legendary musician and producer Brian Eno gave a captivating lecture in 2015 in which he explored the notion that we feel greater trust in others when we feel synchronized with them.[30] It's often an indirect process. We don't ask people to write down their views when we first meet them so that we can cross-tabulate them with our own. We employ meandering discussions about culture, friends, and the news to help us. Eno described his own experience of sitting on a bus and hearing two women talk about an episode of a TV soap opera in which one of the characters was unexpectedly revealed to be a lesbian. The two women were using a shared TV experience as a jumping-off point for an animated discussion. "I realized that because it was a soap opera," Eno observed, "they were able to talk about it in a way they couldn't ever do if it was something that actually was connected to them." He then went on to reference the work of historian William McNeill, who, in Eno's words, "talks about the intense pleasure humans feel in muscular coordination; in dancing, in marching together, in carnivals, in all the things where a lot of people synchronize themselves."

Eno's conclusion was that as intelligent animals, we find calm in the trustful environment that synchronization creates, whether through physical or verbal sync. "I was thinking about that in relation to the two ladies on the bus," he said. "And I was thinking what they're really doing is synchronizing. We live in a culture that is changing so incredibly quickly. Probably in a month of our lifetimes we have about the amount of change that there was in the whole of the fourteenth century. So we have to somehow come to terms with all of that. None of us have the same experiences; you know you might know a lot about what's happening in cars and you might know a lot of what's happening in medicine and you might know something about mathematics and you might know something about fashion. None of us are at all expert on everything that's happening. So we need ways of keeping in sync."

Those who belong to groups that exhibit Sync clearly derive benefits from the experience. Researchers who have looked at choirs have found that their members benefit in ways that are commensurate to taking up exercise or giving up smoking. Daniel Weinstein and his team of researchers found that "feelings of inclusion, connectivity, positive affect, and measures of endorphin release all increased across singing rehearsals."[31] Groups that had achieved the synchrony that singing created also showed a higher tolerance in a pain threshold test—Sync actually made the singers stronger. The researchers found that even groups that superficially appeared to be too large for bonds to be created *were* able to build a sense of cohesion through song. And this could be achieved astonishingly quickly: "Even after only a single session of singing, a large group of unfamiliar individuals can become bonded to the same level as those who are familiar to each other within that group."

A choir may seem a rather extreme example of humans in Sync. But the principles hold for all groups. People who are in supportive relationships are less stressed than those who are not. If there are people around us we trust, they help us to cope: they act as a buffer against stress. A study of American couples who were able to keep their relationships going even when living far apart from each other found that daily small talk, chatting about seemingly trivial matters, was key. Being in Sync through seemingly insubstantial interactions was the secret of a happy marriage—even when the couple in question were living a long way apart.[32] Even more loosely formed social groups can help reduce individual stress levels, whether or not they exist primarily to provide emotional support.[33]

We all have a need to belong. We are stronger, more energized, and more collaborative when we are in Sync with one another. Now let's explore eight ways to build Sync in the workplace.

Sync 1

Move the Coffee Machine

Imagine watching workers in the way you can observe ants interacting in your garden—from above, like a god of work perched where it's possible to see all the hundreds of little interactions that are going on below. Or like a *Sims* fanatic, interacting with an office version of the game in which you can watch the chat, the meetings, the awkward flirting that are all taking place in workplaces around the world.

Well, thanks to the pioneering work of Alex "Sandy" Pentland, a professor at the Massachusetts Institute of Technology, that's close to what we are now able to do. Pentland is a soft-spoken, avuncular figure with a head of shaggy gray hair and a thick beard that must protect him from the long Boston winters. His spark of genius was to combine two existing pieces of technology to create an immensely powerful research tool that brings "big data" and psychology together in a groundbreaking new field that he calls "social physics." First, he and his students took the ID badges that most of us now use to get in and out of our buildings. Then they combined them with something close to the technology that we now find in our smartphones. The resulting sociometric badges allowed him to gather precise information about where people were at any given moment and, thanks to the modified microphones the badges contained, not just who they were conversing with but whether voice intonation indicated a question being asked or an answer being given. (It's worth clarifying that the microphones didn't capture words, just voice tonality.) This vast bank of data—updated every sixteen milliseconds—was then combined with logs of the daily tasks people were undertaking in a whole range of industries and professions. The end result was a precise record of what really happens at work, how groups interact, when and where they are most productive, and how ideas flow from one person to another.[1]

One of the insights that Pentland gleaned should perhaps not come as a particular surprise, given what I've already suggested in Recharges 7 and 10: email may be an invaluable communication tool, but its utility doesn't extend much beyond that. "What we find," Pentland reports, "is email has very little to do with productivity or creative output."[2] He found instead that one of the most important factors determining the success of different organizations was "ideas flow"—the capacity of new thoughts to cross-pollinate with others. And "ideas flow" was largely the product of chatting casually with people (as opposed to talking in meetings). In banks and in call centers, Pentland found, up to 40 percent of the productivity of different groups could be accounted for by the suggestions that flowed from their informal interactions.[3] "I have found that the number of opportunities for social learning, usually through informal face-to-face interactions, is the largest single factor in company productivity," he concluded.[4] In other words, spending time building Sync was contributing between one-third and one-half of a group's productivity. Email added almost nothing to what groups were achieving.

And it wasn't just productivity that rose. Pentland also discovered that some of the best ideas came not from lone geniuses toiling away at their desktops but from groups getting together and talking. "What the data suggests," Pentland argues, "is that most of the time, in most places, innovation is a group phenomenon." People would start out thinking alone in a burst of concentration and focus, but they would then take to their feet and start road testing their thinking with others: "The most creative people are actually people who go around and collect ideas from lots of different people, play with them, bounce them off other people."

In real offices it's small interactions that help shape raw thoughts into great notions: the slight wince from the first person to hear the new idea that tells its champion that it requires reframing. The encouraging smile and wide-eyed nod that suggests that someone is onto something promising. All these facial microexpressions help ideas to be shaped, reshaped, and improved. For Pentland (his badges could "see" people moving from one colleague to another), those who bounce ideas around in a constructive way are similar to musicians improvising with one another: "It's like people playing jazz together; they riff off each other, they respond to each other but you have to bring something to the table to have a good session."

Because workplace dialogue can be such a powerful driver of new ideas, in Pentland's view everything should be done to encourage it. And often it's just a question of how the physical space is organized. In one company, Pentland said, "the simplest way to increase workers' productivity was to make the company's lunch tables longer, thus forcing people who didn't know each other to eat together" (see Recharge 8).[5] A bank's customer service group was moved from its isolated position around a corner when it was discovered that few other staff members were wandering past it and that projects were, in consequence, being badly executed: "By changing the seating plan the bank was able to make sure that everyone, even the previously orphaned customer service group, was in the loop."

Pentland's work has since been taken up and expanded by many of the people who studied under him. One of his students, Ben Waber, for example, has created a new start-up, Humanyze, that sells the sociometric badges to companies to help them pinpoint what is happening in their offices and how things might be improved. Are teams collaborating with each other effectively? Where are the communication bottlenecks?

Like Pentland, Waber and his team have discovered that the fixes required are often very simple ones. Bosses spend days working on team restructures to improve collaboration within the office. Yet they're happy to leave to chance the location of such key gathering points as the water cooler and coffee machine. That's a huge mistake, in Waber's view. "The location of the coffee machine," he told me, "has about as much impact on who talks to who as the org chart."[6]

So, where should you place the coffee machine? Well, it depends on what you're trying to achieve: "If you put it, for example, within one group area, that group will be more internally focused—they will have a very cohesive network. On the other hand, if I put it between two groups they will talk a lot more to each other. If I want that, that's something I should do."

It may be that in your workplace it's not possible to move water coolers and coffee machines. If so, perhaps you should consider moving key teams closer together in a way that they end up sharing the same kitchen. Some companies add TV monitors—showing live news or sports—in softer social spaces between teams. Whatever you choose, that chat over a cup of coffee might well be the source of your company's next big idea.

What You Can Do Next:

» Get people talking to each other. It's the secret of building Sync, and it isn't difficult to do.

» Remember that even small changes that bring teams into closer proximity with one another can build collaboration, trust, and creativity.

» Relocating water coolers and refreshment points is one way to bring together people who you want to interact. If you can't do that, consider moving teams' focal points.

» Experiment with adding TVs, sofas, or other reasons for team members to pause and chat together.

Suggest a Coffee Break

In the previous Sync I touched on the work of Ben Waber, the CEO of WorkTech pioneers Humanyze, which helps companies improve the way they operate by using sociometric badges to plot and identify poor current working methods.

Waber told me about an experiment his company conducted at a Bank of America call center. Call centers are an evolved form of capitalism: everything is structured around maximizing productivity. How can you get a floor of thousands of call handlers to deal with more calls? Especially if you want those calls to have happy resolutions? It's a daily challenge.

You'd be forgiven for thinking that such an individualistic job as a call handler doesn't require any need for teamwork, empathetic Sync, or indeed any team interaction that facilitated ideas flow. Certainly the way in which such centers have evolved would seem to confirm as much. The teams that Waber and his colleagues observed worked autonomously. The workers dealt with their phone calls and then, twice a day—midmorning and midafternoon—headed off one by one for a break to allow them to pause and briefly rest in a lonely break room. Here they would drink something on their own before heading back into the melee of phone calls.

Having observed this, Waber and his colleagues made a tweak. Rather than go separately for a break, colleagues would now be allowed to take time off in teams, spending fifteen minutes together away from the constant barrage of queries and complaints. The result? Well, one outcome should come as no particular revelation: "The groups got about 18 percent more cohesive," Waber told me; "what you'd expect because now I have a break at the same time as everyone on my team I'll talk to them." But it was the other effects that surprised the bank's bosses. First, stress levels (measured by sensors in the sociometric badges I described in Sync 1) fell by 19 percent, largely because colleagues now had the opportunity to chat to others about any difficult calls they'd just had to deal with. Second, from the moment a zero-cost, coordinated fifteen-minute coffee break was introduced, the productive performance of the team went up by 23 percent.[1] Or, putting it another way, the introduction of Sync in a call center caused that center's productivity to increase by nearly one-quarter.

Of course, when you come to think about it, it seems so obvious.

The work in call centers consists of a series of intense phone interactions. Most show society at its anonymous worst. Few are positive or warm, and as a result the average stress levels of the call handlers are way above norms for other jobs. By the end of a session, those taking the calls feel pretty beaten up. They're hearing us in our angriest guise, far angrier, probably, than when we're dealing with family or friends or indeed other work colleagues. Perhaps we want our money back. Or we want something done for free. In many ways we are like novices playing fighting games on a games console: we're not quite sure what button to press to get what we want, but we hope that by hitting them all at the same time we might get somewhere.

So when call center workers take staggered breaks, they wander off into a cafeteria or break area with strangers, sit silently for fifteen minutes, scroll a few hundred screens through their phone, drink their coffee, and then head back onto the vast floor of the center with the echoes of the previous session's phone calls still sounding in their ears. But when they take coordinated breaks, they are able to turn to colleagues and share stories about what just happened—stories that are probably too dull to take home to their partners, or to pollute a night out with friends, but that give them relief when they unburden themselves of them.

And as the power of Sync is unleashed, not only do stress levels decline, but useful, productive hints are also exchanged. "Oh, that happened to me. I answered with this." "I've had a call like that. Why don't you try this?" Through conversations like these, the team members in Waber's study were able to coach each other, to train each other, to solve the problems they were all encountering. Waber's team worked out that the 23 percent uplift was equivalent to the call handlers having ten years' additional experience.[2]

One other very important point needs to be made. These interactions were unplanned. Waber observed that team meetings don't achieve similar levels of synchronization (or, as he often calls it, "cohesion"). The call center conversations worked because they were spontaneous.

In this lesson from the call center floor there's a reminder of what creativity looks like in most workplaces. When the call handlers find a better way to solve a customer's problem, they've been responsible for a spark of creative thinking. We become awed by the concept of creativity, but the truth is that whether we work in a local government office, a supermarket, a law firm, or, yes, a call center, creativity is simply finding a better way to do the job we're trying to do.

The power of a shared break is something that will come as no revelation to people in Sweden. There, the power of *fika* has been understood for generations. The word "fika" is often translated as "coffee and cake," and it may well take the form of a brief fifteen-minute coffee break, but it's as much a state of mind as a dose of caffeine and carbs. Across the country, fika marks the moment when businesses like the Volvo plant halt production for a reenergizing pause. As the IKEA website explains, "More than a coffee break, fika is a time to share, connect and relax with colleagues. Some of the best ideas and decisions happen at fika." Sometimes taken with colleagues or comfortably enjoyed alone, fika is viewed by Swedes as a moment to slow down and reflect. In fact, many Swedish firms now celebrate the chatty walk to the local coffee shop as part of the modern fika experience. Over time, many of us have been made to feel guilty for taking a coffee break. Making a drink and taking it back to our desk, yes—but sitting down and relaxing for fifteen minutes has been made to feel like indolence. Fika shows that it's about refreshing ourselves to give our best thinking and resetting our energy at a higher level.

So it's not just call centers that can benefit from this tweak to the day's routine. Whether you suggest your team set tools down for a midafternoon cup of tea or collectively take a stroll to the nearest coffee shop for a chat, maybe fika is the answer to building more Sync in your team.

What You Can Do Next:

» Experiment. Suggest a break to the people around you. Maybe use your break to walk to a coffee shop—or wander to a kitchen on a different floor of your office. Try initially to take a break two or three times a week and make a note of its impact by Friday.

» Try taking time out with people at the moment when you feel least able to step away from things. Some people report that breaks seem to work most effectively at moments of stress and exhaustion.

Sync 3

Halve Your Meetings

It was like a scene out of Prohibition-era America. Three office workers, smartly dressed but not so much so that they ran the risk of drawing attention to themselves, eased the door closed behind them. Each furtively took a seat, keeping an ever-watchful eye on the world beyond the glass partition—when you're looking out for law enforcement, you need to be confident your opponent isn't creeping up on you. Then one of them slowly opened the luminescent device that up until now he'd managed to keep concealed. Finally, the comfort of a well-designed slide and the calm created by the presence of PowerPoint. *This is safe, this is normal again*, they thought as they collectively exhaled a sigh of relief. They leaned in to gaze at the glowing laptop that sat between them.

And then, in that brief moment of absorption, BANG! The door flew open. In swarmed the Feds. They'd been busted.

Office life in the modern age? Well, perhaps not, but this—give or take a touch of license—was very much the scene at PayPal when its chief operating officer, David Sacks, came on the scene. Striding around an office of seven hundred people like a cop sniffing out speakeasies, he would throw open meeting room doors to break up anything that resembled an unnecessary gathering. As a colleague later recounted, Sacks "enforced an anti-meeting culture—where any meeting that included more than three or four people was deemed suspect and subject to immediate adjournment if he gauged it inefficient."[1] Sacks himself explained that he felt the Meeting Enthusiasts problem was actually a legacy of a recent acquisition that had left the company with twice as many bosses as were necessary. Managers were holding meetings simply to assert their importance in the new power structure.[2]

The PayPal situation may have its peculiar quirks, but what Sacks uncovered is not actually an unusual phenomenon. One of the great challenges of modern office life is finding ways to accurately assess people's capabilities. How do we decide if they're good at their job? You'd think we would try to measure their day-to-day work, their ideas, their ability to operate effectively in a team. In fact, we're just as likely to judge them from their ability to talk or present in meetings, even though there's actually a very limited correlation between meetings and genuine productivity. A get-together to discuss a shared project can, at times, feel energizing and productive. Meetings are, all too often, soul-sapping.

Advertising legend Rory Sutherland, for one, is highly skeptical that such lengthy periods spent sitting in a room with others constitute a sensible use of time, and he compares present practice unfavorably with what prevailed in the past. "In the old 1980s adland," he says, "there were quite a lot of periods where there wasn't much you could do. You put something into the studio and you were waiting for it to come out. The photography had been done and you were waiting for the first retouching to be done or whatever. All those things created an enforced downtime. The enforced downtime was mostly wasted, as all these things are. But then it was wasted in a way which was a special kind of waste. OK, 80 percent of it *was* wasted. But 20 percent of it turned out to be really valuable. You'd have conversations which otherwise wouldn't have happened. . . . I think we've all got to relearn this stuff [how to bring thinking space back to work]," he concludes, "because technology and email arrived so fast there was no time for etiquette or practices or behavioral rules to emerge around it."[3]

To try to get a handle on just why meetings are so unproductive, it's worth taking a look at one of the most interesting experiments in human dynamics to have been conducted in recent years. The marshmallow appears twice in iconic pieces of scientific research (maybe scientists find its squishiness irresistibly compelling). The Marshmallow Test is possibly the more familiar one (children are left in a room with one marshmallow and told they can eat it now or receive two marshmallows if they're prepared to wait five minutes; their ability to delay gratification turns out to be a powerful indicator of whether they will achieve later success in life). But it's the similarly titled Marshmallow *Challenge* that teaches us about power play in meetings.

The challenge, which was devised by Palm Pilot designer Peter Skillman as he explored how groups solve problems, is a very simple one to set up.[4] Volunteers are divided into teams, each of which is then given eighteen minutes to construct the tallest freestanding structure possible out of twenty pieces of dry spaghetti, a yard of sticky tape, a yard of string, and one marshmallow, which has to end up sitting atop the edifice.

It sounds straightforward enough, but Skillman's findings show that different groups of individuals approach the challenge in very different ways and with very different levels of success. Remarkably, the group that consistently performed best for Skillman was made up of preschool-age children. The worst performing, despite their earnest endeavors, were business school students. Psychologist Tom Wujec—who has himself taken on the thought leadership around the challenge—describes what generally happens when teams set about the exercise: "Normally most people begin by orienting themselves to the task. They talk about it, they figure out what it's going to look like, they jockey for power. They spend some time organizing, they lay out spaghetti, they spend the majority of time assembling the sticks into ever growing structures." So far, so familiar. This sounds like the average meeting. "Then finally, just as they are running out of time, someone takes out the marshmallow. They gingerly put it on top. Ta dah! They admire their work. What really happens most of the time is the 'ta dah' turns into an 'uh oh.' The weight of the marshmallow causes the structure to buckle and collapse," just as the clock runs out.

So why are preschool-age children so much better at this challenge, producing not only the most interesting structures but also the tallest ones? In Peter Skillman's words, "None of the kids spend time trying to be CEO of Spaghetti Inc. They don't spend time jockeying for power."[5] What they do instead is interact in a frequently nonverbal way. They grab immediately for materials. They try different things out (what Skillman describes as "prototyping ideas"), often not even bothering to find words to describe their actions. And they quickly discover that the cloudlike fluffiness of the marshmallow is nothing of the sort: it's a dense blob of sugar that weighs enough to collapse anything but the sturdiest structures.

The business school students, by contrast, not only have been schooled to search for the single correct answer but also are focusing at least some of their energy on asserting their position in the group before their anticipated win. Each student wants to be genius discoverer of the perfect correct answer or the leader of the group, or both. Problem solving therefore degenerates into a phony war, where what's really at stake is where each combatant sits within the intellectual hierarchy in the group. Business meetings follow much the same pattern: members of the team may be trying genuinely to solve a problem or trying to assert positions against each other or both.

A colleague of mine encountered a real-life version of the Marshmallow Challenge for herself when she quit a stellar career at Twitter to follow her dream of working in an elite restaurant. Enrolled in the internationally esteemed Leith's Cooking Course, Georgina found that students there were split into three rough groups that largely reflected age. One cohort was made up of those recently out of school (aged nineteen or twenty). Another comprised thirtysomethings. The final one was given over to forty- and fiftysomethings. And what my former colleague soon discovered was that the older the group, the longer it took them to learn. But this wasn't because cognitive ability declines in age: the older groups exhibited just as much of the interest and dedication shown by the youngest class. The problem was that the older groups talked and debated; they discussed and dissected every single thing. Their ability to learn was slowed by members of the group subconsciously asserting their social standing and position.

I mentioned earlier that the anthropologist Robin Dunbar has argued that humans are able to form trusting relationships with at most 150 people (a theory that's sometimes known as "Dunbar's number"). Once we reach that limit, 42 percent of our time is taken up in "social grooming"—namely, building and sustaining trusted relationships with the people we're surrounded with. As I also mentioned earlier when talking about email, meetings play a significant part in this social grooming. We use them to manage our relations with others as we toil away in a complex web of professional relationships. Cass Business School professor André Spicer, talking about the perceived need to get employees in companies to connect, explained: "Meetings help smooth that. They're a social preening ritual—just like monkeys picking the fleas off each other's backs."[6] The problem is that, although such meetings may serve a social purpose, they're deeply unproductive.

The conventional objection at this stage would be to say that there are good meetings and there are bad meetings, and it's wrong to assume that all are a waste of time just because some may be. Devotees of such office gatherings often pipe up to say that the effectiveness of a meeting can be fixed with a strong agenda and clear objectives. They know this because they wrote it down at business school. Almost without exception, these experts are responsible for running dismally life-sapping meetings themselves (and they ban electronic devices from them by way of catty retribution if they think other attendees are looking disengaged). I've been to enough of these business school–inspired meetings with former management consultants to know it's a lie for them to claim that their meetings are better. What they tend to be is exhaustingly earnest (and, as I pointed out in Recharge 8, self-regulation can be mentally exhausting).

In point of fact, regardless of who's in the chair, the evidence for meetings is not encouraging. Ben Waber from Humanyze is emphatic that meetings don't create the kind of cohesion essential to great teams: "The results couldn't have been clearer. Neither formal meetings nor people chatting at their desks encouraged higher cohesion." And Leslie Perlow—trailblazing observer of workplace productivity (mentioned in Recharge 9)—has observed that many of us see meetings as nothing more than a "cultural tax" on a productive working environment. When workers "sacrifice their own time and well-being for meetings," she asserts, "they assume they're doing what's best for the business."[7] It's the perfect description of the average meeting. The problem is that if the objective of the next generation of work is to make us more inventive, then a "necessary tax" on thinking isn't a great place to start.

The great curse of meetings is that they tend to take place just when we could be at our most productive and innovative (see Recharge 1). We give the best time of the day to them, forcing more creative work into our lunch breaks and evenings. We find ourselves making that vital phone call on the journey home or working on that key strategy paper sitting hunched over our laptop at the kitchen table. If you're ever found yourself telling people that you come in early because it's the only time you can get work done, you know how ultimately draining the experience is. You may yourself be guilty of helping to create the problem.

Modern work is filled with so many obstacles in the way of our making progress that we often can't help our attention drifting away. Everyone is familiar with that irrelevant twenty-minute presentation about someone else's part of the business that we've been forced to sit through. If we have to listen to something that doesn't matter to us, to do it once is a kindness, but to do it regularly is a burden. That's why even good people like to get their devices out and try to swipe away a few messages when the spotlight isn't on then. The problem is that—as I've pointed out elsewhere—lots of office behaviors are contagious, particularly if it's the boss leading the way: if a boss does electronic multitasking in a meeting, other attendees are 2.2 times more likely to do so as well.[8] And since no one is as good at multitasking as they think they are, nor is multitasking as productive as its adherents would like to believe (see Recharge 7), it's worth asking the question: what is this meeting achieving if everyone's on their phone?

Put very simply, teams should be small, and meetings smaller. The objective of a good meeting has to be to get as few people in a room as possible to make a rapid decision and to allow others to be aware of the process that went into making that decision. (The "radical transparency" investment firm Bridgewater Associates films all of its meetings so that everyone can, if they wish, find out what happened without getting in the way by attending.) Meetings should also be highly focused—one research paper, for instance, concluded, "Teams that showed more functional interaction, such as problem-solving interaction and action planning, were significantly more satisfied with their meetings."[9] A sense of energy and direction definitely helps, too.

But overall, the best thing we can do is try to halve the amount of time we all spend in meetings, reminding ourselves as we do so that they are unproductive social grooming sessions that all too often involve performance rather than high-quality debate. Meeting for a shorter period of time brings focus to our discussions—and an urgency that is too often lost when we slavishly schedule something to last half an hour or an hour.

Some teams find that it's worth putting a regular meeting or sync time on the calendar but canceling it if there's nothing to discuss. Holding the calendar position ensures that everyone is free. Finding that that particular deathly weekly meeting has been canceled is guaranteed to release a few endorphins.

It's something that one huge British utility company exec I spoke with told me the company was considering testing, the idea being that people could vote on whether there was enough to discuss to make that particular week's meeting worthwhile. The company's ultimate objective was to reduce the time people spend tied up in meetings from several hours a week to just a handful.

Of course, if our bosses don't see things this way, there's little we can do. Proper discussions about the best way to get things done are few and far between. It's nevertheless worth taking it upon yourself to be a gently spoken champion for change. If a discussion can be provoked—and furnished with evidence—about how reducing meetings might help with getting work done, in my experience there's a chance to make progress. Sometimes banning PowerPoint can have this effect (see Buzz 8): when people don't have bulleted text to read, they tend to get their points across in a quicker, more conversational way. In the notes to this chapter there are details of articles that you can print out and share.

The only certainties in life are death and meetings, but be bold; be the agent of change in your office.

What You Can Do Next:

» Start asking questions. Ask the person who runs the meeting if it could be done in less time. Ask the attendees of your own meetings if everyone needs to meet this week. By asking questions you will invite others to question what they might have considered nonnegotiable.

» Suggest to your boss testing a system in which some days are meeting-free. Some companies that have tried this have found that the desk-based chats that take place on those days often accomplish the same objectives as meeting slots but in a more dynamic and energy-filled way.

» Suggest taking the Marshmallow Challenge with your team—
and then leading a discussion about what can be learned from
it. Reminder: you have eighteen minutes to construct the
tallest freestanding structure possible out of twenty pieces of
dry spaghetti, a yard of sticky tape, a yard of string, and one
marshmallow. At the end of the exercise the marshmallow
must sit at the top of the construction. What did you learn
about decision making in your team? (For how others have
fared, see comparative scores in the endnote cited here.)[10]

Sync 4

Create a
Social Meeting

Given that I've suggested you halve the amount of time you spend in meetings, it might seem a little counterintuitive for me to suggest you create another slot in your calendar, but adding a social meeting to the schedule is probably the most essential thing any team can do to increase its Sync.

Most of us work on the assumption that reports, email, and presentations are absolutely key to our performance but that talking to a colleague at the coffee machine is unproductive. "Haven't you got anything to do?" we holler at people we see chatting away as we hurry back to our desks to send that crucial email. But Ben Waber, whose sociometric badges I described in Sync 1, thinks we've got it wrong. All the data he's gathered have convinced him that those casual conversations of which we're so critical have a direct and measurable impact on workplace productivity. He points out, "The whole reason we're in organizations is because together we can do something we couldn't do by ourselves. To do that effectively you need to coordinate. Coordinating effectively means you don't have to redo work." Not to encourage informal conversation runs counter to the business reasons for bringing people together in the first place.

Face-to-face interaction, then, in Waber's view, is a vital but often underestimated trigger of workplace productivity. He found, for example, when he was evaluating software engineers, that those who operated remotely—who didn't interact with others face to face—worked more slowly and made contributions of a lower quality than those who had regular contact with colleagues. "Your code depends on the code of thousands of other people," he argues. "If you don't communicate with them, that's where the bugs pop up." Having looked at decades' worth of research, he has even been able to quantify the shortfall created by remote working among software engineers. "If my code depends on your code and we don't communicate," he says, "it takes us 32 percent longer to complete that code."[1]

A few years ago, the internet firm Yahoo banned its employees from working from home on the grounds that other peer-group companies didn't do it. In Waber's view, this was the right decision, but it was made for the wrong reason. Yahoo, he feels, should have pointed to the clear evidence that remote workers don't talk to others on their teams nearly as often as they should. His figures are stark: an average of 7.8 weekly communications for those working remotely, compared with 38 per week among those in close proximity to one another. When this happens, Waber believes, everything suffers. Work slows. Its quality declines. And costs rise.

Constant communication, then—by which I mean informal, unscheduled chat, not formal, prearranged meetings—is the essential oil that lubricates an enterprise and ensures its smooth running. It's what creates Sync. The question is, what's the best way to ensure that it happens?

Margaret Heffernan found out how the hard way. Heffernan was a wily CEO for hire who proved her adaptable leadership as boss of five different companies (before ultimately becoming a business broadcaster). One of her job moves took her from the United Kingdom to the United States. There, she was confronted with a difference between the way her new team in Boston interacted and the way interactions took place in her previous job on the other side of the Atlantic. "The first company, I did what you'd expect; I hired all sorts of extraordinary and wonderful people and gave them all sorts of hard problems to solve. My observation was that everyone came into work and worked very diligently and went home again. And the thing I chiefly remember is that it didn't *sound* right. There wasn't what I think of as a jolly hum. It certainly didn't sound like companies I'd run in the UK. I thought about this and I was trying to work out 'what's wrong?' I just felt it was all a bit too tasky, too tactical." Having scratched her head as to why this should be so, she hit upon a possible, very simple reason: "What I chiefly remember from my companies in the UK was that at the end of the day—or definitely on a Friday—people would go to the pub to wait for the horrible London rush hour to subside."

This insight led Heffernan to do something that seems in retrospect blindingly simple. She introduced a weekly *social* meeting. At half past four every Friday, everyone would stop work, gather together, and listen as a small handful of their colleagues stood up to say who they were and what they did. At first, as Heffernan is the first to admit, the meetings were "beyond awkward." She nevertheless persisted because she was at her "wits' end" and "didn't know what else to do." And pretty soon the awkwardness and embarrassment became a thing of the past. Colleagues relaxed and started simply to talk to one another. A bond was created. Ultimately, Heffernan says, everyone agreed that the new social meeting was "absolutely transformative": "In any organization, the whole premise of organizational life is that together you can do more than you can do in isolation—but that only works if people are committed to each other—and *that* only works if they trust each other and like each other."[2] This is another reminder that Sync is an advanced way of delivering the sense of belonging I talked about earlier.

The fascinating thing about such social meetings is that many companies end up stumbling into very similar arrangements by accident rather than by design. At Twitter's London office, we have a Friday afternoon meeting called Tea Time. If you asked me to pinpoint what it achieves, I'd struggle. But in terms of energizing the team it is peerless. Someone stumbles to the front of the room and tells a gathered group of two hundred people what their job is. Another person steps up to share a recent project they've been working on that people might not have heard about. To round things off, one of the best storytellers in the team will step forward to share a story relating to Twitter that has taken place that week—sometimes funny, sometimes sad, sometimes a lesson we can learn from. That's it. With a few drink and food options to keep things going.

Biz Stone, Twitter's cofounder, explained to me how this get-together came about: "Tea Time started out when I said we should copy Google—every Friday we should stop work and gather around and talk about the week. What did we ship? What went wrong? And if anyone has anything interesting to show us—whether it's their own work, or some other people's work outside that they find inspiring or interesting or whatever. So let's do it. And Jack [Dorsey, cofounder of Twitter] said, 'Great, and we'll do it at 4:05 p.m. which is teatime, so I'll make tea for everyone.' I bought beer and put it in the fridge. And everyone just drank the beer." Stone explained that there was nothing complicated about this. All they were trying to do was let the team "be a group." "It gets people seeing what happened that week," Stone went on. "Then afterwards I can talk to some sales guys that I never would talk to ever in my normal day at work. It's important to have fun and make fun of the leadership team. You know, everyone's like, 'Oh it's Jack Dorsey, oh my gosh I better look away. I can't sit next to him, he's so important.' I just take the piss out of him all the time. He loves it."

What about the pub approach that Margaret Heffernan commented on? There's no doubt that it has much to commend it. Alcohol plus relaxation often results in the wonderful sound of laughter as colleagues de-stress after a hard day at work and share a subversive take on the previous few hours' nonsense.

But the after-office-hours approach can raise problems. Socializing outside work hours has historically been unfair to working mothers (and the data suggest that yes, it is predominantly women). We might like to think that in this modern age, parental responsibilities are evenly split between partners, but in reality that is very rarely the case. It's telling, for example, that data showing that longer commutes correlate with lower levels of happiness also show that this is particularly the case for women. Why? Because women know that after a long commute they are the ones who are most likely to have to pick up responsibility for domestic duties. (As an aside, it's worth noting that commuting also tends to crowd out the activities that renew our energy—being with friends, exercising, relaxing—a problem that can be mitigated by watching TV shows on our devices, reading, or listening to music.) That's not to say that bars or restaurants aren't sometimes good places for teams to bond, but we should be mindful how we time our visits and take account of other people's nonwork priorities.

A good social meeting, then, is both possible and desirable in an office environment. But just as drink helps break down barriers of reserve in a bar or restaurant, something is needed in the office to help relax people. And I would suggest that that something is food. Claudia Wallace, then head of new business at the advertising agency Young & Rubicam, told me about a weekly ritual at her company called Chip Thursday.[3] The ritual developed organically (as is so often the case with the best ideas), having initially been created by a heroically energizing receptionist. Wallace explained what was involved: "Every Thursday at 4:25 everyone in the agency receives an email from our head receptionist called Gillian saying, 'It's Chip Thursday—it's the best time of the week.' On a long table that runs down the center of the office there are a series of bowls of potato chips. Everyone crowds round, has some snacks and talks about the week (there's often also wine and beers)." To preserve a sense of fun and novelty, each week involves a slightly different theme, so, for example, "a few weeks ago there was a Pringles week and Gillian came dressed as a Pringles can."

"Half past four on a Thursday is a great time," Wallace said. "It's close enough to the end of the day or the week that people feel like they can have a break." But, as she pointed out to me, the occasion is about much more than snacks. It may normally last no more than half an hour, but it creates the ideal environment for those accidental encounters among team members that can prove so invaluable. "In an ad agency it's so important to have these moments where people can have time with people. Sometimes you have conversations there with people you haven't managed to catch up with all week because you haven't managed to put a meeting in for it.

You rely on the fact most people are going to be at Chip Thursday. Sometimes you talk about work, sometimes you don't talk about work at all." It reminds me of what Steve Wozniak—cofounder of Apple—wrote in his memoir about his early years working at Hewlett-Packard.[4] The workday, he recalled, had been made considerably more enjoyable by a cart laden with coffee and cakes that arrived at 10 a.m. and 2 p.m. And those coffee-and-cake breaks were often the occasion for valuable discussions and interchange of ideas.

It doesn't have to be cake or potato chips. Andy Puleston told me of his experiences when he was head of digital at the BBC station Radio 1. "The heartbeat at Radio 1 was the monthly pizza meeting." "Once a month," he recalled, the controller of Radio 1, Andy Parfitt, would lay on pizza and drinks (footing the bill himself), and "as many people as could fit into the board room would pack themselves in (we'd take out the table and chairs)." Puleston's view was that it was the very tightness of the space that gave the regular gathering its unique "all in it together" atmosphere. And with that came a certain degree of magic. "It did have a family feel to it; there's something special about having your work mates up close, rather than spread out in some sort of cavernous meeting space. If you ever put a party on, the size of the venue is critical to whether it works, and having a large amount of people in a small space is much more conducive to having a good time than having a much larger room."[5]

Of course, pizza meetings turned out to be about more than pizza, cramped space, and fun. In Puleston's view, "there was definitely a synchronization part to that meeting. All cultures require synchronization and it's important because it makes knowledge common. The emotional content of that meeting is what made it what it was, and made it so effective." And did food help? "Food is essentially what brings people to the table but then it's all about what you say, and the intent of the meeting." It's worth noting that at the time, Radio 1 topped the BBC's poll of employee satisfaction.

Sandy Pentland from Sync 1 has spent time measuring the impact of these interactions: "Social time turns out to be deeply critical to team performance, often accounting for more than 50 percent of positive changes in communication patterns." This affirms what Margaret Heffernan believes: "The crucial thing is the social bonds between people." If you want people to work well with one another, you have to give them the opportunity to meet informally, to get to know each other properly, and to swap thoughts and ideas. "If you really believe that the value of collaboration lies in the aggregation and compounding of talent and creativity then you have to have an environment in which people are really willing to help each other. And people are only really going to be willing to help each other if they in turn believe that they will be helped when they need it."[6]

So go out, buy five tubes of Pringles, and give a social meeting a go.

What You Can Do Next:

» Ignore the cynics and try to organize a social meeting.

» Work with and around your organization's rules, just as Radio 1 did by getting the boss to buy the pizzas. It may be, for example, that you're not allowed to drink on-site. If that's the case, do a charity bake or just grab a cup of coffee with colleagues and decamp to a meeting room.

» Remind the naysayers that researchers have found time and time again that teams experience Sync at its best when they meet in a social way.

» At first, you may need to incentivize people by adding a quirky or entertaining element to the enterprise.

Sync 5

Laugh

How can some people appear not to love laughing? Kids love to laugh. Why, then, do their adult selves often seem so unsmiling? How did they go from early giggling to stern-faced misery? Yes, of course, the world can be a cruel place, but that transition from smiling to frowning seems a great tragedy.

And not simply because it's fun to laugh and see others laugh; humor is a very powerful tool for helping us to cope and stay sane. Writers such as Laurence Gonzales and Al Siebert have studied the effect that laughter can have on us, suggesting that laughing cements a sense of positivity, of resilience. It's often been noted that those who are caught up in traumatic situations but who can find humor in their predicament cope better than those who experience only anxiety and stress. All the evidence suggests, for example, those who have emerged from a plane crash in the jungle are not those who stayed in sober focus but rather those who admitted strange moments of levity in their despair. They inexplicably found themselves experiencing moments of amusement about their apparently hopeless plight. Similarly, those who do very dangerous or highly stressful jobs cope best when there's humor around. Gonzales, who has also studied the survival mentality observed in the dark humor of fighter pilots, notes that this is observable even during routine daily briefings in combat situations: "In a true survival situation you are by definition looking death in the face and if you can't find something droll and even something wondrous and inspiring in it you are already in a world of hurt."[1]

Studies of army field hospitals report that these places are filled with laughter: "It's just something that allows them to get on with the job."[2] Mark de Rond, an ethnographer who spent six weeks embedded in a field hospital in Camp Bastion in Afghanistan, told me that in his first week alone he observed 174 casualties, 6 of whom were dead on arrival. But despite all this, he said, there was a morbid humor to their team dynamic—they would laugh all day, every day.[3] In *The Survivor Personality*, Al Siebert characterizes those with a survival mentality as people who "laugh at threats, playing and laughing go together. Playing keeps the person in contact with what is happening around him."[4] Humor in such situations is, in Laurence Gonzales's words, a "de-escalating emotional response" that helps those who do manage to survive catastrophes to move from the paralysis of fear to a far more constructive state of mind.

Admittedly, an office is not exactly the same as a war room or an army field hospital. But even so, humor has its part to play here, too. And the evidence suggests that it plays a much more sophisticated role than you might think. Quite simply, it helps us to Sync.

Psychologist Robert Provine, who has taken a keen interest in laughter as humankind's way to synchronize with each other, has provided invaluable insights into office life and culture and, in particular, into one of humanity's great pleasures.[5] He started his investigation of laughter with an invitation for people to watch comedy videos in his lab in groups of three while he observed them. To his frustration and annoyance, no one laughed. But he'd nevertheless stumbled upon an important discovery that we can probably all recognize: strangers plus comedy films is not a great formula for laughter. Next, he turned off his videos, put on his coat, and headed out for the street. And as he wandered around shopping centers, offices, and campuses he eavesdropped on people, waiting for that moment when they broke into laugher, and scribbling down what he observed as they did so. It strikes me as a research method that was not without risk, but fortunately no one ever summoned a passing police officer.

Having immersed himself in mirth, Provine reached a conclusion that was, superficially, at least, a very simple one. "Laughter," he argued, "can be regarded as an aesthetically and sonically impoverished 'human song.'"[6] Just as birds sing to each other, or dogs in neighboring backyards bark at each other, or wolves howl together, so humans laugh to connect with one another, to achieve synchronization. "Laughter is the quintessential human social signal. Laughter is about relationships. . . . Think of the last time you sat in an audience, laughing and letting waves of laughter wash over you," Provine wrote. "A pleasant experience—one of life's best. But consider now the primal nature of the animal chorus and the way the members of an audience synchronize their noises."[7]

"Synchronize their noises" is not a phrase that we would naturally associate with laughter. We think of the roar of the crowd as they respond to a comedian's killer punchline. She delivers the payoff line and the audience responds in a euphoric wave of hilarity. But actually, what Provine is talking about here is something different. It's not about laughing because a joke is funny. It's about laughing as a form of social bonding and group coordination.

By stepping inside offices, Provine was able to study and record over a thousand laughter episodes. And what he discovered was that laughter wasn't triggered by humor or hilarious jokes but by seemingly innocuous comments:

"I'll see you guys later."

"We can handle this."

"I think I'm done."

"I told you so."

"There you go."

"Must be nice."

Laughter here wasn't a response to humor (nor was it meant sarcastically or facetiously). It was a human means to warm a room, to lift the mood, to create a sense of connection. It was accomplishing something that we observe in animals. Just as birds in a forest join one another in song, so we laugh together to come together. The urge to join in transcends the humor of the moment. "You know, in hindsight, it wasn't actually that funny, but . . ."

If you're skeptical about this, watch a comedy special on your own on Netflix tonight. Laughter (as opposed to a sense of amusement) needs more than humor to get it going. When others aren't there, we laugh less because we're not attempting to synchronize with them. Provine's critical point is this: "We tend to overlook the fact that laughter evolved because of its effect on others, not to improve our mood or health." Just as Eno's pensioners on the bus achieved a moment of synchronization through a conversation about a TV soap opera (see p. 126), laughter has precisely the same effect. It signals that we're in agreement; we're in Sync.

And, by the same token, it indicates that we feel we're in a safe and secure environment. Professor Sophie Scott from University College London points out that scientists have observed that many mammals exhibit laughter-type reactions but that these can be easily stopped by a negative stimulus. "Rats stop laughing if they feel anxious," she says. "Humans do the same thing." On the other hand, a moment of laughter is an indication that we feel relaxed and safe, that we can afford to let our protective guard down. Or, as Professor Scott put it: "It's a sign if people are laughing that they're not in that anxious state. It's a marker that the group is in a good place."[8]

When dogs play, they initially lean down on their front legs to signal that what's about to happen is not for real—it's just a game. Their body language (a literal downward dog position, yoga fans) says, "This isn't a genuine chase or fight." For Scott, laughter does the same for humans. It signals, "No harm will pass here." "Groups that laugh together can be more cohesive," Scott argues, and she picks up on that link between humor and stress that I mentioned earlier: "There is literature on workplace humour for professions that have quite stressful jobs like doctors, police and nurses. They tend to be characterized by quite dark humour that's quite exclusive. If you're not part of that group you can be surprised they're laughing at that. But for that group it works because it's just a reason to share laughter in situations where they need to make it better."

An inability to laugh suggests that there may be something wrong: that people feel wary of others, that they don't trust them, that they don't feel they can risk letting their guard down. James Comey, the former FBI director fired by President Trump, observed that he found it remarkable that he'd never seen Trump laugh. Nor could he find any clips on YouTube that showed the president in a relaxed, laughing mood. For Comey, laughter in a leader is a signal of openness and a willingness to show vulnerability. "The mark of a great leader is a combination of things that seem contradictory:

enough confidence to be humble."[9] Insecure people, by contrast, "can't take joy in the achievements of the people around them and a marker of that balance between confidence and humility is humor. If you are insecure you cannot laugh. . . . Engaging in a humorous encounter is a risk for an insecure leader because I might have to acknowledge you, that you've said something funny that I didn't say." Comey recalled that he'd seen Presidents Bush and Obama use humor to relax people, "to get to the truth."

There's something else to bear in mind, too: firsthand accounts suggest that the relaxation brought about by laughter opens our minds to creative thinking. When in 2017 Nobel Prize–winning economist Daniel Kahneman drew back the curtain on the working methods he and his late partner Amos Tversky developed as they collaborated on research into human decision making that is now viewed as groundbreaking and revolutionary, he said that what he recalled vividly was not so much earnest endeavor as laughter. And the pair's *most* creative time together, he went on to say, was also the most laughter filled. "Amos was always very funny," he recalled, "and in his presence I became funny as well, so we spent hours of solid work in continuous amusement."[10]

Amusement, in other words, isn't just a frivolous waste of time. The looseness of thought that laughter provokes triggers our creative juices, encouraging free association of ideas. John Kounios from Drexel University and Mark Beeman from Northwestern University demonstrated as much when they invited volunteers to watch a video of Robin Williams delivering comedy zingers in a stand-up routine and then asked them to solve a series of tricky logic puzzles. What they discovered was that a short laugh at a comedy clip improved people's puzzle-solving ability by 20 percent. Why should this be the case? Well, it appears that laughter triggers the superior anterior temporal gyrus—an area of the brain, just above the right ear, associated with connecting distantly linked ideas. When rigid concentration isn't the answer, it would appear that the distraction caused by laughter can prove invaluable.[11]

Laughter, then, performs numerous functions. It builds trust, it helps us bond with one another, it creates Sync. And as our creative guards come down, it helps us have better ideas. Teams who laugh and joke together tend to be better able to open up and share challenges with each other—which is particularly important for coping with stress and enhancing creative problem solving.[12] So much is clear. But how do we go about laughing more at work without appearing to have gone insane or to have joined some freakish cult?

There's no avoiding the fact that, for some, fully fledged seriousness is what work is about. Such people regard laughter skeptically, suspecting it may simply indicate that some people around the place don't have enough to do. They believe in what is sometimes called "performative busyness." I vividly remember a colleague at my first job advising me that the most appropriate response to being late was to "dump your coat in the accounts department, grab a sheet of paper and walk to your desk looking angry." It's the same mind-set as that of the person who assumes that a serious face silently communicates the message "Yes, I've been in since 7 a.m. working on a special project, and no, I'm not allowed to tell you about it."

So how do we unlock these benefits of laughter in our workplaces? Provine's suggestion is that we should try to adopt a "laugh-ready attitude": "You can voluntarily choose to laugh more by lowering your threshold for amusement," he argues. "Just be willing and prepared to laugh." And one of the ways he suggests that we do this is to arrange more social events—meetings and gatherings in your company intended simply to get people together. In Sync 4,

I made the case for social meetings. Here, I am suggesting that it's just these kinds of get-togethers where laughter can thrive.

It's not always easy to find the right approach to this. The cleaning products company Method has a slot in its weekly meeting in which new employees are introduced and then asked how they propose to "keep Method weird." I'm not going to lie. It makes my stomach clench just thinking about it. A former boss of mine at Twitter used to ask new starters to share their impressions before joining the company, share their first impressions since joining, and then do an impression. A more excruciating welcome I can't begin to imagine. I'm mortally embarrassed that it took us six months to get it abolished.

But the critical thing is to find something that works for your team—and stick to it. Former head of digital at BBC Radio 1 Andy Puleston told me that one ritual the station observed was epic send-off speeches. They felt no sense of shame that someone might be choosing to move on. Instead, they wanted to celebrate the Radio 1 stage of the employee's career through funny, emotion-filled speeches. "We placed a huge amount of importance on leaving speeches," he told me, "because of the culture transference power they had on new joiners. Nothing demonstrates the sort of people and workplace you are joining than witnessing how teams celebrate and bid farewell to the leavers. For those who had been with us a long time, I saw these moments as a chance to acknowledge the entirety of their contribution to work and the team, a living eulogy if you like." Andy would spend time gathering memories, jokes, and photos from teammates and coworkers to give a fully rounded tribute to the leaver. Through those tributes everyone in the team would be more vividly aware of what they were part of; Andy said the room was always filled with "a lot of laughter."

In straitened economic times, the notion of prioritizing discussion and laughter as one of the most important things to do as a team might seem superfluous and trivial—if not to yourself, then to others. But if people say as much to you, remind them of Nobel Prize–winning Daniel Kahneman. Maybe next time inspiration strikes, it will find you laughing.

What You Can Do Next:

» Find time for laughter in your meetings—a social meeting is a good space for this, but so are send-off speeches, milestone work anniversaries, and the like.

» If there's someone on the team who is funny, celebrate it. There is no shame in recognizing that some people have more of a skill here.

» What applies in teams also applies to customers—if laughter builds affiliation and Sync, then why not use humor to build a tighter rapport with the people you do business with?

» People laughing in the office isn't something only for the good times. Laughter isn't just for Christmas; it's for life.

Sync 6

Energize Onboardings

First impressions count, as we're constantly reminded from childhood onward. But as much as we're aware of this truth, we tend to forget it when it really matters. And it does. When TripAdvisor got going a few years back, the hotel industry was suddenly and rudely awakened to the fact that the impression a hotel makes at the point of check-in disproportionately influences the review that people subsequently leave. Hotels eventually took notice and started an arms race of giving warmer welcomes: waiting areas filled with sumptuous sofas, drinks at check-in, wet towels to wipe oneself down in humid climates, Jacuzzis by the elevators, furry animals to cuddle, and so on.

But while some in the hospitality sector may have learned the lesson, it's not one that has had much of an impact with the average business. True, larger companies—with more new starters—tend to be better than most at building basic welcome programs that explain who does what and how to find one's way around. They're less good, however, when it comes to providing any kind of emotional orientation that might help newcomers do their jobs better. A 2018 survey by the workplace technology company Kronos concluded that most companies view onboarding as a way of informing new starters of rules and regulations. They may pay lip service to the cultural aspects of the firm, but they don't give much time to it when workers are most receptive.[1]

So would a more imaginative approach to the onboarding process help? This is what London Business School professor Dan Cable and his colleagues set out to determine in an experiment they ran with a call center in a tech firm called Wipro. New joiners were divided into three groups of fifteen to twenty-five people. One group was given the company's standard orientation. The second was reminded of Wipro's accomplishments in a morale-boosting operation that "focused on the elements of the company that made them proud to be part of the organization." The final group was treated slightly differently: they were asked to reflect on times in previous jobs when they had felt proudest of their achievements, and to chat about these with others in the group. "What is unique about you that leads to your happiest times and best performance at work? Reflect on a specific time—perhaps on a job, perhaps at home—when you were acting in the way that you were 'born to act.'"[2] It was a forty-one-word question, and people were given fifteen minutes to think about it and discuss it.

Given how little time the third group spent on the question, it's tempting to assume that it wasn't much more than a nice icebreaker. Yet it had a transformative influence on their experience of their job. Those new starters who had been invited to share their achievements immediately felt more at home at Wipro. What's more, after six months they were far more likely still to be in their job, in a sector traditionally associated with high staff turnover. Indeed, they were 32 percent less likely to have resigned than their colleagues in either of the other two groups.[3] Perhaps most extraordinary of all, encouraging people to present a positive version of themselves didn't just transform their attitude toward their new job; it also had a measurable impact on the happiness of their customers. The employees who went through the other two onboarding processes scored 61 percent in customer satisfaction polls. Those who had had the "best self" start scored 72 percent. Or, put in other words, fifteen minutes and forty-one words led to an 18 percent improvement in customer satisfaction. For zero cost. Cable noted that despite this energizing impact, "in all my years of working with companies, I have not seen a company use this approach to onboarding."[4]

Other companies have tried other approaches. Stanford business professor Chip Heath and his coauthor brother, Dan, describe how new employees at the heavy machinery manufacturer John Deere receive a friendly email the day before they start work in which they are buddied up with a current member of the staff. Their assigned friend duly introduces himself, gives a few tips on what to wear and where it's best to park, and promises that he will be waiting in reception for the new employee on the first day. The following day, the work friend is there to say hello and to take the new starter to his desk, which has been decorated with a welcome banner. Other small, friendly acts follow.[5] John Deere knows that the more quickly new employees feel at home, the better the work they will do.

So, thinking about how we welcome workers into their jobs is vital. It's easy to get consumed in orientations that offer either a litany of traffic rules or a list of the mundane aspects of the job. But onboarding should be a colorful moment of engagement. If we want to encourage new employees to be their best real selves, let's do that from day one.

What You Can Do Next:

» Try a "best self" onboarding. Think about how you can encourage new starters to feel more at home, more quickly.

» The better the welcome, the sooner new joiners will be delivering results for your team. First impressions count.

Sync 7

Don't Be a
Bad Boss

Let's not mince words. There are some people who end up being cultural icons who behave like dickheads. Fortunately for them, amid the legends of their great products or pioneering successes, we're prepared either to airbrush out their rudeness or (worse) assume that being mean to people is part and parcel of being a genius. But whatever excuses we make for them, they nevertheless remain dickheads. One such person was Steve Jobs.

The iPod was the product that changed Apple's fortunes, setting the company on a path that saw its value increase fifty times. The development stages were long and complex and involved the construction of multimillion-dollar prototypes. On one occasion, according to tech writer Nick Bilton, the expectant engineering team went to Jobs's office to show him their progress on the latest and slickest model. Proffering the miraculous device, they told him, "This is the thinnest we can get it." "Jobs stood there and looked at it, asked a bunch of questions," Bilton explained. "Then he walked over to the fish tank and dropped this $3 million prototype into the fish tank." I know what you're thinking: what kind of jerk has a fish tank in his office? Let's just remind ourselves that it was 2001 and there were still a few corporate fish tanks knocking around. Meanwhile, the team stood around in shock at what Jobs had just done. "Look, there's bubbles coming out of it," Jobs said. "There's still room to make it smaller."

It's pretty clear how your mom would have reacted at this point if you'd done this. "I'm not suggesting you didn't make an interesting point," she would have said, "but you didn't have to make it in that way." Your mom is dead right. Don't have a fish tank, don't drop things in your fish tank, and don't be a dickhead to people next to your fish tank, Steve Jobs.[1]

Whether you're the new recruit or the old lag who has been evading being found out for a couple of decades, it's certain that you have a boss. All of us—even CEOs—are accountable to someone. And nothing affects what we think about our job more than our relationship with our boss. There's an old truism that people "resign from their managers, not their job." The evidence bears that out. If you want to stem the flood of people resigning from a team, the first action you should take is to look at the manager.

Bad managers are, unfortunately, everywhere. (According to Professor Robert Hogan from the University of Tulsa, three-quarters of American adults say the worst aspect of their job is their immediate boss.)[2] Psychologist Teresa Amabile, whom we first met in Recharge 1 and who tracked office workers' daily routines via the diaries she got them to keep, observed that most of the time when managers were mentioned, it was generally in the context of *de*motivating someone in their work. People think they have a bad job if they have a bad manager. Bad management is one of the easiest ways to destroy Sync in a team.

The findings of renowned Nobel laureate Daniel Kahneman are arguably even bleaker. He and a team of collaborators wanted to get a handle on those times when we feel the greatest satisfaction in our lives, so they set out to measure the good and bad moods (positive and negative affect) volunteers felt at different moments of the day and to discover what caused these shifting feelings.[3] Not surprisingly, they found that there was a gulf between the enjoyment people felt while commuting (3.45 out of a possible maximum 6) and the enjoyment they experienced when relaxing with friends (4.59)—a 1.14-point differential on their scale. When it came to the workplace, pressure or tiredness could easily shift happiness down a point on the scale (in fact, tiredness could bring even the single most enjoyable experience, "intimate relations"—in other words, sex—down from a 5.1 to a score lower than the 3.1 recorded for people who were on their daily commute but who felt well rested).

	Positive Affect Rating (Out of 6)	When Under Time Pressure (Out of 6)	When Tired (Out of 6)
Intimate relations	5.10	0.74	3.09
Socializing	4.59	1.20	2.33
Eating	4.34	0.95	2.55
Watching TV	4.19	1.02	3.54
Preparing food	3.93	1.54	3.11
Taking care of children	3.86	1.95	3.56
Working	3.62	2.70	2.42
Commuting	3.45	2.60	2.75
Interacting with friends	4.36	1.61	2.59
Interacting with spouse	4.11	1.53	3.46
Interacting with boss	3.52	2.82	2.44

There are two massive headlines that come out of Kahneman and his colleagues' work. Being with our bosses is our least favored interaction of our day (beaten only by commuting)—but additionally it's worth noting that every single thing in our lives is made considerably worse by time pressure and tiredness. These headlines incidentally point to the truth of Recharge 4—that hurry sickness is toxic, and Recharge 11—that sleep is essential. In the context of this disdain for our bosses, it should come as no surprise that when researchers at the University of Warwick asked people how much more they would have to be paid to be prepared to work with a bad manager, the response was that a 150 percent increase in wages would be required to compensate for the stress and unhappiness caused.[4]

So what is it that bad bosses do? According to Tulsa University professor Robert Hogan, the "misery" and "stress" they cause attacks people's health and immune systems to the point where they are actually sick ("bad managers create enormous health costs," he said).[5] One vast survey that tracked over three thousand Swedish men across a ten-year span of their working lives found that bad managerial practice led to a 60 percent increase in the incidence of heart attacks (on the positive side, those men who had good managers were 40 percent less likely to have heart problems). Four particular trigger traits were identified: incompetence, lack of consideration, secretiveness, and uncommunicativeness.[6]

Of course, there are those who would argue that the factors that help workers rise to the level of being bosses (ambition, drive, resilience to setbacks) are the very personality traits that cause them to be hopeless, unempathetic managers. It's worth noting, though, that none of those traits appeared among the list that the Swedish researchers identified as defining a bad manager. You can be ambitious and resilient without being a terrible boss.

Poor managers tend to blame their teams. "Forget about bad managers," they say; "what about bad workers?" Or "If only I could just get rid of the moaners, we'd be happy." What they tend to forget, though, is that *everyone* hates working for a bad manager. When researchers at Warwick University crunched years of data from the United Kingdom and the United States to try to understand how much of our happiness at work was related to the performance of our bosses, they discovered that whether those involved were moaners ("drains") or genuine assets ("radiators"), the views expressed were exactly the same. Bad managers make us all unhappy.[7]

What, then, makes a good boss? Two principal guiding stars seem to be involved. One, quite simply, is to "be supportive." Such is our desire to be valued by our managers that even if all they appear to do is to say how amazing we are, that can actually help improve our workplace performance because it encourages our sense of engagement. Researchers who studied people working for very generous bosses who, if anything, tended to overrate their teams, found that praise inflation invariably worked: "that vote of confidence made them more optimistic about future improvement." Those, by contrast, whose bosses were more critical often ended up quitting their teams, "confused or discouraged—often both." They tended to interpret negative feedback not as a spur to improve but as a brake on likely future success.[8] Such findings are very much in line with the research into unmarried couples in relationships I mentioned earlier (see pp. 113, 125). "Positive illusion"—the belief that someone is amazing, regardless—is extraordinarily powerful. It keeps couples together.[9] At work, the belief that someone values us highly overcomes almost everything else. If we believe that our bosses love us, we are more likely to feel we're happy in our job.

Indeed, good managers have more impact than higher salaries. That, at least, is the conclusion that was drawn following a role-play experiment carried out in Spain and the United States in which teams were given a challenge and managers were instructed to direct them as they saw fit. It was found that those managers who communicated motivationally were more effective than those who offered rewards. In the view of the researchers, the best thing that managers can do is to tell the team to work hard, remind them that they are well paid, and then get out of the way![10] It's a not dissimilar view to that expressed by happiness expert Richard Reeves, who reckons that managers should try to stay out of the way as much as possible. "Do no harm," he recommends. "That's an incredibly important principle. What are the things that make people unhappy? Stop doing them."[11] If a boss feels uncertain what to do to help, doing less is better than getting involved.

Of course, keeping out of the way is desirable only if a boss isn't very capable. There's no doubt that an elite manager doesn't just stay out of the way but provides high-quality coaching and support. And that brings me to an assessment of what a good boss does to separate himself or herself from a bad one: the evidence suggests it's best to have a good working knowledge of what you expect the members of your team to be doing.

While I'm always reluctant to share examples from the world of sports, as they tend to be based on small data sets and obscured by anecdotes, in this instance this is something that the sporting world has long known about. "The best basketball players really do become the best coaches," Amanda Goodall, an associate professor at Cass Business School, told me.[12] And she found precisely the same picture when she looked at Formula One auto racing: "We identified four general types of team leaders (Principals as they are called in F1): managers, engineers, mechanics and former drivers. We found that the former drivers go on to be the best Principals." In the world of everyday work, in Goodall's view, similar rules apply: people respond best to someone who understands the nuances of their job. She argued, "If their boss had worked their way up through the organization or started the organization, if that boss was capable of doing the job of an employee, and if the employee considered their boss to be competent... these were incredibly strong predictors of high job satisfaction among employees."[13] The more connected a boss is to the intricate details of the job, the more likely their advice will be helpful.

It's worth adding that there's an innate danger here. A "been there, posted the photo" mentality is never going to help if a boss is exclusively bringing learning from a previous generation of work. Experience and empathy are a vital combination.

Goodall's findings should serve as a warning to those who think an MBA in management is all you need, and that the specifics of a sector are less important for a boss than general notions of strategy and leadership. Fortunately, some organizations have woken up to this. These days, companies such as McDonald's send their bosses back to the shop floor once a year to make sure they understand what it is they are expecting their frontline troops to do. Nothing builds empathy more quickly for those doing a job than actually having to do it yourself.

Tom Leitch, the engineering director for the international food delivery app Deliveroo, is certainly one who believes this. He explained to me that everyone on his team is also registered as a delivery driver on the app and that they have to make the time to do a delivery or two themselves every week. "We just end up understanding some of the things that go through a real driver's mind far more completely," he argues. "For example, we found that our drivers in Hong Kong are preoccupied with finding parking spaces for their bikes way before they get to a restaurant. Hong Kong is basically on a mountain, so what looks like short walking distances on a map can be huge hills. A parking spot that looks like a minute away can actually add five minutes to a trip."[14] Understanding such crucial details—which might otherwise seem irrelevant annoyances back at the office—transforms the relationship between managers and employees and eliminates the danger of a knowledge gap opening up between the shop floor and those who are making the decisions.

In other words, an expert is not the same as a know-it-all—expert managers know a lot, and they build trust and empathy on the basis of that knowledge. But they don't have to be the sort of person who could claim to do someone else's job better than them. Indeed, if they think that, real danger lurks.

Mastering the computer systems that your team uses, seeing every mundane stage of a process, knowing how something is made—all these things can help bridge the gap of understanding that will otherwise gradually build up between bosses and workers in our jobs and can create that essential bond. It's often the case, too, that once a boss understands how a job is done, she will become more sympathetic to, say, allowing flexible hours or eliminating that meeting everyone else knows is a waste of time. "If your manager is an expert boss, they create the right working environment for you," Goodall reminds us. "We find that good bosses understand the nature of our work."[15] This understanding leads to more trust. By contrast, when managers don't fully comprehend the roles, they might be tempted to intervene. As Goodall puts it, a bad manager would say, " 'I think I'm going to get them to fill out this form before they go to a meeting to keep my arse clear in case [they're] lying.' If you've walked the walk, you don't have to put in loads of managerial processes." It's why Goodall's advice is that all managers "have to start off with humility—knowing what they don't know." The best people "go in asking questions . . . they go in and listen to the experts who are doing the job."

And once that happens, the performance of the whole firm improves. Researchers at the University of Sheffield found that companies that enjoy higher levels of trust in their management achieve better results than those that don't.[16] The conclusion? If employees feel that they are being treated fairly and are being led well by good managers, they will invest more in what they do. If we think we're working for a fair company, we more than compensate by working harder for it. Management alone can't create Sync, but poor management is very capable of destroying it.

Badly run companies, by contrast, hemorrhage workers, and in the process they ratchet up all the costs this involves, spending money on recruitment while losing money via the temporary loss of productivity and expertise.

The rules for good bosses are clear: empathic knowledge and support. If you can't be good, be supportive. It's time to stop being a bad boss.

What You Can Do Next:

» "Do no harm" is the golden rule of management.

» Empathizing with the challenges and realities of a job is vital for managers. If your team complains about a software system you've never used, it's possible that you'll dismiss their concerns about it; the only way to fully understand is to spend a week in their shoes.

» The best bosses generally have done the job they are managing. If you've never done the job, then going out of your way to fully understand it bridges the gap with a team.

Sync 8

Know When to Leave People Alone

"Most inventors and engineers I've met are like me . . . they live in their heads. They're almost like artists. In fact, the very best of them are artists. And artists work best alone. . . . I'm going to give you some advice that might be hard to take. That advice is: work alone. . . . Not on a committee. Not on a team." Apple co-founder Steve Wozniak's view of how the best ideas are created may come as something of a shock after everything I've said about the need for teamwork.[1] It certainly contradicts how Steve Jobs viewed things. According to his biographer Walter Isaacson, Jobs agonized over the design of Pixar's office space precisely because he was convinced that people shouldn't be working alone. "He obsessed over ways to structure the atrium, and even where to locate the bathrooms, so that serendipitous personal encounters would occur," Isaacson wrote.[2]

So which is it? Do you leave your finest inventive minds well alone? Or do you embed them in a group and seek to create a brilliantly inventive team?

The answer is that it entirely depends on what stage you are at and what you are seeking to do. In the early days of a project or in-itiative, you should leave people to their own devices, to dream up ideas and play around with them in their heads. But when it comes to polishing and finessing those ideas, or to solving problems and bottlenecks, the team needs to be there to help. It's not a ques-tion of either leaving people alone or bringing them together. It's a question of knowing *when* to leave them alone and when to bring them together.

Certainly, the evidence suggests that getting a team involved too early in proceedings can be counterproductive. It's become clear over the past few years that the ultimate expression of the collective imagination—the brainstorm—doesn't really work, or, at least, that it is far less effective than we once wanted to be-lieve. People may think they're throwing brilliant ideas about, but as in all meetings (see Sync 3), a lot of wasted effort is actually going into social positioning and one-upmanship. Additionally, as one researcher, Charlan Nemeth, a professor of psychology at the University of California, Berkeley, points out, one of the norms of brainstorming—"no idea is a bad idea"—is also one of the reasons why it doesn't work. It's simply not the case, she says, that "the most important thing to do when working together is stay positive and get along, to not hurt anyone's feelings. That's just wrong. Maybe debate is going to be less pleasant, but it will always be more pro-ductive. True creativity requires some trade-offs."[3] The friction of saying why a suggestion is lame is far more likely to produce a creative spark in a group. Interestingly, scientists have found that brainstorming sessions work best when people are first given the opportunity to come up with their own ideas. If they do that and the group then comes together to pool its thoughts, the result is often a doubling of creative suggestions.[4]

Susan Cain, writer of *Quiet*, believes that the reason we like to believe in the power of the brainstorm is that the groupthink of the modern age celebrates the habits of extroverts at the expense of the less evident actions of introverts. She argues that the rise of performative arts and culture that we witnessed through the twentieth century resulted in a favoring of the skills of the half of society who are extroverted over the other half who are too embarrassed to admit they prefer to work alone.

And yet, Cain says, if you look closely at how even famously collaborative teams have worked, it's clear that their great ideas started with individuals. Take two of the most successful songwriters of all time: John Lennon and Paul McCartney. Many of their greatest songs, credited to the Lennon-McCartney brand throughout the life span of the Beatles' career, weren't the fruits of a full-time partnership but arose from the comparing of notes after periods of intense individual invention. Elsewhere in the world of songwriting, Elton John once said of his fifty-plus-year collaboration with Bernie Taupin that their success came down to writing in two separate rooms. "We've never written a song in the same room, ever," he told *Music Week*.[5] Once, they communicated via fax machine. These days, Taupin says, he emails lyrics to John, John composes a melody, and they then meet up to hammer out the details together.

Even though we're familiar with the idea of TV shows emanating from writers' rooms filled with talented minds, often the first work of a script is done by a lone writer—and then it is appraised by the group. Bruce Miller, the showrunner for *The Handmaid's Tale*, explained that for the show, one writer was sent away to construct a script before a second group was then asked to appraise and improve it.[6] Robert Carlock, producer of the Netflix smash *Unbreakable Kimmy Schmidt*, explained his team's approach: "We send an individual off to write an outline. . . . When the draft comes back, we all discuss it, take it apart, put it back together, and then rewrite in a small group. We rewrite a lot."[7] We're not all song or television writers. But the basic principle applies everywhere.

In Sync 4, I described how computer programmers need to work together and talk to each other if they are to iron out bugs in the code, but these connections with one another act as punctuations to blocks of quiet work. Sync isn't achieved by constant dialogue; rather, conversation and solitude act as the vital light and shade of productive working.

It was the power of solitude that emerged from an experiment called the "Coding War Games." The Coding War Games took six hundred developers from almost one hundred different companies and paired them into three hundred teams of two (working at their individual desks), who were given the task of creating a medium-size program to perform a specific task. Teams were allowed considerable autonomy: they could choose to complete the task in whatever coding language they felt to be most suitable, and the researchers were careful to make note of such variables as experience and salary.[8] The one stipulation was that the programmers should perform their task in precisely the same conditions in which they carried out their normal jobs.[9]

As it turned out, the best teams performed far, far better than the worst—by a factor of 10. They also outperformed the average by 2.5 times. The reason? It was whether people felt they were able to get work done in peace. Sixty-two percent of the top performers said their work space was "acceptably private." Seventy-five percent of the bottom performers, by contrast, said they worked in locations that subjected them to constant interruptions. I've already discussed the negative impact of open-plan offices on performance (see Recharge 1). It would appear that it's not good for creative thinking either. But more to the point, those programmers who performed best did so because they were able to incubate their ideas on their own.

If effective working means getting lots done in calm tranquility, does that mean that working from home is the best solution? I'm very aware what a godsend telecommuting can be for people who are challenged by the demands of balancing domestic and work life. But through gritted teeth, I have to share the news that the evidence for working from home isn't great. Yes, we seem to get blocks of work done, but the loss of Sync outweighs any productivity upside. When Elena Rocco from the University of Michigan explored the different outcomes from colocated and remote workers, she found that remote workers saw a gradual breakdown of mutual trust, which ended up impacting the quality of their collaboration.[10] Home workers report that without a regular feedback loop, their initial productivity boost quickly starts to wane. Here's Ben Waber from Humanyze on the subject: "When you work from home it doesn't just affect you. You dramatically reduce the performance of people you work with by being at home."[11] Waber believes that the reduction in ideas flow caused by working from home reduces the collective intelligence of teams. Staying at the kitchen table is not the answer. You need a balance.

As a workplace tries to build Sync and collaboration among individuals, it's tempting to assume that the next stage is to get teams together to actually come up with ideas. "We've got the team liking each other, there's a good rapport between everyone—now let's come up with some suggestions for next year." Beware of falling into this trap. Sync is about people working together in harmony— but no amount of Sync will change the power of individuals applying gray matter to difficult problems alone. Creativity is about thinking and then discussion—a team in Sync will make sure it's doing both.

What You Can Do Next:

» Remember that creative ideas are sparked and nurtured in one person's brain. The group's role is to shape and improve the initial idea—feedback loops will make it better.

» Monk Mode Mornings or moments of quiet reflection are a vital part of the creative process.

Part 3

Buzz

THE TEN SECRETS OF ENERGIZED TEAMS

Introduction

Making Your Work Buzz

Having discussed ways to Recharge and to Sync with your team, I'll now suggest some ways to achieve the most elevated state of work: Buzz. Earlier, I described how successful teams have forged a state of synchronization. Buzz is the next step up—a sense of engagement and positive energy, created through a combination of two well-recognized phenomena: positive affect and psychological safety.

Positive Affect

Imagine that you're sitting at home one evening and the phone rings. You answer and promptly discover that the person at the other hand has misdialed: she'd been hoping to talk to her friend Victor; instead she's got you. And she's also got a problem because that wrong number means that she has just used up the last of her call credits and, as she tells you in a panic, she has no immediate way of topping them up. She sounds desperate, but in her frustration she doesn't suggest a solution.

What do you do?

It may come as no surprise to learn that it very much depends on how you're feeling. As pioneering psychologist Alice Isen from Cornell University demonstrated, if you're in a good mood, you'll be more inclined to offer to call Victor yourself to relay a message; if you're in a bad (or neutral) mood, you'll be far less likely to offer to help.[1] The technical term for the former frame of mind is "positive affect," and it's a mental state that shapes how we think about almost every situation we encounter in life. More than that, it has a strong influence on how we tackle that situation. As Isen wrote, "Positive affect facilitates creativity, cognitive flexibility, innovative responding, and openness to information."[2] When we're at work, positive affect helps us do a better job.

Positive affect is in many ways what a layperson would call a good mood. And, as with a good mood, it doesn't necessarily have to be associated with a beaming smile, an energized gait, and a hat tip to a stranger. It simply means that at that moment, one has a positive, forward-looking view of the world. That said, positive affect and good mood are not quite the same thing. Whereas a good mood can be attributed to a particular cause (it's a sunny day; you passed an exam), positive affect is more nebulous: as the psychologist Barbara Fredrickson put it, "Affect is often free-floating or objectless."[3] You may feel positive affect without knowing quite what triggered it—in fact, you may be unaware that you *are* feeling it.

Nevertheless, it's a powerful force. Even mild positive affect can make us "approach and explore novel objects, people, or situations" with an open mind.[4] Take the art of negotiation. We tend to assume that when we're trying to achieve a particular outcome we should emulate movie and TV protagonists who adopt a prickly, hostile position to clinch a better result. But actually, we're more likely to succeed if we're in the positive affect zone. As Isen wrote, "There is reason to believe that, even in a potentially hostile situation, positive affect facilitates cognitive flexibility, the ability to switch perspectives and see things in multiple ways and come up with viable solutions, and the ability to cope with potential problems and avoid conflict."[5] In other words, when we know that success in negotiations is usually about creating new and unexpected variables, positive affect puts us in the mind-set to imagine those variables.

The knowledge that positive affect can lead to a good overall outcome is now so well established that many enterprises try to capitalize on it. Why do restaurants give you a mint when they present you with the bill? Because they know that this "present" will make you view the bill more favorably and therefore tip more generously. It's a classic stimulus. According to a study published in the *Journal of Applied Social Psychology*, servers who delivered the check with mints (and then returned with more as a bonus) found that their tips increased by 21 percent.[6]

Positive affect works in a more indirect way, too, as Alice Isen demonstrated when she visited shopping malls and offered passersby a free, no-strings-attached gift in the form of a pair of nail clippers. Since nail clippers are a gift of no more than token significance, you'd expect recipients to be briefly pleased but hardly elated. Isen, however, was interested in how the gift affected their subsequent mood. She therefore arranged for those same passersby to be stopped later and, in an apparently unrelated exercise, asked to give their opinions on their household appliances. What she found was that the recipients of free nail clippers invariably expressed greater satisfaction with their freezers and washing machines than did those who were asked the same questions but who hadn't previously been given a gift. Positive affect is a powerful force.

It also shapes our ability to do things—and from an astonishingly early age. In one experiment, researchers gathered together some four-year-olds and split them into two groups. Both were given a shape-sorting task. Before they started, however, the children in one group were asked, "Can you remember something that happened to you that made you feel so happy that you just wanted to jump up and down?" They were then given just thirty seconds to reflect on their joyful memory. As the shape sorting proceeded, it became clear that the children who had been prompted to recall happy events performed much better at the task than those who hadn't been put in a similarly good mood beforehand.[7]

Maybe there's something to be said for carrying a bag of candies with you and handing them out to people on your travels—at least, that's what you'd conclude when you consider other evidence Isen put together to support her thesis. In one study, for example, she looked at the way positive affect works with hospital doctors. First, she presented each doctor with a patient's case file, containing a full medical history and details of any lab tests carried out. Following this, she gave half the group a paper bag filled with six hard candies and four chocolate miniatures (they were asked to put the gift away for later, so that the experiment would not be affected by random sugar rushes). All the doctors were then asked to do two tests. In the initial one, they were presented with a Remote Associates Test (RAT) in which they were given a series of three words—for example, "room," "blood," "salts"—and asked each time to come up with a fourth word that linked them (it's a test often used to measure creative thinking).[8] After that, they were asked to offer a diagnosis of the patient whose file they had been given. Those doctors who had been given the bag of candies achieved a significantly better set of results in the RAT and arrived at more rounded conclusions in the case study than did the doctors who had come to both tasks unprimed. Isen noted that "doctors in the positive-affect condition realized that the symptoms might suggest liver disease, and considered [the] liver, significantly earlier in their protocols than control participants." They didn't jump to conclusions, she said, but their minds were more engaged and curious. Quite simply, the gentle nudge toward positive affect provided by the candy caused them to do a better job.[9]

So what exactly is going on when we experience positive affect? According to researchers at the University of Toronto, positive affect triggers particular regions of the brain in a particular way. In their experiment, they showed volunteers a series of photos, each of which featured a general view of a house on which a face had been superimposed, asked them to judge whether the face was that of a male or female, and told them to ignore everything else.[10] Since it's been established that there's a region of the brain that is activated by faces and a separate region that responds to places, it came as no surprise to discover that a request to focus on faces resulted in the "face" region of the brain being activated. However, this was not universally the case. The brains of participants who had first been brought into a state of positive affect (normally achieved with a small gift) showed activity not only in the "face" region but also in the "place" one.[11] In other words, because they were experiencing positive affect, they had much broader awareness than did those who hadn't achieved the same mental state. Positive affect opens us up.[12]

For Isen, this opening up was a very powerful force. "Positive affect," she argued, "leads to helping, generosity, and interpersonal understanding." It also improves our judgment.[13] And the surge of dopamine that positive affect stimulates in the brain's frontal cortical areas (specifically, the prefrontal cortex and anterior cingulate cortex) not only better enables us to cope with stress and anxiety but also enhances our creativity.

In Alice Isen's view, the links with creativity are threefold. First, positive affect increases the number of "cognitive elements" available for association—in everyday parlance, it gets more of our brain cells tingling with thought. In word association tests, for example, a good mood has been shown to generate far more imaginative ideas than a bad or neutral state of mind.[14] Second, it leads to defocused attention of the kind advertising executive James Webb Young was so keen to promote (see Recharge 3). That is to say, it

encourages us not to obsess about something but to let it perco-
late in the back of our mind until—seemingly miraculously—we
make a breakthrough. (Unfocused thinking explains why three-
quarters of us say that we often have our best creative ideas while
we're in the shower.[15] Aaron Sorkin, the writer of screen hits such
as *The West Wing* and *The Social Network*, is one creative mind
who's learned to harness the power of this unfocused thinking; he
proudly claims to shower six to eight times a day: "I'm not a germa-
phobe [but] when writing isn't going well . . . I will shower, change
into new clothes and start again."[16])

Finally, positive affect increases cognitive flexibility, increasing the probability that different ideas (cognitive elements) will
be activated. In Sync 5, I noted that people who watched a Robin
Williams comedy routine proved better at puzzle solving than
those who didn't. When our brain is relaxed, we're more likely to
think innovatively.

Having said that, it's worth acknowledging that many of us can
recall an experience when a moment of heightened stress—or an
urgent deadline—helped focus our mind to its sharpest. Negative
affect has a part to play in our lives, too. Barbara Fredrickson, who
has devoted her career to studying the effects of these forces on
the human psyche, explained: "The negative emotion, fear, is associated with the urge to escape. The negative emotion, anger, is associated with the urge to attack."[17] We need our negative emotions
at times. Brief moments of stress, for example, have been shown
to help focus the mind. The problem comes when we're exposed to
such feelings for a prolonged period. A quick pump of adrenaline
might help us get something urgent achieved, but stress over the
longer term is a debilitating force. Living with a sense of constant,
gnawing stress has a measurably adverse impact on our ability to
do our best work.[18]

Barbara Fredrickson's view is that positive affect not only offers immediate benefits but also builds momentum, creating what amounts to a virtuous spiral. "Individuals who achieve such upward spirals," she believes, "not only enjoy improved emotional well-being, but also build their coping arsenal for handling future adversities."[19] In other words, not only do Fredrickson and her coauthors view positive affect as the way for individuals to bounce back from setbacks and stressful experiences,[20] they also argue that it creates a "broaden-and-build" frame of mind whereby a moment or stretch of happiness becomes a self-perpetuating and growing force of positivity.[21] In creative terms, this can be astonishingly powerful. If you've ever patted yourself on the back during a particularly productive day at work and said "I'm on a roll," you'll know what I mean. Good ideas spawn good ideas because we're in precisely the right mental zone to create them. "Certain discrete positive emotions," Fredrickson wrote, "including joy, interest, contentment, pride, and love . . . all share the ability to broaden people's momentary thought-action repertoires. . . . Joy, for instance, broadens by creating the urge to play, push the limits, and be creative. These urges are evident not only in social and physical behavior, but also in intellectual and artistic behavior." And, of course, that mood then becomes contagious. As I argued earlier, the positive affect we project carries others forward, too. They become a part of the broaden-and-build effect.[22]

It follows, then, that if we could stimulate positive affect at work, the outcome would be both a better working environment and increased levels of inventiveness and creativity. And this is where the dozen changes I suggested in the Recharge section come in. They should help you feel better physically and improve your mental state. Taking proper breaks, not working ridiculous hours, avoiding unnecessary distractions, getting a decent night's sleep—all these things have been shown in scores of scientific papers to have a huge impact on how upbeat a view of the world we have and how enthusiastic we feel about work. And the positive affect created radiates out to the people we work with, helping them to do their best work, too. Conversely, if we don't take enough breaks, if we don't allow ourselves sufficient recovery time, our mental state suffers and we experience negative affect, damaging ourselves and others in the process.[23] The courses of action I proposed in Recharge aren't "nice to haves"; they're essential to protecting our workplace mojo and putting us in the best place to build team Buzz.

Psychological Safety

Perhaps the best way to demonstrate the other component of Buzz is to imagine another important phone call. This time, however, conceive of a rather different scenario in which you're not taking a call but wondering whether to make one. You're working a night shift at a busy city hospital, you've just noticed that the drug dosage you're supposed to be giving a patient seems unusually high, and you wonder whether to question it. The problem is that the doctor who prescribed the medicine has now gone home, and you have a strong suspicion that she won't take kindly to being disturbed with a suggestion that she might have made a mistake, particularly given that she has been critical of your work in the past. So do you go with your concern and make the call, or do you resist picking up the phone? How comfortable do you feel in taking the action that you suspect is the right one?

This has to do with what the experts term *psychological safety*.

If we're trying to achieve the workplace Buzz that will help us as individuals and as team members to enthusiastically do our best work, we need not only to be in the right mind-set ourselves but also to feel comfortable and safe among our colleagues.

This is something that Amy Edmondson, a professor at Harvard Business School, has looked at closely. Hoping to prove the simple hypothesis that cohesive teams achieve better results, she gathered performance data on different hospital teams and then sent nurse investigators to visit their units to check for prescription errors. Her hunch was that the best teams would clock up fewer mistakes.

Initially, it seemed, she couldn't have been more wrong. Far from great teams making fewer mistakes, the best ones actually made *more* errors than the worst. The first-class team at what she styled "Memorial Hospital 1" was making nearly 24 drug errors per 1,000 patient days, while the seemingly less impressive staff at "Memorial 3" was making one-tenth of those mistakes, at 2.34 errors per 1,000 patient days.

How could this possibly be? Were her data inaccurate, or was the entire premise of her experiment at fault? As she worked through the data, the answer became apparent. "In a blinding flash of the obvious," Edmondson said, "I thought, maybe the better teams aren't making more mistakes; maybe they're more willing to discuss them. What if the better teams have a climate of openness that allows them to report and even get to the bottom of these things?"[24]

Which indeed turned out to be the case. The best hospital teams were far more willing to discuss problems, and their simple statistical ranking suffered as a result. The less good teams bottled things up and therefore appeared to the outside world to be more competent. Edmondson went on to demonstrate that those hospitals that were more willing to admit and discuss errors performed far better.

At work, we're obsessed with what Edmondson calls "self-protection": worried that we're being constantly assessed by others, we carefully manage the image that we project of ourselves. The last thing any of us wants is to appear ignorant, incompetent, or excessively negative—and we take steps to protect ourselves accordingly. If we don't want to look ignorant, we simply don't ask questions or suggest ideas that might reveal our ignorance. If we don't want to look incompetent, we don't admit to weaknesses or mistakes. If we don't want to look negative, we don't criticize or question decisions made by others.

As Edmondson found, the best-performing teams do challenge all these things. They're able to do so because they have created an atmosphere in which people feel comfortable to question and to admit fallibility. In a hospital, that mind-set saves lives.

The environment where this basic truism has been very fully demonstrated is another life-or-death one—aviation. When news breaks of a terrible crash, people's first instinct is to speculate what mechanical fault might have been responsible. Did an engine fail? Was there structural damage to one of the wings? In fact, a catastrophic technical failure is almost never to blame. Most planes that crash do so because their all-too-human crews have made a mistake. Back in 1978, ten passengers died aboard United Airlines flight 173 because the captain ignored the junior pilot when he gently informed him that they had insufficient fuel to continue circling the airport ("Fifteen minutes is going to really run us low on fuel here," he timidly suggested).

In the case of the terrible disaster of Air France flight 447, which crashed on June 1, 2009, en route from Paris to Rio de Janeiro, with the loss of all 228 people aboard, an initial technical glitch turned into a full-blown emergency when a highly experienced crew made a series of wrong calls after the autopilot disconnected, causing the plane to stall and plunge into the sea.

Fortunately, these days plane crashes are rare, a fact attributable not so much to technical improvements as to an important step taken to reduce pilot error after a series of particularly appalling accidents in the 1970s. Known as CRM, or crew resource management, it's a standardized training program that sets out how crew members should raise and share concerns if something untoward appears to be occurring. "Hey, Captain, it seems we have only an hour's worth of fuel left. How about I radio and ask for an urgent landing slot. Does that sound good?" is an example of CRM at work. In those twenty-eight nonaggressive, nonpanicked words are an opening, an expression of concern, an outlining of the problem, a suggested solution, and an invitation to agreement. It's a five-point format that everyone is trained to understand. It creates a psychologically safe zone in which people can openly say what is worrying them without fear that they will be slapped down or ignored.

It should come as no surprise that the safest crews on the planet tend to be the ones who know each other best. Organizational psychologist Adam Grant pointed out that "over 75 percent of airline accidents happen the first time a crew is flying together." He also noted that, according to a NASA simulation, "if you had a crew flying together for the first time, they made more errors than a sleep-deprived crew that had just pulled an all-nighter but had flown together before."[25] Familiarity doesn't breed contempt in such environments. It builds a safe zone in which people are prepared to speak up and question each other's decisions.[26] It also helps people avoid the risks that too great a degree of deference in hierarchies can create. The writer Malcolm Gladwell, seeking to explain why Korean Air experienced more crashes than any other airline in the late 1990s, put it this way: "When we think of airline crashes, we think, 'Oh, they must have had old planes. They must have had badly trained pilots.' No. What they were struggling with was a cultural legacy, that Korean culture is hierarchical."[27]

It's perhaps no coincidence, therefore, that one of the people responsible for helping to bring greater levels of safety to the United Kingdom's National Health Service should be a man who happens to be an airline pilot. On March 29, 2009, Martin Bromiley and his two children, aged just five and six, waved goodbye to Martin's wife, Elaine, as she went into surgery to have a routine procedure performed on her sinuses. So routine, indeed, that having dropped her off, Martin zipped back home with the kids.

What happened next was that nightmare we all fear. Martin had just gotten home when he received a phone call from the consultant: "Your wife isn't waking up after surgery—you need to return to the hospital immediately." On arriving, he was informed that the medical team had struggled to keep his wife's airway open after the anesthetic was administered, and as a result her oxygen supply had fallen to critically low levels. A straightforward operation had become a medical disaster. Now Elaine was in intensive care with severe brain damage. She lingered in a medically induced coma for a few days, but before long Bromiley was being asked to support a decision to switch off her life support. Less than two weeks after her routine operation, Elaine Bromiley died.

As a pilot who knew all about the rigors of CRM and the discipline of postincident review, Martin Bromiley assumed that what would happen next would be a full investigation. But he quickly discovered that was not something hospitals carried out as a matter of routine. Thanks, however, to insistent but respectful probing on his part, the hospital agreed to ask a well-respected anesthetist to take a look at what had taken place.

The report that followed diverged completely from what Martin had been led to believe by the hospital. He had understood that his wife's death was a very unfortunate accident. In fact, the report's author said, it was due to the most simple of mistakes, a mistake that some of those present at the operation had actually spotted but had been unable to communicate to senior members of the team. A highly qualified group of experts with over sixty years of experience between them had failed to talk to each other—and the outcome was that a healthy thirty-seven-year-old woman died.

Let's take a closer look at what happened in the operating room that day. The first sign of danger came within two minutes of the start of the operation, when the anesthetic consultant observed that Elaine's airway had collapsed. There's a standard procedure for dealing with such eventualities: because oxygen deprivation can lead to irreversible brain damage within ten minutes, it's customary that if you "can't intubate, can't ventilate," you make an incision in the trachea, and, once you've performed this tracheotomy, you admit the patient to intensive care. Everyone in the operating room that day would have known this, and the moment they realized that Elaine's airways had collapsed, they should have gotten a tube down her throat within a matter of minutes or, if that procedure appeared to be problematic, carried out the emergency procedure as soon as possible. As it was, the team spent twenty-five minutes getting a tube down Elaine's throat, during which time her face became blue (a sure sign of oxygen starvation) and her heart rate fell dangerously low.

The nurses saw the warning signs—Elaine's troubled breathing, the blueness of her face, her erratic blood pressure, bodily convulsions (another indication that the body is in a state of oxygen-deprived trauma)—but still the senior surgical team was so focused on getting a tube into her trachea that they ignored the danger signals. One nurse was sufficiently concerned to get a tracheotomy set. The doctors didn't acknowledge what she'd done. According to a subsequent report in *New Statesman* magazine, "Another nurse phoned the intensive-care unit and told them to prepare a bed immediately. When she informed the doctors of her action they looked at her, she said later, as if she was overreacting."[28] The lead anesthetist later accepted that he had simply lost control of the situation.

That's true as far as it goes, but the broader problem was that there had been a catastrophic breakdown in communication. Those in senior positions, experienced as they were, ignored what others were telling them and, in the process, reduced the collective intelligence of the group. Individuals did draw attention to what was going wrong. They even suggested ways of dealing with it (for example, the nurse producing the tracheotomy equipment). But they lacked the psychological safety of being confident that they could speak up without either being ignored or slapped down.

In Martin Bromiley's view, the hospital was living in an outdated world dominated by hierarchy. The surgeons were the dominant figures—aggressive, almost always male, and unwilling to contemplate weakness or ask questions. Then came the anesthetists, accepting of their supporting role and prepared to play a subordinate role in the operating room. At the bottom of the heap were the nurses, key to the hospital's success yet all too often treated in a brusque, dismissive manner. In a world where academic excellence was used as a benchmark for human worth, the nurses lacked the particular qualifications that would have won them the esteem of their boorish peers.

Yet, as Martin Bromiley has calmly shown, unless teams are open to continual feedback, they won't perform to the sum of their talents. "To be a learning organisation, you need to be open to experiences and perspectives," he argued.[29] The reason people go along with things they know to be wrong is that they feel it necessary to conform to the social pressures a fixed hierarchy imposes. They don't want to rock the boat, and they certainly don't want to be called out in front of others. Amy Edmondson reported in her survey that a nurse told her she had been "made to feel like a two year old" when reporting a drug error. Another said, "[If you make a mistake here] doctors bite your head off."[30] People working in great teams, on the other hand, are willing to challenge each other, not in a hostile way but in the knowledge that their views will be given their proper weight.

This is where psychological safety comes in. You need to know that you are accountable for your decisions, but you also need to know that your colleagues won't bite your head off when you make your views known. Senior voices carry weight by virtue of their position at the top of the food chain. Junior voices, however, need to be heard. They may not always have the life-and-death control of nurses in a hospital, but their views and opinions are nevertheless key to an organization's ability to make great, imaginative decisions.

So psychological safety and positive affect are two vital twin pillars of a successful enterprise. When they are brought together, they create what I would call Buzz. And when you get Buzz, the result can be both magical and transformative.

	Negative or Neutral Affect	Positive Affect
High	**GRIND** A rare condition. Characterized by straight talk but lacking in warmth, it's found in workplaces that believe in the power of radical transparency but not in an accompanying warmth. Grind can also be found in situations in which safety checklists and procedures take a very high priority (e.g., aviation). Work environments that are in the Grind state are candid but clinical.	**BUZZ** A combination of honest dialogue grounded in trust and sustained motivating positivity. Buzz is found in creative environments in which candor and high output go hand in hand.
Low	**SURVIVAL** A very common workplace condition. "Keep your head down and get on with your work." Survival involves putting in the hours (or at least being seen to put in the hours) and hoping to avoid exposure to risky projects.	**ISOLATION** A workplace culture in which people feel that they will be rewarded if they achieve great things individually, but there's little sense of teamwork. Such a culture is often highly political and engenders a sense of job insecurity. Workplaces that carry out "stack ranking" of employees' performance but that also provide good benefits can find themselves creating this sense of isolation.

Psychological Safety (vertical axis label)

Bringing Together the Elements of Buzz

Positive Affect + Psychological Safety = Buzz

As should be clear by now, psychological safety and positive affect can operate independently of each other. But it's when they are simultaneously present that workplaces achieve their vibrant, energized creative potential. This is when work reaches a Buzz state.

The simple model presented on page 209 demonstrates the different ways in which psychological safety and positive affect can coexist. The grid moves vertically from high to low psychological safety and horizontally from negative to positive affect. I've opted not to differentiate between different levels of neutral or negative affect. My focus instead is on the various proven benefits of the upside.

Now let's look at these in a little more detail.

Survival
(Low Psychological Safety, Negative or Neutral Affect)

This is common in some public-sector roles and in enterprises that offer workers low-benefit "zero hours contracts." Such workplaces tend to constrain individual jobs within very tightly prescribed purviews, removing individual autonomy and with it any sense on the part of individuals that they can express themselves or make even minor decisions. If they are allowed to act autonomously, the chances are that they will be so anxious that they will indulge in what is sometimes called "defensive decision making" (it's become very prevalent in the worlds of medicine and teaching). Advertising executive Rory Sutherland explained, "A doctor knows that you can get sued for inaction much more easily than you can for action. So it leads to excessive intervention in medicine. 'I'll put this person in for this exploratory operation because there's a 1 percent chance it's something serious.' The operation itself carries a degree of risk. But let's face it, I can't get sued for it; I've handed it over to a consultant—it's someone else's problem. Whereas if I say, 'Look, to be honest, if you just go home, wrap up warm—you'll be fine in three days...' Over-prescription of antibiotics for kids I'm sure is absolutely rampant because of the same effect."[31]

Unionized workplaces also often operate in a state of Survival, though the dynamics here are a little different. Workers are safe inasmuch as they are protected from the whims of the boardroom, but they are not psychologically safe, lacking a real say in their jobs or the ability to say how things might be differently or better managed. As a result, they can often feel profoundly dissatisfied. And because job protection is a very different thing from real trust, there's often a culture of game playing and an atmosphere of mutual suspicion. This isn't to say for one moment that workers shouldn't be protected from the capricious decisions of firms, but because of the way unionized workplaces have developed over time, their workforces can often feel unmotivated.

Isolation
(Low Psychological Safety, Positive Affect)

The researcher Kurt Dirks once performed a very telling experiment with groups of students to determine to what degree trust shapes team effectiveness. In the first part of the test, students in groups of three were given individually colored blocks and asked to build as tall a tower as possible in a short period of time. Points were then awarded for both individual and collective achievement. But then Dirks staged an intervention. To create a degree of doubt in the participants' minds about the motivations of their team members, he asked each participant to adopt a particular character trait and told them that the other participants were going to be playing either trustworthy or untrustworthy characters. After that, he got the groups to replay the tower-building exercise.

What he discovered was that even when people just played at having a particular type of personality, if they believed the others to be less reliable, the tower-building dynamic changed. Where high levels of trust were noted—if the participants had been told the others would be playing reliable characters—better results were recorded in collaborative tower building. Where low levels of trust were identified, people often performed very well individually but the overall team achievement was less impressive.[32]

The state of isolation I've described is not necessarily a disastrous one, particularly for those who customarily work on their own. Journalists, doctors in private practice, and salespeople out in the field don't always need a team dynamic to perform their job well. And at times the independence that comes with isolation is clearly invaluable. Nevertheless, even here something is lost when group trust evaporates, however motivated the individuals concerned may be. If you don't work in cooperation with others, you will miss out on those occasions when a better solution to a problem or a more imaginative innovation might have come through the swapping of ideas with like-minded people. And when people in an organization work wholly independently of one another, that organization will lose out if they leave because there will have been no collective learning: the know-how gathered by individuals will go when they go.

There's another problem, too. Even if people feel content with their jobs, if there is a low level of psychological safety, they won't take the dynamic chances that lead to real advances and breakthroughs. In their desire to avoid risks, they will try to cover themselves before seeking to innovate. As Rory Sutherland put it, "I worry sometimes that quite a lot of market research is really done, not for the illumination that it brings, but essentially to defend people from personal consequences if what they're engaged in goes wrong. One of the problems about fear is it's a huge restriction on imagination because it's much, much easier to be fired for being illogical than it is for being unimaginative."[33] Sutherland says this is why individuals try to make safe, easily understood decisions rather than do anything that might appear to rock the boat: "We disguise our decisions as non-decisions," Sutherland says; "it's why huge committees exist to give people the confidence of feeling that they won't be held solely accountable for a decision. It's effectively burying accountability so that you distance yourself as far as possible from the consequences of your actions. It reaches its apotheosis in heavy bureaucracies where in—say—a very bad civil service environment it's simply a rule: 'don't mess up and you've got a job for life.'"

Grind
(High Psychological Safety, Negative or Neutral Affect)

There aren't many workplaces that fit this profile—and it's pretty clear that there's an apparent contradiction between the two parts of the equation. How can someone feel safe and protected in speaking their thoughts but not simultaneously be in a warm and motivating environment? Bridgewater Associates is a world-renowned investment banking firm created by Ray Dalio, a man who, in his book *Principles*, spent plenty of time sorting through press clippings that called him "the Steve Jobs of investing." Dalio believes that the secret of his success is using data to evaluate every single aspect of the investment process, even asking team members to give scores to meeting attendees, including himself. "Ray, you deserve a 'D–' for your performance in the meeting," is the email that Ray proudly waves as a proof that this culture is alive and well in his organization.

The fact that across his book, interviews, and TED Talk, Dalio returns to this single story is enough to start the smoke alarm. One story of him getting a low score? I can't help feeling that if you scratch beneath the surface, any potential benefits of brutal honesty are likely to be more than offset by the cutthroat atmosphere that appears to coexist with it. The high turnover of staff reported at Bridgewater Associates points to what is clear to see. Quite simply, it just doesn't seem a fun place to work. The daily grind of blunt directness does help staff in their pursuit of candid debate, but because it lacks positive affect, a lot of people end up deciding "life's too short for this"—and leave.

As a rule, neutral affect and psychological safety can coexist only when workplaces have worked very hard to achieve the latter without too much regard for building a happy environment. CRM in aviation, mandated safety procedures in mountaineering, operating guidelines in certain hospitals: these are guardrails that enlightened industries and workplaces implement to ensure that safety exists regardless of the people—and egos—involved.

Buzz
(High Psychological Safety, Positive Affect)

Teams who are in a buoyant mood and who also feel free to speak their mind are unconquerable. Ideas flow. Nothing looks as though it could stand in their way. That is the state of Buzz—a combination of psychological safety and positive affect.

Of course, it's easier said than done. Getting that balance of straight talk and enthusiasm is a tricky endeavor that requires constant effort and monitoring. Allow the two component parts to get slightly out of line and the benefits vanish swiftly. But that's not to say that it isn't a goal worth shooting for or, indeed, that it's not achievable.

In his wonderful memoir of the history of Pixar, the company's current president, Ed Catmull, described a powerful method the company discovered to deliver straight feedback to senior people (psychological safety) while sustaining the wonderful positive affect that permeated its early culture. The method took the form of a review meeting called the Braintrust. Its aim, as Catmull explained in *Creativity, Inc.*, is to "put smart, passionate people in a room together, charge them with identifying and solving problems, and encourage them to be candid." But there are very clear rules in place to ensure that the candor does not become destructive (far from it—Catmull says the results have been "phenomenal").[34] The key rule is that the authority of the project (and the project leader) must never be undermined. The whole Pixar team is invited into a rough cut movie screening (sometimes of sketches, sometimes of early edit material) and asked to identify problems and to be candid. Anyone can offer comments on the storyboard or film clip under review, but no one is allowed to make suggestions. "The Braintrust's notes . . . are intended to bring the true causes of problems to the surface—not to demand a specific remedy." It's easy, isn't it, whether in work or home life, to find ourselves going into solving mode? Telling people what they need to do. But the Braintrust avoids that. No solutions, just comments. That's how Pixar ensures that a dose of real talk doesn't end up killing the energized creative fizz of positive affect.

When Bob Iger led the Walt Disney Company's acquisition of Pixar, he brought the smaller company's leadership team over to bring the Braintrust approach to Disney (though it's styled Story Trust at Disney).[35] The process helped shape some of the movie moments you've grown to love. In Disney's case, it allowed Princess Elsa to find her happily ever after in the sorority and love of her sister rather than the annoying moonfaced woodman Kristoff—before the Trust came along, Anna and Elsa weren't even sisters.[36] The Trust method works to challenge things that don't feel right but leaves it to the team to apply their own creativity to fix them.

Creating an environment where difficult questions are encouraged doesn't have to mean that the mood created is a negative one. As Amy Edmonson says, "Psychological safety means no one will be punished or humiliated for errors, questions, or requests for help," and if that is the case, then people will take comments in the constructive spirit in which they are meant and will be inspired to do their very best work. In the Buzz sections that follow, we'll look at methods that will bring about this state of working. Edmonson suggests that the basic rule should be that everyone has to be allowed to ask questions and to express doubt: "I need to hear from you because I'm likely to miss things."

Most of us face tiny risks at work every day. Whether we're recommending *this* or selling someone *that*, we're putting our reputations on the line—if only to a very small extent. The fear that we may have it wrong shapes the way we approach our job. If we're particularly paranoid, we live in constant fear of being fired (or perhaps even being prosecuted, in certain jobs). Feeling confident that we're safe will shape how good a job we do.

Someone told me recently about the relatively new senior boss of a pretty well-known tech firm who had to step in and address the troops when the company's usual manager, Jerry, happened to be away. "If things don't improve pretty quickly, Jerry needs to know I'm going to fire him," he said in answer to one question. I suspect if we sat him down and asked him to talk us through the postmatch video of that moment he'd tell us that the line was a joke, a quip. Perhaps it was. But there's all the difference in the world between message sent and message received, and in that transmission gap can live a festering quagmire of gossip, rumors, and doubt. Whether he meant it as a joke or not, that senior boss immediately signaled to the team that this particular workplace was not one where psychological safety was at home.

Some companies make this approach a conscious strategy. The "Netflix Culture Deck" became a sensation when it was first released on the web in 2009 for its stark honesty. As the document makes clear, if Netflix employees do a reasonably good job, they should be in no doubt they will be fired: "Adequate performance gets a generous severance package."[37] This is one reason why former Netflix chief talent officer Patty McCord refused to use the word "family" in reference to great teams. No matter how bad Thanksgiving dinner is, you aren't going to fire your mom; your brother can tread mud all through the house, but his name will remain in the family text group. We know work isn't family, but for psychological safety to exist we need to know people will accept us without prejudgment or rejection. Because psychological safety is such a hard-to-reach nirvana, some businesses choose not to try to achieve it at all.

It's certainly hard to reach the Buzz state, but when a firm can achieve the combination of psychological safety and positive affect, the results are breathtaking. Now it's time to look at proven ways to bring Buzz to your team.

Buzz 1

Frame Work
as a Problem
You're Solving

In just six years, between 2008 and 2014, the cell phone giant Nokia suffered one of the most spectacular reversals of fortune in corporate history. With around 40 percent global market share (more than double that of its nearest rival), the company had seemed unassailable. True, the iPhone, Android, and the BlackBerry were eating into Nokia's dominance of the luxury, basic, and business segments of the mobile phone market. But the Finnish colossus was confident that its new Symbian operating system was going to chase off the competitors snapping at its heels. Then everything went wrong.

The problem, according to Cass Business School professor André Spicer, was easy to identify: Symbian sucked—it was slow and seemed generations behind Apple's new iPhone. Nokia staff were fully aware that it sucked. The category of smartphones was exploding with innovation, and Nokia's offering wasn't competitive. However, they decided not to say anything. Spicer explained why. "They feared communicating the bad news up the hierarchy," he wrote, "because they didn't want to appear to be negative. They had got the message: if you wanted to keep your division open, it was imperative to be only upbeat and pass on positive news."[1] The result? In 2014, with Nokia's market share down by almost three-quarters, the company was barely hanging on in feature phones and had been vanquished in smartphones. That year, the once-pioneering company was sold to Microsoft as a last hope.[2]

Sometimes we find it easier to go along with things, even when we suspect they are wrong. It's all a question of how we frame the challenge that faces us.

If we approach it with the mind-set that we have to keep those at the top happy, we're framing the challenge around them, not around it. If, on the other hand, we frame the challenge as a problem that we all need to solve (and solve with a degree of open-minded humility), we're far more likely to emerge intact at the other end. "Framing," as the term suggests, entirely shapes the way we view things. Amy Edmondson has even gone so far as to suggest that it can be a lifesaver. She argued, for example, that the reason the Austrian neurologist and psychiatrist Viktor Frankl was able to endure the horrors of Auschwitz was that he framed his experience in terms of needing to capture the stories of courage he observed and then surviving so that he could share these stories with the world.[3] Laurence Gonzales, who spent years studying those who survived terrible disasters, came to the conclusion that their odds of survival were strongly determined by the way in which they had framed their predicament. According to survivors, their companions who saw their situation as unjust misfortune struggled to cope and often succumbed. Those who framed it as a problem that they needed to solve with open-minded humility were far more likely to make it through.[4]

A study Edmondson conducted of heart surgery at some of

America's biggest hospitals powerfully illustrates the point. Until comparatively recently, the standard procedure used by surgeons was both effective and pretty brutal: the patient's breastbone would be split open and the rib cage pulled apart so that the heart could easily be reached. Since 2009, however, a technique has been available that involves gaining access *between* the ribs, in what is effectively keyhole surgery.[5] The advantage of this approach is, of course, that it's far less invasive and that recovery time is therefore dramatically reduced. But it's also far more complex. The surgeon reaches the heart not directly, as before, but through arteries and veins in the groin. "The most difficult thing about [the new method]," one nurse said, "is that you can't see. If there is a bleeding artery or something unusual, I can't see it. In an open chest I can see."

The team that pioneered the new approach estimated that practiced surgeons would need to perform this new technique around eight times before they became familiar with it. As it turned out, it took most teams forty operations to master the procedure.

But what's interesting in the context of framing is that success and speed of success were very much bound up with how individual surgical teams approached the challenge. Some adopted the classic top-down method, whereby the head surgeon would take the lead and others would observe. Often the lead surgeon would refuse to wear a head camera (which would allow others to observe what he or she was doing, but obviously offered no direct benefits to the wearer of the camera) and proved reluctant to enter into a long discussion of what precisely was going on (lead surgeons tended to instruct those with queries to talk first to the junior doctors present).

Other teams, however, went for what Edmondson styled the "learning approach"—often after they had tried and failed with the top-down one. With the learning approach, the lead surgeon would choose a deputy but then delegate the selection of the rest of the team to the lead specialists in the various fields required. When it came to performing an operation using the new technique, lead surgeons would emphasize that it would be a challenge, but instead of framing this challenge purely in personal terms ("I have to master this technique") they would treat it as a team challenge, talking everyone through the intricacies of what was about to follow and making it clear that everyone had a part to play ("You guys have got to make this thing work," one surgeon was quoted as saying).

After twenty operations that employed the new surgical procedure, one of the top-down approach surgeons commented: "It doesn't seem like we're getting that much better." Sure enough, shortly afterward, the top-down hospital abandoned the innovative approach altogether. Those who had adopted the learning approach, by contrast, were enjoying marked success. After the forty-operation mark, the lead learning approach surgeon started accepting even more challenging cases. Edmondson also noted how enthusiastic and motivated these teams had become. "I can see these patients doing so well," one nurse told her. "It is such a rewarding experience. I am so grateful I was picked." In addition, they developed a real sense of team rapport. "He's very accessible," one team member said of the team's lead surgeon. "He's in his office, always just two seconds away. He can always take five minutes to explain something, and he never makes you feel stupid." "There's a free and open environment with input from everybody," a nurse said. No one behaved as though they alone had all the answers. The lead surgeon would use the head camera to help the team and invite feedback and queries from all.

The rapport that was built up in the operating room transferred itself to the wards, too. Everyone involved, in fact, developed a real sense of motivating purpose ("we're doing this for the patients"), as well as collectively learning how to solve a problem.

Obviously, most of us rarely, if ever, find ourselves in such life-and-death situations. But that framing technique Edmondson talked about has the widest possible application. Instead of framing things in narrow or personal terms, we need to zoom out. "Tell yourself that the project is different from anything you've done before and presents a challenging and exciting opportunity to try out new approaches and learn from them," Edmondson advised. In doing so, we will also quickly realize that we need a team around us. "See yourself as vitally important to a successful outcome and, at the same time, as unable to achieve this alone—without the willing participation of others."

This is where the psychological safety comes in that I discussed earlier (see p. 201). If you're going to frame challenges and problems in terms of a team, you need to ensure that everybody on that team feels able to speak up freely without fear of being ridiculed, slighted, or slapped down. Amy Edmondson suggested that there are three ways to ensure this. First, in order to "frame the work as a learning problem, not as an execution problem," we need to introduce a clear sense of uncertainty into the room. So often at work we feel we have to display conviction and certainty, and we tend to assume that the person who offers a clear, unambiguous answer is always right. If we really want to make progress, though, our starting point has to be that we don't have all the answers and that we need everybody's input.[6] Allied to this is Edmondson's second piece of advice: we must acknowledge our own fallibility. Leaders should practice telling the group, "I need to hear from you because I'm likely to miss things." It's comments like this that invite others to speak up. Third, and finally, Edmondson said we should openly demonstrate curiosity and encourage others to do so as well.[7]

As witnessed by the top-down hospital in Edmondson's work, psychological safety is immensely hard to achieve. If reaching it were about university qualifications and intellect, that accomplished team would never have failed. But achieving this state is reliant on cultivating a sense of openness and humility. Our natural instinct in work and in life is to move toward certainty; we feel secure when someone appears to have the answers. But to be in the state of psychological safety, teams need to share uncertainties and vocalize their doubts. It can feel unnatural to us; it can feel as though we're deliberately creating instability, but the consequence of it is an increase in trust.

What You Can Do Next:

» Try scrapping the team meeting agenda one week and have a discussion instead about what ultimate goal you are all trying to achieve.

» Practice saying (and encourage others to say), "I don't know."

» Don't be afraid to look at things from a different angle. "What could go wrong here?" is a valuable question to ask.

» Encourage the team to look at something completely new together and to ask a few questions about each component part of it. Emphasize that this is an exercise in discovery, not opinion: you're trying to build a list of questions that will open up a topic to exploration.

Buzz 2

Admit When You've Messed Up

I've talked extensively about how essential it is to have a positive atmosphere at work and about the ways in which this state of Buzz radiates out and inspires and motivates others. But you have to be very careful how you go about creating it. Seeking to mandate how people should feel never works; all it does is invite cynicism. You can't tell people to be happy or to embrace a sense of fun. You can, however, create an environment in which a positive mood can thrive (see Syncs 4 and 5, for example).

The same is true when it comes to building the culture of openness and honest feedback to which all companies say they aspire. There's cause to be skeptical of organizations that put openness and honesty in their statement of values but don't specifically explain how that will work in practice. But for teams wanting to achieve this honesty, there is a relatively simple way to ensure that feedback can be given without causing collateral damage.

A while back, I was fortunate enough to be able to spend time with Jonathan, a squadron leader in the UK Special Forces (something close to a British Navy SEAL). I had hoped to interview him on my podcast, but the cloak of secrecy that necessarily surrounds these elite military forces—and the fear that his identity could be revealed through vocal recognition software—unfortunately made that impossible. Members of the Special Forces not only are subjected to a rigorous process of selection (at the end of the selection regime, the failure rate is in excess of 90 percent) but also are instilled with a very powerful set of values.[1] Those values, however, Jonathan explained, tend to be defined at the team level in a squadron, not imposed from above. In that way, he said, they feel more organic and authentic.

There's a common assumption that the army is all about hierarchies and commands. In fact, its motto—"Serve to Lead"— suggests something rather more subtle, and Jonathan took pains to explain to me that the perception that "in the armed forces all we do is give orders" is wrong. "In truth," he said, "we never give orders in the military."

And perhaps nowhere is the fallacy of a simple top-down command structure more clearly shown than when it comes to giving regular feedback—or, as Jonathan termed it, the daily "hot debrief." When he was stationed at Camp Bastion in Afghanistan's Helmand Province, he told me, troops would be sent out each day from the dust cloud–shrouded camp to patrol the area and to engage, when necessary, with the enemy. Once back at camp, the assault leader would review what had happened over the previous hours, but he would then say what he personally felt he could have done better. After that, others would join in a broader discussion about operational improvements that could be made for the future. While the hot debrief wouldn't go on for hours, it would nevertheless be exhaustive and all participants would have an opportunity to share their thoughts. To wrap things up, the leader would summarize what had just been said and would outline what the squadron would do differently in the future.

It's a simple enough procedure, but it contains several elements that make it a highly effective one. In the first place, it's immediate—there's no delay between completing a day's work and reviewing it. "We often find ourselves in situations where we come out of meetings or presentations where our first action is to head to our transport home," Jonathan told me. "We exchange a few words on email. By the time we come to discuss the outcome of the meeting it lacks specificity or freshness. 'It went well' becomes the only thing of value we can assert with conviction." A hot debrief, by contrast, takes place then and there.

Second, everyone—not least the officer in command—talks about what they might have gotten wrong and what they think they could do better next time. "Taking a moment to confess where we personally have messed up is a powerful component of learning," Jonathan said, before going on to explain: "Training is everything to us. Our elite military calls this approach 'world-class basics.' We spend years on it. A one-year course at Sandhurst Military Academy isn't seen as training; it's seen as part of the selection process." He concluded, "That's why we subscribe to the Navy SEAL saying, 'Under pressure you don't rise to the occasion; you sink to your level of training.'"

The act of sharing views in a nonconfrontational way is crucial, too, because it builds trust within the group—that vital belief that team members will "do the right thing under pressure." And because people trust each other, it's therefore possible to "delegate decisions to the lowest level possible. . . . There's a trust that if a squadron is well prepared they will be in the best position of anyone to make the correct decision."

It's not just the military that has engaged with the power of hot debriefs. The best sports teams follow a similar approach, using any breaks in a game to discuss what is working, what isn't working, and how best to adapt to the situation they currently face.[2] It works in business, too. Researcher Connie Gersick found that at the midpoint of time-constrained projects, team members often exhibited a greater willingness to question their own methods and revise their plan. Her view was that just as the halfway stage in a sports game was an obvious time for strategic reappraisal—many sports have a halftime at exactly that point—so the midway point in projects at hospitals, banks, management consulting firms, and universities could be a valuable trigger for a moment of collective reflection.[3]

A hot debrief allows a team to pause and honestly evaluate what they have just experienced. In our relentlessly fast-paced world, taking a moment to say, "This is what just happened, and I'm sorry for what I did wrong" is incredibly powerful. "Sorry" is a word that, by expressing vulnerability, creates an environment in which psychological safety can take root, with all the advantages that flow from it.

What You Can Do Next:

» Talk about issues and problems right away.

» Make sure the leader begins the debrief by saying what he or she did wrong or might have done better.

» Encourage everyone to speak up.

» Never say, "Sorry, but." That's the opposite of an apology. If you're hiding an excuse behind an apology, then it's time to grow up and start being honest.

Buzz 3

Keep Teams Lean

When Yale professor Stanley Eisenstat was asked by his students how long their coursework ought to take them, he had no idea. His curiosity piqued, and eager to be in a position to offer guidance to future undergraduates, he decided to investigate and find out precisely how long existing students were taking to finish the tasks he gave them. What he discovered surprised him deeply. Some students, he established, were able to complete their assignments in one-tenth of the time that others devoted to them. This wasn't necessarily because they were more able: they were simply more efficient. What's more, he discovered, there was no ultimate correlation between time spent and grades earned.

Eisenstat's findings so intrigued software developer Jeff Sutherland that he decided to apply the same investigation to the world of work. If a fast student can complete her tasks ten times quicker than a slow one, he asked himself, how much more swiftly can an efficient team deliver a project than a run-of-the-mill one? If the answer also turned out to be ten times faster, that would mean that the fastest teams achieve in a week what a slow team labors over for two and one-half months—a worrying differential and one that, at scale, would have a material impact on the productivity of different companies. Sutherland accordingly looked at studies covering 3,800 different projects—from accounting to software development to tech jobs at firms such as IBM. And he discovered that the times-ten factor was way off. Once you allowed for the complexities of teams, discussions, presentations, status chats, email and reviews, he discovered, the time spent on a badly organized project seemed to increase exponentially. "It actually didn't take the slow team ten weeks to do what the best team could do in one week," Sutherland concluded. "Rather, it took them *2,000* weeks."

That's a line that makes you reread the last paragraph, isn't it? It can't be right. What did you miss? That 2,000-fold difference between the best and worst teams is so extreme that at first it seems hard to believe it can really be true. But then think about some of the big infrastructure projects we all read about in the papers. Why was it that X seemed to go so swiftly and finished on budget? Why, by contrast, was Z dogged from the start and cost a fortune? And why—until Jeff Sutherland and his colleagues came along— were software projects notorious for always running late, going over budget, and being of poor quality?

We've complicated work to such an extent that even simple projects ("design a logo," "draft a new brochure for customers," "build a new ordering process for the website") become complicated and constipated by excessive procrastination. We get caught up in endless reviews and discussions—or become victims of the defensive decision making mentioned by Rory Sutherland (no relation to Jeff; p. 210).[1]

It was Jeff Sutherland's shock at finding how badly so many teams performed that led him to devise a new methodology called "Scrum." The Scrum framework is a system (a little like the subsequent "Agile" approaches) that empowers small teams of developers to collaborate to achieve an agreed goal. At first, it was employed to deal with delays in complex software projects, and now it's used by some of the biggest names in web development (including Google and Facebook). But its utility extends much further: from the US military (where, among other things, it's used to get warships built) to such organizations as the BBC and British Telecom.[2] Its word-of-mouth success is due to the fact that the system's results speak for themselves. "Scrum teams that work well are able to achieve what we call 'hyperproductivity,'" Sutherland wrote. "It's hard to believe, but we regularly see somewhere between a 300- to 400-percent improvement in productivity among groups that implement Scrum well. The best teams can achieve productivity increases of up to 800 percent and replicate that success over and over again. They also end up more than doubling the *quality* of the work."

This isn't the place to go into detail about the Scrum methodology, other than to say that at its heart it involves team members regularly coming together to review any backlogs and to agree what pieces of work urgently need to be done, before then setting about the completion of their agreed set of tasks in a short period of time ("a sprint"—typically between a week and a month). But two particular features are worth calling out. The first is effectively a mirror image of the hot debrief I described in Buzz 2. A hot debrief is a kind of postmortem, conducted as soon as possible after the event or project it seeks to review. Sutherland's meeting is sort of a pre-mortem (see Buzz 9), held at the same time each day and designed to give people quick feedback on how things are going, what the focus now needs to be on, and which things require particular focus. It need last no longer than a quarter of an hour, and, like the hot debrief, it should involve a series of uncomplicated questions that will yield simple, executable answers. What did you do yesterday to help the team finish the sprint? What will you do today to help the team finish the sprint? What obstacles are getting in the team's way?

The other striking feature of Scrum is its emphasis on team size. Throwing people at a problem, while tempting, is rarely the answer. Instead, Sutherland believes, teams should be kept as tight as possible—ideally to around seven people, give or take one or two. In support of this, he cites Brooks's Law (coined by the US software engineer Fred Brooks back in 1975), which states that "adding human resources to a late software project makes it later."

Most of us have found ourselves in that classic situation where it seems easier just to do the job ourselves than to take the time to explain it to someone else. But Sutherland's argument in favor of small teams is more fundamental than that. The problem with adding a person to a team, he argues, is that it multiplies the lines of communication. There's even a formula for it. Sutherland says, "If you want to calculate the impact of group size, you take the number of people on a team, multiply by 'that number minus one,' and divide by two"—in other words, communication channels = $n(n-1)/2$. Or, put more simply:

Team Size	Communication Channels
5 people	10
6 people	15
7 people	21
8 people	28
9 people	36
10 people	45

Once team sizes are assessed in light of the number of communication channels involved, the problems inherent in a large team become immediately apparent. All too quickly a sense of overload prevails, which can lead all too easily to confusion. In Sutherland's words, "Our brains simply can't keep up with that many people at once. We don't know what everyone is doing. And we slow down as we try to figure it out." This holds true not just for groups working on a particular project but for every type of work gathering. Meetings, for example, inevitably slow down when more people than necessary are involved. It's tempting to be inclusive, but the danger is that what might otherwise have been a five-minute face-to-face chat or a ten-minute catch-up snowballs into an hour-long presentation, complete with slides and endless requests for questions when you have a whole group of people sitting there. In the course of his career, Sutherland has observed thousands of such ill-judged gatherings. By making things bigger and more formal, we've multiplied the time consumed by simple activities: "Meetings that took minutes now take hours."

For Patrick Lencioni, a world-renowned coach to some of the world's most senior business management teams, this fundamental principle extends right to the top. If large project teams are inefficient, so too are large management teams. Equally important, in Lencioni's view, their very size precludes their members from speaking truth to power. The psychological safety I talked about earlier (see p. 201) is more likely to exist in a small group where people feel that they can safely challenge the views of the leader (in this case, the CEO) if they feel it is necessary to do so. If they can't do that, Lencioni has noticed, they tend to voice their frustrations to the team that reports to them, often in the form of sarcastic asides that have a corrosive effect. They do this in part because instead of regarding themselves as a member of the management team, they view their reports as their "real team." In Lencioni's view, "When leadership team members avoid discomfort among themselves, they only transfer it in greater quantities to larger groups of people through the organization they're supposed to be servicing." He argues that while it's tempting to reward good managers by promoting them to a crowded top table, it makes far more sense to restrict leadership teams to no more than eight or nine people: "When more than eight or nine people are on a team, members tend to advocate a heck of a lot more than they inquire."[3] Clearly, Sutherland's team size law applies throughout an organization.

The Scrum approach has been validated by countless software development teams. Indeed, Sutherland says some teams have reported an eightfold increase in productivity once they eliminated the drag caused by big meetings and big teams. It's a finding that is very much aligned with Amy Edmondson's study of hospital teams that I mentioned earlier (see p. 202). The best, she found, had "quick, task-focused updates" in which problems were brought immediately to the table and promptly dealt with.[4]

So, next time you call a meeting, check whether you really need all those regular attendees to come along. When you're putting a project together, don't make the mistake of assuming that the more people you add, the more important it will seem. By keeping groups small and meetings short, you might be adding the magic touch that makes them succeed.

What You Can Do Next:

» Ask yourself whether your big meetings are too big. Might occasional brief updates to noncore people make more sense?

» Assess how much "work about work" your team does. What could you easily stop doing?

» Remember that the best teams rarely contain more than eight or nine people.

Buzz 4

Focus on the Issue, Not the People

General Electric is credited with almost single-handedly creating modern management. Along the way, back in the 1980s, Jack Welch, its legendary CEO, introduced a new and rather brutal form of staff evaluation to his company. Known as "stack ranking" or "forced ranking," it scores employees on their performance. And because Welch knew that there's a limited pool of truly great workers, a much larger one of competent employees, and a small one of people who struggle, he insisted that the scores needed to be consistent with the shape of a bell curve, his rule of thumb being that 20 percent should be judged excellent, 70 percent perfectly competent, and 10 percent below par.

Part of the rationale for the exercise was, of course, to identify future potential leaders. But it was also designed to quickly get rid of the worst performers. Indeed, Welch's view—and he was helped here by American labor laws—was that every year, that bottom 10 percent should be let go. His approach soon found favor with other organizations. It's been estimated that up to one-third of companies have introduced stack ranking at some stage in the time since Welch first championed it.

The ethos of stack ranking received a boost when Netflix's culture document was released on an unsuspecting world. Co-created by Patty McCord, it's become a viral hit—shared, like the "Gangnam Style" of SlideShare, millions of times online and becoming in the process the One Ring That Rules all other culture slide decks. Its philosophy is candidly hypercapitalistic. Employees, it states in its dour Helvetica font, should expect to work with "stunningly talented" colleagues. And that means that the less than "stunningly talented" have to go: "Unlike many companies, we practice: 'adequate performance gets a generous severance package.'" Or, as McCord explained to me, someone delivering a B-grade performance should be told that they will be leaving the company.

Netflix is a great company. But is this a great way to operate? Notions of elite assessment clearly make sense in such fields as sport. But all the evidence is that this inflexible view of the talented and the not-so-talented is self-defeating when we're talking about the world of work. Apart from the two hundred hours it's estimated that US companies spend stack ranking each employee each year,[1] leaving people feeling as though they are working in a Dunder Mifflin–based version of *The Hunger Games* is not exactly inspiring.[2] More important, as the uncertainty that goes with feeling closely scrutinized and compared with others rises, so is lost the psychological safety that is so essential to the key virtues of trust and collaboration. "If you give employees incentives to cooperate, they will share information and take time to train their colleagues instead of thinking [only about] themselves," says Peter Kuhn, an economics professor at the University of California.[3] But if you pit them against each other in a kind of Darwinian struggle for survival, that key virtue will disappear. It should therefore come as no particular surprise that workplaces that put too much emphasis on individual performance find themselves achieving worse results.

There's a delicate balance to be struck here, as I mentioned earlier. You need straight talk in an organization (as Amy Edmondson says, "Using direct, actionable language . . . contributes to an effective learning process"),[4] but if that is achieved at the expense of psychological safety, you end up in a state of Grind (see p. 213). Telling individuals in a group that they might not cut it is not great for team building. It also introduces a false element into any group discussion. Teams are there to achieve things, not to criticize each other. The tips I offered in Buzzes 1 and 2 will certainly help here. But there's also something else that is worth trying.

Bjarke Ingels is a dazzlingly talented architect, acclaimed by industry website Dezeen in 2016 as the second hottest talent in the world (the top slot was reserved in tribute for the late Zaha Hadid, who passed away that year, with obvious implications for Ingels's true standing).[5] Ingels started out with imaginative but low-cost housing projects in his native Denmark and quickly found himself being courted to build fantastical constructions around the world, including, recently, such subverted reinterpretations of New York skyscrapers as the squashed pyramid of Via 57 in midtown Manhattan and an ambitious project styled XI that is placing two twisted towers containing 236 apartments next to the city's High Line attraction.

The pressure on this young rock-star architect, working with multibillion-dollar liabilities, must be impossibly intense. But he has a very effective way of ensuring that it doesn't get to him or his team and that the inevitable disagreements that do arise when so much is at stake don't degenerate into personal ones. When he's presenting or discussing his work with others, he always makes sure that he has sketches and models at hand. That may seem a blindingly obvious approach for an architect to take. But what's interesting is his rationale. "I tend to think," he argues, "that the best way to facilitate an open collaboration between many people—and the way you avoid it becoming about my idea or your idea—is if that idea is always present in the form of a model or a sketch or drawing or statement. Then if someone is criticizing it they're not criticizing me or the person who came up with the idea. They're criticizing the idea because the idea is there, it's on the table between us."[6]

One of the challenges any architectural practice faces, Ingels told me, is that nineteen out of twenty projects that they work on never come to pass. They might fail to make it through the competitive bid process, or clients might change their mind, or planning permission may be denied. Given the odds stacked against them, it would be highly possible for risk aversion to creep into the space created by failure and rejection. But Ingels knows that he has to keep his practice's thinking fresh if his team is to work at the level of creativity that brought them success in the first place. A candid exchange of views is therefore critical. "Architects are probably privileged by the fact that the work we do is so physically present in our work environments . . . the models that you create, the pictures that you create," he told me. "In a way, the best way to open up a creative process for incorporating input from the many is to make the idea as physical and as physically present as possible. Because then the conversation becomes about it, not about what you said or what I said."

Not all discussions lend themselves as easily to the visual as the architectural ones that Ingels outlined. But it's not hard to see how scribbling down a flow diagram for a particular project or a rough sketch for a suggested new process might help. Remove the personal element and encourage people to focus on the work at hand rather than the individuals involved. Most teams find the challenge of reaching psychological safety elusive; testing new approaches like the one Ingels uses could be the method that clicks for you.

What You Can Do Next:

» Try to find ways to ensure that discussions are about issues, not people.

» It might be worth getting team members to present problems and issues in diagram form so that others focus on the message rather than the messenger.

Introduce a
Hack Week

What can we learn about creative thinking from two playful knights? I mentioned earlier (see p. 123) the idea that our satisfaction at work comes from having autonomy (the freedom to get things done and to have a personal impact), mastery (a sense that we are getting better at it), purpose (an understanding of why we are doing a job), and a voice (a say in what happens). But while most of us might seek to map out our jobs to look like this, the actual work often gets in the way. "Work is what happens while we're busy making other plans," as the wise man so nearly told us. And that's why hitting Pause on the day-to-day can be the most effective way to amp up creativity in our work.

It's become the stuff of company culture legend that from its inception, Google asserted it would be giving its engineers the scope to allocate their time on a "70-20-10" basis: 70 percent on their main job, 20 percent "working on what they think will most benefit Google," and 10 percent on anything they chose. "This empowers them to be more creative and innovative," the Google founders stated in their IPO letter. "Many of our significant advances have happened in this manner." The company cited examples such as Gmail and Google Maps as the offspring of this flexibility.[1]

It sounds great. The only problem with it is that the 70-20-10 allocation never really existed. In my four years at Google, I often asked engineers if they did 20 percent or 10 percent time. The question always elicited a laugh. "Yes of course, 20 percent time—we call it Saturday," one told me. "I've got to tell you the dirty little secret of Google's 20 percent time. It's really 120 percent time," said Marissa Mayer (employee number twenty at the company).[2] I have a strong suspicion that any new recruit who declined a meeting because they'd allocated that time slot to the 20 percent portion of their week would have been promptly upbraided. The 20 percent principle may have been widely discussed outside the company, but inside, it was laughed at. That's not to say that working on projects on a Saturday isn't a workable—possibly an essential—approach during the start-up stage of a company. It's not, however, a viable way to drive long-term performance at most companies.

Yet it would be foolish to throw the baby out with the bath-water. The problem with the 20 percent rule was not the thinking behind it but the number that got attached to that thinking. "Twenty percent time was—from its inception—almost too big a bite at the apple," writer Daniel Pink told me. "It was too much." A less ambitious percentage, on the other hand, is definitely worth considering.[3]

Pink told me about Andre Geim and Konstantin Novoselov, two professors at the University of Manchester who won the Nobel Prize in Physics in 2010 for isolating something called graphene. Graphene is a truly remarkable substance. Almost transparent, a single layer of it is so impossibly thin that we can't see it; it's the strongest material humans have ever discovered; and it conducts electricity. In the future it will be employed to filter the salt out of seawater, to help us create batteries that can be charged five times faster than the ones around today, to facilitate targeted drug delivery, and much more. And how did (the subsequently knighted) Andre Geim and Konstantin Novoselov discover how to manufacture this magical substance? By playing around with whimsical ideas in their downtime.

The two men had found that the demands of their responsibilities (writing papers, fulfilling the terms of scientific grants, teaching) threatened to take the joy out of their jobs. So they instigated an informal "Friday-night experiments" session. Every Friday for just two or three hours they would bounce thoughts and ideas back and forth, their only (informal) rules being that they wouldn't work on what they had funding for or on what they were planning to produce a paper on.

One Friday evening, they found themselves playfully and repeatedly applying sticky tape to a block of carbon graphite. Each application of tape removed a few flakes of graphite. After a while, the flakes of graphite had become a solid strip just a few atoms thick—this was graphene.[4] The two men then started to test the properties of what they had created and immediately realized that the discovery could well prove to have almost limitless applications.

The point here, as Daniel Pink says, is that these two men made an extraordinary breakthrough not by devoting vast swaths of time to it but by setting aside a block of time about as long as a movie. I'm not suggesting for a moment that we'll all win Nobel Prizes if we retire to the garden shed for an hour or two each week, but it is nevertheless remarkable what we can achieve when we set aside even a short period of time to ponder, exchange ideas, and experiment. Ten or 20 percent of the workweek devoted to such activities is, in truth, not a practical option in our busy, overcommitted lives. A few hours here and there, on the other hand, very definitely is.

And that's where the thinking behind taking a Hack Week comes in. A kind of concentrated short burst of thinking aloud, it's something that many companies have experimented with. However, it's perhaps worth sharing the Twitter experience of a Hack Week because it's so ingrained in the fabric of the company. "Twitter was born from a Hack Week," cofounder Biz Stone told me.[5] "It's very important that we do this every year because it's part of our culture; it's part of our DNA." To say that Twitter emerged from a Hack Week is no exaggeration. Back in 2006, Ev Williams, who had founded Blogger, sold it to Google. Biz Stone was one of the Blogger team members who went with Ev to set up a new start-up called Odeo, where they hired Jack Dorsey. Odeo had seen an opportunity in the first iPods to invent a podcasting platform that would do for the spoken word what Blogger had done for text.

Things were gradually progressing at Odeo until one morning Apple announced its plans to build podcast feeds into iTunes. At a stroke, the very reason for Odeo's existence had been swept away. Founders and staff alike were despondent. There seemed no reason at all to carry on with Odeo. But CEO Ev Williams refused to be defeated. He announced that a skeleton crew would keep Odeo going, and, according to Biz, he also "suggested a hackathon, mostly as a morale booster. . . . We would team up in pairs," he recalls, "and would have two weeks to build anything we wanted." No restrictions were placed on what people could do.

For their part, Biz and developer Jack Dorsey got together to work on "something simple and elegant." It emerged, as they were chatting, that both had been impressed by the status bar on AOL

Instant Messenger. How would it be, they mused, if they created a text-based service that would allow people to send short status updates so that others knew what they were up to?[6] Some pondering later and Twitter was born. It's scarcely surprising that there's an immense fondness for Hack Weeks at Twitter.

Biz explained to me that today Hack Weeks are guided by certain basic principles. First of all, to avoid the danger of people's thinking becoming too random, each week has a theme. In my time at the company there have been Hack Weeks dedicated to nonprofits (charities), location, conversation, news, sports, fixing broken functions. Once the theme has been announced, teams start self-organizing in a kind of tribal way, bringing in allies and helpers as they need them. "What they do is they say, 'This is my hack and we need iOS developers and backend engineers,'" Biz says. "And you can join a team if you didn't make your own one. There are a lot of great projects put forth and then all this week people just go to work on hacks."

Engineers, designers, and salespeople all step forward with their flights of fantasy. Ideas that they never thought might possibly become a reality. "I've had my latest hack idea since 2002," Biz told me. "And I finally realized how it could be put into Twitter—because alone I don't think it would ever get the traction or it would never work as a stand-alone app. But if it were to be built into something hundreds of millions of people use every day . . . now we're talking!"

Twitter stages a Hack Week twice a year, usually immediately after the New Year (that depressing week when people are struggling to get their mojo going anyhow) and again before staff take their summer break. When a Hack Week is in progress, all regular meetings stop and routine one-to-ones are canceled. And on

Friday, people get together to celebrate that week's ideas in a sort of raucous fiesta that acknowledges the audacity and ingenuity of our colleagues.

Given that there is *always* something urgent to do at Twitter, it's sometimes tempting to cancel a Hack Week (as, indeed, happened once a few years back). But just as we kid ourselves that if we skip our lunch break we will be more productive (see Recharge 8), so is eliminating a Hack Week a false economy. By defocusing, by switching to a different problem, by letting ourselves be distracted for a period of time that is long enough to allow our minds to wander but not so long that they will wander aimlessly, we can dream up fresh ideas and simultaneously bring a sense of renewal to our everyday jobs.

The power of Hack Weeks isn't just that they provide distraction and creativity in our repetitive jobs. The interruption from routine certainly prompts fresh thinking and renewal in our patterns of thought, but above all, as with Friday night experiments, it often acts as the moment of brilliant creation. Dozens of very visible improvements at Twitter have come about as the direct consequence of Hack Weeks: Twitter Moments, threaded conversations, better suggestions of whom to follow, smart ways to tackle abuse, and the function that lets you download your tweet archive, among them. Alongside these have been dozens of other minor tweaks that the outside world will never notice: small adjustments to the user interface of the app, better spreadsheet sales reports, and clever new macros for Microsoft Excel.

As Dan Pink has shown, setting time aside for innovation makes that innovation more likely to happen. Ten or 20 percent of each day is simply not practical, but a week every six months (equivalent to two hours a week)—or even a day or two—is eminently achievable, and the results can be extraordinary.

What You Can Do Next:

» Set up a Hack Week—or a Hack Day—for two months' time. Consider what it could look like, and then plan back from it.

» Set yourself realistic goals. Don't expect to produce something that will become the new iPhone, but treat the defocusing of attention as a way to freshen everyone's approach to their day jobs.

» Review the Hack Week or Hack Day fully afterward. What improvements could be made next time?

» Schedule another Hack Week.

Buzz 6

Ban Phones
from Meetings

In barely more than a year, Susan Fowler went from the high of joining one of the world's hottest start-ups as an engineer to the low of leaving in a state of disillusioned despondency. The problems, she reported in a blog post in February 2017, began very early on at her career at Uber. After a couple of weeks of training, she had moved to the team that specialized in her area of expertise. But she almost immediately found herself the unwilling recipient of a stream of pings from her manager via the company's Gchat instant messaging system that informed her that he was in an open relationship and "really looking for a woman to have sex with."[1]

This was bad enough. The situation was, however, compounded by what happened next. When Fowler reported this amateurishly disguised proposition to human resources, she was informed that her manager had an outstanding track record and that this was his first offense. She was then told that she could therefore either move to a team less suited to her specific skills or stay put and accept that her boss would probably give her "a poor performance review when review time came around."[2] It was an appalling choice. From a professional point of view it made no sense to move teams, and yet to stay where she was left her in an almost impossible situation. Eventually, she decided that moving was the less bad of two terrible options.

It wasn't long before she heard, in the course of a lunchtime chat, that this wasn't the first time that manager had behaved in this way. Soon after that, she heard of another boss who had behaved inappropriately but whose wronged colleague had similarly been told that it was his "first offense." Fowler herself was to experience further microaggressions in the course of the year, not least of which were managers threatening her with dismissal if she reported anything to HR. She quickly came to realize that the entire Uber culture was toxic: "There was a *Game of Thrones* political war raging within the ranks of upper management. . . . It seemed like every manager was fighting their peers and attempting to undermine their direct supervisor so that they could have their job." She recalled one meeting where "one of the directors boasted to our team that he had withheld business-critical information from one of the executives so that he could curry favor with other executives."

By the end of 2016, Fowler had had enough. She left Uber and found another job. In her spare time she wrote up her experiences in blog form, as much as an act of catharsis as in the belief that her thoughts would elicit any response (she was a junior engineer, after all). The impact of her decision to press Publish on February 19, 2017, was nevertheless seismic. Four months later, Uber's CEO resigned—in no small part because of the storm that had been precipitated by Fowler's blog. Susan Fowler ended the year sharing *Time* magazine's Person of the Year Award (recognized as part of the #MeToo movement, which gathered momentum that year). She also won the same accolade from the *Financial Times*. Meanwhile, Uber's woes continued. Prior to his resignation, CEO

Travis Kalanick had been caught on camera disparaging a driver, and Uber employees had been revealed to have built a "God mode" that allowed them to watch where celebrities such as Beyoncé were being taken in their cars.[3] For her part, Fowler reported that someone was paying a private investigator to contact her friends and family with a view to discrediting her.

It was amid this feverish atmosphere that Harvard business professor Frances Frei was invited to step into a senior executive role to rebuild the culture at Uber. Clearly, there was much to fix. But in her view, Frei's first priority was to build a bond of trust, both internally with management and externally with customers.

"It takes many good deeds to build a good reputation, and only one bad one to lose it," founding father Benjamin Franklin said. Rebuilding a reputation is correspondingly difficult to achieve. Frei's view was that it would take three things: authenticity, logical rigor, and empathy. "If you sense that I am being authentic," she argued, "you are much more likely to trust me. If you sense that I have real rigor in my logic, you are far more likely to trust me. And if you believe that my empathy is directed towards you, you are far more likely to trust me."[4]

Fine words, but what did that mean in practice? Well, interestingly, one of Frei's first steps was to discourage the use of phones and laptops during discussions. I've already talked about the dangers of sending email during meetings (see Recharge 10 and Sync 3). Quite simply, they are a terrible distraction. One recent experiment, which involved getting people either to place their phone face-down in front of them, keep it in their bag, or leave it in a different room before being asked to do a test, found that those who left their devices in another room performed substantially better. As the lead researcher explained, "Your conscious mind isn't thinking about your smartphone, but the process of requiring yourself to not think about something uses up some of your limited cognitive resources. It's a brain drain."[5] And, of course, that was when people had no intention of using their phones. The drain on "limited cognitive resources" is inevitably much more marked when we're switching between our screens and the real people in the room. (Incidentally, research elsewhere suggests that taking notes by hand during a meeting or lecture is more effective than using a laptop because we tend to think more and abbreviate with handwritten notes and think less and transcribe more using a keyboard.)[6]

I've discussed the harmful nature of distraction caused by our phones, but for Frei at Uber, there was another compelling and more immediate reason to restrict the use of devices. In Uber's toxic days, some people had taken to pinging each other during meetings with critical messages about others in the room. Electronic dissing had seeped into the culture. What she urgently needed to do, she felt, was to get the devices out of the way and encourage people to connect properly with one another. Once that happened, there would be real scope for open dialogue and an honest exchange of views and, with those, a slow rebuilding of empathy and trust. "If you do nothing else," she argues, "put away your cell phone. It is the largest distraction magnet yet to be made, and it is super difficult to create empathy and trust in its presence."[7] Aside from the sniping that Uber employees were practicing, the very presence of the distraction was reducing the quality of the human connection in the room.

Those who routinely work away from the office might feel that this advice isn't especially helpful to them—their devices are their means to connect. But it's worth taking a moment to spotlight the very particular challenge for organizations that routinely use remote workers. A United Nations report in 2017, which highlighted that 25 percent of all office workers reported experiencing stress, also pointed out that among remote workers the proportion was considerably higher: 41 percent.[8] Office-bound nine-to-fivers may falsely assume that their remote counterparts operate in a calm serenity, an environment where uninterrupted Deep Work is the order of the day, but the fact is that remote workers are more likely to feel isolated and alone. Remote workers also have a widespread tendency to worry that colleagues are talking about them negatively, according to research by business authors David Maxfield and Joseph Grenny, published in the *Harvard Business Review*.[9]

If we're face to face, we must put away our devices. If we're interacting remotely, we have to find ways to connect that optimize human interaction. The way that many organizations have tried to connect geographically disparate groups is by the use of long calls or video meetings. Anyone who has endured one of these will know that the default form of someone robotically reading PowerPoint slides can lead even the best-intentioned participant to zone out. If achieving a degree of synchronicity works for couples who have to live away from each other for extended periods of time (see p. 128), then making time for some small talk and general chat will reap dividends for teams that are operating from different bases. Injecting human Sync into professional discourse is essential.

To my mind, that makes Frances Frei's approach of seeking trusted connection all the more convincing—and relevant for remote workers. According to Maxfield and Grenny, remote workers "report that workplace politics are more pervasive and difficult, and when conflicts arise they have a harder time resolving them." Their findings demonstrate in an extreme form just how essential it is to talk to one another without distractions if we are to achieve true Sync at work.

Ben Waber, CEO of Humanyze, once told me that even when he was traveling he made a point of picking up the phone to have a five-minute conversation with all his direct reports. My old boss, Adam Bain at Twitter, used to do the same with me—calling from eight thousand miles away to ask how the day was going. It's surprising how powerful the connection with someone can be when we're simply shooting the breeze.

People often look at their phones in meetings not out of malacious intent (as per Uber) but because so many meetings are life-sappingly monotonous. Unless we can find a better way to run them (see Sync 3), attendees will be unlikely to want to agree to a phone ban. But connecting at a human level is vital if everyone is to achieve that state of psychological safety that is so essential. Whether it takes the form of an undistracted face-to-face meeting or a friendly chat on the phone, proper human contact is the only way to achieve a state of workplace Buzz.

What You Can Do Next:

» Turn meetings into genuine face-to-face interactions.

» Discourage distractions, such as phones. They interfere with our powers of concentration, and they reduce trust within teams.

» Find ways to reach out to remote workers. Everybody needs human Sync to build trust and forge a sense of belonging— especially those who are separated by distance.

Buzz 7

Champion Diversity

American "frat houses" have acquired a notorious reputation for hard drinking, heavy socializing, and a toxic attitude toward women. Whether that matches the reality or not, it's certainly the case that they tend to have strong, almost tribal senses of group identity and belonging. Their composition both is self-selecting and requires group approval. People have to believe that they will fit in and then prove that they do fit in. And because of that, their cultures tend to be very homogeneous. Like attracts like.

All of which clearly makes life more comfortable for the average resident of a frat house. It's easy to be with people who are similar to you and appear to be on the same wavelength. But does the lack of variety carry disadvantages, too? This is something that a group of researchers decided to test. They therefore set groups of frat house members a test in the form of a murder mystery puzzle. First off, each student had to spend twenty minutes alone with a dossier of evidence. Then they were joined by two other members of their fraternity group for a twenty-minute discussion. Five minutes into their chat, either another member of their fraternity group or someone previously unknown to them was brought in to help them.

The results were unequivocal. Those groups composed entirely of people from the same frat house found the experience far more enjoyable than those who had been joined by an outsider. They were also more confident and much happier about the conclusion they finally came to. There was just one snag. Whereas the groups with the interloper got the answer correct 60 percent of the time, for the homogenous groups the figure was just 29 percent—they were half as successful.[1]

And this shows one of the challenges of group diversity. It doesn't always feel easy. It seems so much more straightforward for us to have team members around who adhere to whatever it happens to be that we think constitutes the "norm." Yet this is dangerous. The fact is that it's the inclusion of a different perspective that will militate against the lazy groupthink we're so often guilty of.

It's something the psychologist Sam Sommers observed when he set out to establish what impact ethnic diversity has on jury deliberations. In one experiment he split a couple hundred participants into mock juries, each consisting of six members. Some juries were all white, and some were composed of four white and two black jurors. Each mock jury was then shown a video of the trial of a black defendant charged with a sexual assault. That even before discussion with other jurors the diverse groups were 10 percent less likely to presume the defendant's guilt than the all-white juries is perhaps not particularly surprising.[2] As Sommers explained, members of the mixed group were more alive to the dangers of possible racial bias. But what is fascinating is that the diverse juries were also more thorough. On average they spent eleven minutes longer discussing the case than the all-white groups, and along the way they made fewer errors as they sifted the evidence.

Diversity is obviously about much more than garnering different perspectives, and it takes numerous forms: social background, gender, sexual orientation, political outlook, and ethnicity among them. But purely from the narrow, practical business view of what creates the best outcomes, it is worth noting that companies whose workforce comes from a spread of backgrounds generally produce better results. A rigorous survey in 2015 by the consulting firm McKinsey found a correlation between companies in the top 25 percent of ethnic and gender diversity and above-average financial returns for their sector. The figures were even more impressive for those in the top quartile of racial and ethnic diversity (35 percent higher financial returns than the average) and the top quartile of gender diversity (15 percent higher).[3] Of course, correlation here is not the same thing as causation. It might be that the best workers just like being in diverse companies, rather than that diversity creates the best results. But the basic truth that a mix of different perspectives can set us on the way to making better decisions seems unassailable.

Achieving a balance of people from different backgrounds and with different outlooks is challenging. Humans have a tendency to be tribal, as anyone can confirm who has ever observed a group of expatriates. They may have left the country they grew up in, presumably because they were hungry for new experiences, but they still tend to spend time with others from their homeland. It's just easier to hang around with people who are the same as us. We share the same cultural reference points and often the same opinions and the same sense of humor. We don't have to make an effort.

There's nothing new about this. But there's also nothing new about accepting that we benefit from associating with people who are not like us. Back in 1848, the philosopher John Stuart Mill wrote, "It is hardly possible to overrate the value . . . of placing human beings in contact with persons dissimilar to themselves, and with modes of thought and action unlike those with which they are familiar. . . . Such communication has always been, and is peculiarly in the present age, one of the primary sources of progress."[4]

What You Can Do Next:

» Don't select team members according to how similar they are to you. That way you will end up with groupthink.

» Remember that the best businesses seek to include people from as many different backgrounds as possible. The world is not homogeneous. Companies shouldn't be, either.

Buzz 8

Replace Presenting with Reading

"We try to create teams that are no larger than can be fed by two pizzas. We call that the two-pizza team rule," says Amazon founder Jeff Bezos. And it's a wonder that anyone bothers to listen to him past that point. As we all know, the number of people that two pizzas feeds is two. As we also know, highly effective teams can contain up to eight or nine members (see Buzz 3). Had Bezos called it the eight-pizza team rule, he might have been onto something. But two pizzas, no.

There is, however, something else that Bezos does that I definitely think is worth considering: at Amazon they start every meeting in silence as each attendee reads a document that has been specially prepared for subsequent discussion. "We don't do PowerPoint presentations at Amazon," Bezos proclaimed in a letter to shareholders.[1] "Instead we write narratively structured six-page memos. It has real sentences, and verbs, and nouns—it's not just bullet points." Bezos explains that the memos often take days and weeks to produce: "They simply can't be done in a day or two."[2] They're never circulated in advance. Bezos thinks that if they were, people would simply skim them and then bluff (alternatively, they might feel too embarrassed to speak up). "We read those memos, silently, during the meeting," he says. "It's like a study hall. Everybody sits around the table, and we read silently, for usually about half an hour, however long it takes us to read the document. And then we discuss it."

At one level, this sounds horrific. Suddenly, we're back at school, sitting in the exam hall, unnerved by the alpha kid next to us who thrusts his hand up to request more paper as we nervously turn the first page. But dismissing an idea simply because it sounds as though it might be a little embarrassing to put into practice doesn't really cut it. And the fact is that there is a compelling practical case for the silent read approach. Big presentations at meetings are all about bluff and bluster, bombast and bold fonts. Agenda-driven meetings favor those who speak most confidently, not necessarily those who know most. A memo may just be facts on a page, but these come alive when, having taken time to read and study them, we can then discuss them. It's hard to look at Amazon's outstanding performance and not believe that it's the thoughtful culture symbolized and promoted by such an approach that has helped the company make so many astute decisions over the past fifteen years.

A few years back, a team from Carnegie Mellon, MIT, and Union College set about trying to establish whether a group of people in a meeting could display measurable "collective intelligence."[3] They constructed a field trial that involved splitting nearly seven hundred people into small groups and giving them a series of different puzzles to solve. Each puzzle was calibrated to measure a different aspect of thinking. Some were creative challenges ("Suggest different ways you could use this item"); some were logic problems ("Plan a shopping trip where you can only drive a certain number of miles"); some were negotiations.

Two key findings emerged. The first was that the groups that performed well on one task tended to do well on all of them—and, vice versa, bad groups tended to tank at everything. The second was that individual intelligence didn't have a direct impact on how each team performed. You could have an astonishingly brainy person on your team, but that didn't in itself guarantee overall success.

What *was* important, though, was how team members treated each other. The unsuccessful teams tended to be dominated by one or two powerful members. The successful groups were characterized by their democracy: each person spoke in roughly equal measure, or, as the researchers put it, there was an "equality in distribution of conversational turn-taking." "As long as everyone got a chance to talk," the lead researcher, Anita Williams Woolley, said, "the team did well. But if only one person or a small group spoke all the time, the collective intelligence declined. . . . Teams that have a more equal distribution of communication tend to have higher collective intelligence because you're hearing from everybody, we're getting information and input and effort from everybody if they're all contributing."

These successful teams displayed high levels of "social sensitivity"—in other words, their members were good at reading the nonverbal responses of others to what was being said, could gauge what people were thinking, and adapted their behavior accordingly. There was no danger of confident team members domineeringly talking over others, or good ideas being lost because their advocates felt too intimidated to speak up.

One way in which the social sensitivity of individuals was assessed during the experiment was via a test originally created to screen people for autism. Those on the autism spectrum usually find it difficult to read facial cues that reveal what others are feeling. The clinical psychologist Simon Baron-Cohen therefore devised the "Reading the Mind in the Eyes" test, which involves showing people three dozen photographs of people featured in magazines in the 1990s and asking them to try to assess the emotional state of each subject. It's a test you can try yourself in full online, or in part with the couple of examples I've included below. In each case, choose one word from the four next to the image that you think best describes the emotion being expressed. For the correct answers, see the endnote.[4]

Figure 1

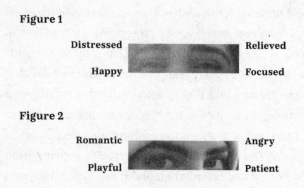

Distressed   Relieved

Happy   Focused

Figure 2

Romantic   Angry

Playful   Patient

When Williams Woolley and her colleagues got the volunteers in their experiment to try the test, they found that an ability to intuit the emotion shown in each image correlated strongly with being a good contributor to collective intelligence. "It's something that comes out of the tradition in cognitive psychology, the general ability to understand somebody else's perspective and anticipate how they're going to react to something, to understand how they're thinking or feeling based on subtle cues," she told me.[5]

It's also worth noting that the ability to intuit is stronger in women than it is in men. So, in the collective intelligence test, it was invariably the case that the groups with the highest levels of collective intelligence were the ones that included a fair proportion of women, with those in which women made up over half the total contingent scoring particularly high. When women were in the minority, they tended to be crowded out of the discussion. "It's only when women are in the majority that most of the women tend to contribute a lot more," Williams Woolley told me. "The men continue to contribute a lot even though they're no longer in the majority—so you have the highest levels of participation when you have teams that are gender diverse with a tilt toward having more women."

Interestingly, these empathetic skills worked online as well as face to face. "Online and off," Williams Woolley said, "some teams consistently worked smarter than others. More surprisingly, the most important ingredients for a smart team remained constant regardless of its mode of interaction: members who communicated a lot, participated equally and possessed good emotion-reading skills."[6] You may have noticed how some teams just seem to be more alive and interactive than others: they all jump in with ideas; they feel so comfortable with one another that they may even finish each other's sentences. In Williams Woolley's view, such groups have achieved what she calls a "burstiness" of creative contribution. All have something to contribute; all know that their contributions will be welcomed; all are in a state of positive affect (see p. 193) and feel a sense of psychological safety (see p. 201). There's a genuine feeling of Buzz.

So where does that leave us with Bezos's long silence? Well, by removing the grandstanding possibilities of the PowerPoint presentation and the conventional agenda-driven meeting, and by substituting a period of reflection and thoughtfulness, he has leveled the playing field. He has invited the sort of turn-taking that Anita Williams Woolley and her colleagues discovered to be such a powerful driver of collective intelligence. Good meetings should engage everyone, and everyone should feel prepared and confident to contribute. If those ideal conditions are there and yet some still don't contribute—well, perhaps they shouldn't be at that particular meeting.

The driving force of decision making and problem solving at meetings is engaged discussion. Those meetings that don't achieve that probably aren't worth having.

What You Can Do Next:

» Try the silent memo format of meetings. It's excruciating at first, so you will have to be prepared to stick with it for some time before you can establish whether it will work for you.

» Avoid meetings that favor the single charismatic voice.

Buzz 9

Conduct a Pre-mortem

On October 30, 1935, Boeing proudly unveiled the B-17, nicknamed the Flying Fortress, to a crowd consisting of the elite of the US military. Representing an incredible leap forward, it was faster and could fly twice as far as previous bombers and was capable of carrying five times as many bombs as the army had requested.[1] On the long-planned day of launch, the shiny new plane sailed down the runway, took off perfectly, but then, within seconds, stalled. It banked in midair, smashed into the airfield, and burst into flames. The pilot and one other person aboard died as a result of their injuries. The copilot and two other crew members had to be dragged from the burning wreckage, but fortunately they survived.

The subsequent investigation found that the plane had been in perfect working order. Human error—the pilot, Peter Hill, had forgotten to disengage the plane's gust locks—had been to blame. But his mistake, it was decided, was due to the inherent complexity of the plane's design—indeed, it was suggested that, bearing in mind the limitations of human memory, the B-17 was simply "too complex" to fly.[2] Development work nevertheless continued, and the B-17 finally went into service two years later. It proved its worth in the Second World War, and it is reckoned that, all told, B-17s clocked up 2 million miles in the air.

What ultimately ensured that the B-17 experienced no further disasters was a very simple innovation: a preflight inventory of the tasks that had to be ticked off as the crew readied themselves for departure. These days, of course, such checklists are ubiquitous. All US combat pilots carry one in their thigh pocket that specifies what they should do if things go wrong. And we're all familiar with the mantra "Cabin crews, doors to manual and cross check" aboard commercial flights. In fact, there is scarcely an area of life involving some degree of complexity that doesn't have its accompanying checklist. It makes complete sense. If our brains are overloaded with too much information, we can't process what is being asked of us. At such moments, the clarifying power of having a simple set of bullet points to refer to is immense. The congested clutter of what we previously tried to juggle in our working memories becomes a straightforward list of actions that need to be performed.

There's a further advantage to checklists. When tasks take the form of a simple list, it's far less likely that egos will get in the way. There are jobs to be done; people don't have to squabble over who decides what they are and what order they should be carried out in. The evidence suggests, too, that in spheres such as aviation and surgery, the use of checklists not only reduces the number of errors and omissions but also lessens the chances of blame being handed around when they are spotted. Members of the team do not feel that they are being judged, and the chasm between workers and managers is narrowed, thus helping to lessen one of the most common causes of dysfunction in teams.

Checklists clearly don't apply in every situation. In scenarios where a checkbox approach isn't appropriate, a simple tool that provides the same degree of efficiency and psychological safety is the pre-mortem. We're all familiar with the concept of a postmortem. Some blancmange-faced corpse has been fished out of a lake, with the telltale marks on his earlobes showing that the Earlobe Murderer has struck again; our hero goes down to the morgue to see the body rolled out on one of those strange sliding drawers by a mortuary attendant who is borderline psychopathic and delivers a couple of cutting sarcastic barbs. Work postmortems are similarly unpleasant and do much the same job: establish what happened and what went wrong (though work postmortems conducted after six months have a tendency merely to prove that hindsight is always twenty-twenty).

Pre-mortems in the business world are much more constructive. Rather than inviting us to wring our hands over something that's gone wrong, at a point when there's nothing we can do about it, they ask us to imagine how something might turn out, and then to plan for it. Members of a team might, for example, be invited to jot down a list of things that might go wrong with a project over the following year and the reasons why. As with a checklist, there's no attaching of blame here—people are simply being invited to do a bit of crystal ball gazing; they're putting themselves in a disassociated future state where they can candidly talk about their fears and thus pinpoint potential difficulties and challenges without having to worry about being blamed or considered negative. And yet, despite their apparent simplicity, premortems have been shown to be a very powerful tool. When Wharton School's Deborah Mitchell and her colleagues looked into them, they found that simply asking "What could go wrong with this plan?" resulted in a 30 percent improvement in predicting the outcomes. One Fortune 500 company correctly surmised that its billion-dollar environmental sustainability project might fail when its figurehead CEO retired. Another realized that a change to a government agency policy might well undermine the business case for a new venture.[3]

Key to the success of a pre-mortem is a culture of curiosity. Unfortunately, it's a commodity that is in short supply in the modern workplace. When Francesca Gino at the Harvard Business School conducted a survey across a wide range of sectors, she discovered that 70 percent of employees felt that they faced barriers to asking questions at work—in part, she suggested, because employers worried that if they allowed people to explore their own interests discipline would break down, and in part because they valued efficiency over exploration.[4] And yet, as Gino argued, curiosity is so important: "When our curiosity is triggered, we are less likely to fall prey to confirmation bias (looking for information that supports our beliefs rather than for evidence suggesting we are wrong)." What's more, as Spencer Harrison, now at INSEAD, discovered when he and his collaborators were studying the high staff turnover environment of call centers, curiosity quite simply helps us do our jobs better. His survey of new starters at ten different companies discovered that workers with inquiring minds elicited more useful information from their coworkers and became measurably better at dealing with customers' problems.[5] It should come as no surprise, therefore, that 92 percent of the three thousand people surveyed by Gino believed that those on their teams who were curious about things ended up contributing ideas.

It's not just that workplace curiosity is quite rare; there's also evidence to suggest that, at the individual level, it declines over time. In the course of her study, Gino looked at 250 people who had recently started a new job and found their levels of curiosity declined on average more than 20 percent in their first six months: they had simply become too busy to ask questions.[6]

So creating the culture of inquisitiveness that will, among other things, make your pre-mortems better requires a lot of work. But it's not work that is difficult or challenging. All it involves is encouraging and rewarding those who ask questions. When I worked at publishing company Emap, the unassuming CEO, Sir Robin Miller, used to go from office to office, pull up a chair at the desk of an unsuspecting worker, and simply ask what they were doing. Gino found that when she prompted workers with the eleven-word text message "What is one topic or activity you are curious about today?" for four weeks, it translated into the workers scoring higher marks for demonstrating innovative behaviors in their jobs. Another route is to adopt the learning approach I outlined earlier (see Buzz 1) in which things become a group issue that the whole group is encouraged to tackle.

If, then, you want an honest conversation with people about a project—a conversation in which they will speak up without feeling they have to worry about the consequences—a pre-mortem can be a very useful way to go. And if you can cultivate a culture that celebrates curiosity and the asking of questions, then your pre-mortems will become even more productive.

What You Can Do Next:

» Whenever you are faced with an immediate task that is complex or involves various stages, draw up a checklist. It will give you a sense of security and will also ensure that key elements don't get overlooked.

» If you're working on something that is complex or involves various stages that will be completed over weeks or months rather than days, consider conducting a pre-mortem. At the very least, it might yield a few useful ideas. At best, it provides a powerful last glance behind before you jump out of the plane.

Buzz 10

Relax

By now, I hope, you will have a clear sense of some of the ways work can be made more enjoyable and rewarding. There are twelve simple Recharges any of us can try to restore our energy, enthusiasm, and creativity. There are strategies we can adopt to help us work better as a team, enhancing our powers of collaboration and building our collective intelligence to the point where we achieve Sync. Finally, as we discover how much more we can achieve as a group than as disparate individuals, we can seek to reach that state of positive affect and psychological state where teams really start to excel. This is when they enter what I've called the Buzz state.

But there's one other piece to the Buzz jigsaw that I haven't yet talked about. In the course of explaining how we can achieve Sync, I argued that laughter has the power to connect and bond us, to forge resilience, create trust, and open up the imagination. Now I want to explore the ways in which laughter has a crucial part to play in activating the Buzz state as well.

One reason why Buzz so often seems to be beyond our grasp is that we're not good at being ourselves. As children, we may have been influenced by one of those mothers whose voice turned elegant and polished when she answered the phone. As teenagers, we self-consciously edited ourselves so as to create a better impression and help us navigate life with less fear of disapproval. And as serious adults in a serious workplace, we're desperate to make the right impression, and so, as Professor Amy Edmondson at Harvard Business School has pointed out, we moderate what we say and do to ensure that we appear to best advantage.

It's not just that we know we won't get very far if we loudly burp in briefings the way we're happy to do at home. It's that we're so aware of performance reviews and stack ranking and endless email and meetings and being judged that we adapt our behavior so as not to draw too much attention to ourselves. In the process, our personalities are sanded, the rough edges are knocked off, and, just as our mothers adopted a phone voice to avoid someone else's lazy judgment, we adopt a work persona to fit in better with what we assume our bosses and our coworkers want to have around them. At home, we're ourselves, complete with jogging pants and sloppy T-shirts. At work we're a different person.

Mark de Rond, an ethnographer who works at the Judge Business School (part of Cambridge University) has spent weeks and months embedded with teams, to the point where he just seems an ever-present face in the background and so is able to gain an extraordinarily accurate picture of the conditions that create outstanding teamwork. And his work with the winning 2007 Cambridge Boat Race team serves as a crucial reminder of the power of laughter to unlock trust.

Rowing is a sport where everything gets analyzed. The rowers' performance, for example, is measured in terms of their power, stamina, maximum strength, and how they do in head-to-head tests. But there's a psychological aspect to the sport as well. De Rond noted that prospective crew members indulged in mind games as they battled for a seat in the boat. A spirit of collaboration might be crucial for the final lineup, but as the rowers competed to be selected, de Rond noted that they behaved very much as "calculating individuals."

And at the end of it all, de Rond told me, "It's not the best six rowers that made the boat." For the 2007 crew, and against the coach's advice, the team elected to play a wild card: he "wasn't the best," according to de Rond, but he was "absolutely hilarious." And because he was funny, he helped bring connection and trust to a brutally tough environment.[1]

Whether that team member's ability to instill psychological safety and positive affect was responsible for what happened next is impossible to say, but ten days before the 2007 Cambridge Boat Race the crew felt confident enough to make a radical decision that constituted an eye-popping departure from the norms of race preparation. They had just disappointingly lost a race against Molesey Boat Club. And they promptly concluded that they needed to change things around. After a frank discussion, they therefore decided to let their cox, Russ Glenn, go and appointed a replacement—in the process, effectively overruling their coach again.[2] Less than two weeks later the replacement cox, Rebecca Dowbiggin, led Cambridge to their first win in three years.

Unpacking everything that happened here is not straightforward. But I think there can be no question that the positive affect radiated by the "hilarious" crew member helped build a strong sense of psychological safety that allowed difficult conversations to be had and radical decisions to be made. The result speaks for itself.

If the Cambridge rowing example shows a direct link between humor and positive affect and an indirect one between humor and psychological safety, an academic team from Oxford University and University College London demonstrated that that latter bond can be a direct one, too. Robin Dunbar, Brian Parkinson, and Alan Gray were interested to see whether laughter has an impact on people's willingness to collaborate. As I've said before, laughter is not something that people tend to associate with the workplace. The myth that children laugh hundreds of times a day but adults only a handful has led us to assume that grown-ups have to be more serious. It's not difficult to see why. Because you don't want to be judged or dismissed when you're at work, you don't like to let your guard down. You don't relax. And you certainly don't laugh.

The experiment that Dunbar and his team conducted involved getting people to watch comedy excerpts together in groups of four (as I pointed out in Sync 5, people are more likely to laugh when they're with others than when they're on their own). Having watched the clips (which featured Michael McIntyre), each person was asked to write a description of themselves for their watching buddies "so they can get to know you better."[3] The researchers gave each description a score, depending on how much the individual involved was prepared to reveal about themselves. High scores for real contributions were elicited by such revelations as "In January I broke my collarbone falling off a pole while pole dancing" or "I'm currently living in squalor (with mice!)."

What the researchers found was that those who had laughed together were significantly more likely to share intimate details with one another, and to be closer to their real selves, than those in a nonlaughing control group. There was a physiological reason for this. "One likely reason why the comedy condition elicited significantly more intimate disclosures than the neutral condition," the researchers argued, "is that the higher laughing rate led to an increase in endorphin activation. . . . The opioid effect of endorphins makes individuals more relaxed about what they communicate." They went on: "Endorphins may serve to facilitate interaction through reducing self-directed attention; alleviating concerns about disclosing too much information or coming across as 'weird' or unlikable, and, in turn, promoting the exchange of intimacies." Quite simply, when we laugh we're willing to show our truest selves to others and be more open to the quirkiness of others.

Why does that matter from a work point of view? Well, it would appear that teams are more likely to reach the "burstiness" of collective participation (see Buzz 8) when they feel relaxed and are able to laugh. They stop worrying that they or their ideas might be dismissed by others, that a suggestion they make will be met with the sort of chilliness one associates with a proposal to one's family that next year's Christmas could perhaps be done in a different way. In the introduction to Part 3, I looked at Amy Edmondson's study of hospital operating rooms and described how nervous some nurses were about offering suggestions to intimidating surgeons. That's the kind of shutdown you get when people lack psychological safety.

Laughter creates a safer space. It allows us to be a bit freer with our ideas. As Dunbar said, "Laughter reduces self-focus, and this in turn reduces awareness of how intimately one is disclosing." And, of course, it's when we enable unconventional thinking that our best ideas emerge, because we're not simultaneously worrying about how we come across to others. Those surgical teams in Amy Edmondson's study that offered psychological safety came up with smart suggestions. One nurse, for example, managed to solve a challenge created by the new heart surgery procedure by arguing for the use of a long-forgotten piece of equipment—a clamp nicknamed the "iron intern."[4]

Trevor Noah, the host of Comedy Central's *The Daily Show*, was once asked to explain the importance of laughter to his team's creative process. "When I'm in a writers' room," he replied, "I'm looking for what we're going to be doing on the show that day.... I believe that laughter is absorbed just like second-hand cigarette smoke into the very fabric of who we are as human beings."[5] When our teams are comfortable, when we've allowed positive affect, when we've achieved psychological safety—that's when our best ideas are revealed. It's when the boat crew can speak up, it's when the nurses can make suggestions to surgeons, it's when the members of the research study dropped their guard and shared their real lives. Laughter isn't a luxury—it's both a cause and a product of Buzz.

What You Can Do Next:

» Sometimes the secret to unlocking laughter within a group is finding the quirky soul who can catalyze it.

» Remember that laughter creates the conditions for positive affect and psychological safety that are essential to Buzz.

Epilogue

#LoveWhereYouWork

A year or so into setting up our Twitter London office, something happened that changed us all. Our team was small but rapidly expanding, working out of a rickety office on Great Titchfield Street. Software engineers, salespeople, and marketers competed for space in a working environment far removed from the glamour that people might associate with Silicon Valley start-ups. As with other teams that start as six people, then grow to twenty, then step up to forty, there was still that feeling of personal connection with everyone in the team and a sense that we were all pulling in the same direction. It was the sort of place where everyone bundles off to the local pub a couple of times a week.

The sense of energy and determination was palpable. Things were going well. We were seeing pacesetting audience growth and supercharged revenue advertising. And all this despite our chaotic surroundings. Dara Nasr—then the head of sales, now the UK managing director—chose to have the worst desk in the office—a work surface the size of a tea tray in a space that was partly dissected by a masonry pillar, a space so bad he couldn't type while sitting down. It was a symbolic choice: if he had a seat that partly cut off the circulation in his limbs, no one else could come and complain about their own lack of a window view. Nobody did. Things were rocking.

But then one day in the late summer our beloved marketing manager emailed in sick. Lucy Mosley was a bionic-strength member of our small team. She would never have claimed to have superpowers of imagination or creativity. Instead she quietly occupied the role of head of inquisitiveness, constantly picking the brains of her colleagues. "What did you think of that? What did you like about this?" Her great skill lay in having a bright-eyed interest in others' thoughts. Every day she sifted through mountains of chaff to find specks of gold. Having called in sick, on doctor's advice, Lucy had a small operation and—at the office's collective insistence—only gradually started easing herself into work after a month's rest. Then, one Friday lunchtime, Lucy discreetly closed her laptop screen and quietly left for home. Most of us never saw her again.

That Sunday morning I received a phone call. Lucy had been diagnosed with an aggressive cancer that had spread through her body. She was in the hospital, and it was more than likely that she had only a few days to live. The brutality of stage four cancer is overwhelming. Victims may be constantly reminded of how others have overcome their illness and how the great secret is to "never stop fighting." But for some, like Lucy, their very strength means that they're a long way down the road before they realize that they're sick. She had no time to fight because the disease was everywhere. That nonnegotiability added to the blunt brutality of the diagnosis.

The hospital ward Lucy was taken to had strict rules: no flowers (because of the risks of a pollen allergy) and no sugary treats (because sugar feeds the cancer). And because Lucy's fiancé very understandably wanted Lucy to be free from day-to-day stresses and excitements, he asked that people not text, tweet, or visit. In these circumstances, how do you send someone a message of love without breaking the rules?

And then, as we wrestled with the logistics of sky painting, one ingenious colleague, Lyndsay, suggested that we all knit Lucy a vast woolen blanket. It was a brilliant idea—with just one drawback. We'd all reached the state of adulthood united by our inability to knit. But we decided not to allow that small consideration to get in our way. Knitting lessons were hastily arranged for after work that Monday, and everyone committed to deliver at least twenty lines of knit stitch. In a race against time, the work began.

The click-clack of size-eleven needles became figurative healing, baby-soft wool bonded into a strong sheet. It felt as though we were crafting a spell. We dreamed that each and every stitch was helping to mend someone we loved. Remarkably, within a few days our band of unschooled amateurs had stitched together an eight-foot tapestry that might not have won any prizes but emanated affectionate care.

Bruce Daisley
@brucedaisley

Today's meetings have featured knitting. Lots of knitting.

6:36 PM · 14 Oct 2013

1 Retweet 11 Likes

Bruce Daisley
@brucedaisley

When you're reminded that you work with the best people in the world... Our week's work for someone we truly love.

6:58 PM · 18 Oct 2013

6 Retweets 66 Likes

We had the blanket urgently dry-cleaned and boxed up, along with a beautiful book of photographs and messages. Having received a call telling us that Lucy's battle was nearing its end, filled with what felt like foolish hope rather than certainty that our message would arrive in time, we couriered the blanket over to the hospice that was now her home. Morning turned to afternoon, afternoon to evening. At just after seven o'clock that night Lucy sent us a message—her first tweet in weeks:

Lucy Mosley @LucyCDMosley · 21 Oct 2013
Keeping cosy with my @TwitterUK @Twitter blanket
#LoveWhereYouWork #Family

That night, if they were anything like me, my colleagues would have let out a sob of tear-sodden joy. We might not have been able to be with Lucy, but it was a joy to know she finally felt our love, that she was enveloped in our amateurishly created quilt.

The reason why I want to share this story is that I feel that with her use of the #LoveWhereYouWork hashtag, Lucy started a movement for us. Like all companies there have definitely been moments that felt like Twitter UK is a truly joyful place to work (and plenty of moments when it hasn't), but through those times people have used Lucy's hashtag in moments of connection to share what they felt.

When people ask their friends what it's like to work at Twitter, colleagues have been known to say, "Check out the tweets using the hashtag #LoveWhereYouWork." It's become something we've had to justify, too: journalists are sometimes understandably skeptical when they hear of offices emblazoned with signs that profess collective affection. It could all so easily be construed as a corporate mind-control plan—rather than as part of an organic movement of togetherness. Those outside Twitter regularly say "What the hell is this?" and so they should: it was never intended as something to be worn like a badge.

If you click on the #LoveWhereYouWork hashtag today you will find trivial things. Perhaps someone at a Twitter office somewhere has had a cup of coffee made for them and they're joking about it. Perhaps something a little more special has happened—a team giving up their evening to help local kids, for example.

Lucy Mosley
@LucyCDMosley
Following

Keeping cosy with my @TwitterUK @Twitter blanket #LoveWhereYouWork #Family

7:01 PM - 21 Oct 2013

16 Retweets 214 Likes

60   16   214

For me it's also turned into something else. #LoveWhereYou-Work has become a standard I have to live up to. It reminds me of my duty as a boss to help create the conditions in which people can do their best jobs, leave work on Friday evening feeling proud, and be unashamed to say "I love where I work." There have been times since Lucy's tweet when it didn't feel as though my colleagues loved their jobs—their faces would be grim, and they would trudge heavily out the door at the end of the day. But if I didn't always feel a sense of achievement, I did feel a sense of aspiration.

Everyone wants to do a job that they are proud of. We all love the sense of delight that comes from laughing with colleagues. Through my podcast, with this book, with the discussions I love having with people on Twitter and on LinkedIn, I have sought to explore the secrets of improving our jobs. I've reveled in finding evidence that will silence the bullies who say lunch breaks are for wimps, or who think workplaces should be filled with fear and anxiety rather than chat and laughter. The sadness is that so much of this evidence tends to be hidden away in specialist publications and research papers. What I've set out to do here is to share it.

I hope that you will try at least some of the thirty ideas I've outlined and that you will get yourself on the way to enjoying work again. If you do, please get in touch, on Twitter (@brucedaisley or @eatsleepwkrpt) or email (brucedaisley@gmail.com).

Let me know how you started to #LoveWhereYouWork again.

Bibliography

Books

Amabile, Teresa. *The Progress Principle: Using Small Wins to Ignite Joy, Engagement, and Creativity at Work*. Harvard Business Review Press, 2011.

Archer, Laura. *Gone for Lunch: 52 Things to Do in Your Lunch Break*. Quadrille, 2017.

Cable, Daniel M. *Alive at Work: The Neuroscience of Helping Your People Love What They Do*. Harvard Business Review Press, 2018.

Cain, Susan. *Quiet: The Power of Introverts in a World That Can't Stop Talking*. Penguin, 2013.

Catmull, Ed, and Amy Wallace. *Creativity, Inc.: Overcoming the Unseen Forces That Stand in the Way of True Inspiration*. Bantam Press, 2014.

Colgan, Stevyn. *One Step Ahead: Notes from the Problem Solving Unit*. Unbound, 2018.

Currey, Mason. *Daily Rituals: How Great Minds Make Time, Find Inspiration, and Get to Work*. Picador, 2014.

Dalio, Ray. *Principles: Life and Work*. Simon & Schuster, 2017.

DeMarco, Tom, and Timothy Lister. *Peopleware: Productive Projects and Teams*, 3rd ed. Addison-Wesley, 2016.

de Rond, Mark. *Doctors at War: Life and Death in a Field Hospital*. ILR Press, 2017.

de Rond, Mark. *The Last Amateurs: To Hell and Back with the Cambridge Boat Race Crew*. Icon Books, 2009.

Dolan, Paul. *Happiness by Design: Finding Pleasure and Purpose in Everyday Life*. Penguin, 2015.

Drenth, Pieter J. D., Henk Thierry, and Charles J. de Wolff, eds. *Work Psychology*. Vol. 2 of *A Handbook of Work and Organizational Psychology*, 2nd ed. Psychology Press, 1998.

Dunbar, Robin. *Grooming, Gossip, and the Evolution of Language*. Faber & Faber, 2004.

Feldman Barrett, Lisa. *How Emotions Are Made: The Secret Life of the Brain*. Pan, 2018.

Foster, Dawn. *Lean Out*. Watkins, 2016.

Fried, Jason, and David Heinemeier Hansson. *Rework: Change the Way You Work Forever*. Vermilion, 2010.

Gawande, Atul. *The Checklist Manifesto: How to Get Things Right*. Profile, 2011.

Gawdat, Mo. *Solve for Happy: Engineer Your Path to Joy*. Bluebird, 2017.

Gonzales, Laurence. *Deep Survival: Who Lives, Who Dies, and Why*. W. W. Norton, 2017.

Grant, Adam. *Give and Take: Why Helping Others Drives Our Success*. W&N, 2014.

Grant, Adam. *Originals: How Non-conformists Change the World*. W. H. Allen, 2017.

Heath, Chip, and Dan Heath. *The Power of Moments: Why Certain Experiences Have Extraordinary Impacts*. Bantam Press, 2017.

Ingels, Bjarke. *YES Is More: An Archicomic on Architectural Evolution*. Taschen, 2009.

Ito, Joi, and Jeff Howe. *Whiplash: How to Survive Our Faster Future*. Hachette USA, 2016.

Kay, John. *Obliquity: Why Our Goals Are Best Achieved Indirectly*. Profile Books, 2011.

Layard, Richard. *Happiness: Lessons from a New Science*. Penguin, 2011.

Lencioni, Patrick. *The Advantage: Why Organizational Health Trumps Everything Else in Business*. John Wiley & Sons, 2012.

Levitin, Daniel. *The Organized Mind: Thinking Straight in the Age of Information Overload*. Penguin, 2015.

Lundin, Stephen, Harry Paul, and John Christensen. *Fish! A Remarkable Way to Boost Morale and Improve Results*. Hodder & Stoughton, 2014.

Lyons, Dan. *Disrupted: Ludicrous Misadventures in the Tech Start-up Bubble*. Atlantic Books, 2017.

McCord, Patty. *Powerful: Building a Culture of Freedom and Responsibility*. Silicon Guild, 2018.

Mill, John Stuart. *Principles of Political Economy*, reprint ed. Oxford University Press, 2008.

Moore, Bert S., and Alice M. Isen, eds. *Affect and Social Behavior*. Cambridge University Press, 1990.

Newport, Cal. *Deep Work: Rules for Focused Success in a Distracted World*. Piatkus, 2016.

Pentland, Alex. *Honest Signals: How They Shape Our World*. MIT Press, 2010.

Pentland, Alex. *Social Physics: How Social Networks Can Make Us Smarter*. Penguin Random House USA, 2015.

Pfeffer, Jeffrey. *Power: Why Some People Have It—and Others Don't*. HarperBusiness, 2010.

Pink, Daniel H. *Drive: The Surprising Truth About What Motivates Us*. Canongate Books, 2011.

Pink, Daniel H. *When: The Scientific Secrets of Perfect Timing*. Canongate Books, 2018.

Provine, Robert R. *Laughter: A Scientific Investigation*. Penguin, 2001.

Reed, Richard. *A Book About Innocent: Our Story and Some Things We've Learned*. Penguin, 2009.

Reeves, Richard. *Happy Mondays: Putting the Pleasure Back into Work*. Momentum, 2001.

Ressler, Cali, and Jody Thompson. *Why Work Sucks and How to Fix It: The Results-Only Revolution*. Portfolio, 2011.

Sandberg, Sheryl. *Lean In: Women, Work, and the Will to Lead*. W. H. Allen, 2015.

Schwartz, Tony. *The Way We're Working Isn't Working*. Simon & Schuster, 2016.

Seligman, Martin. *Learned Optimism: How to Change Your Mind and Your Life*. Nicholas Brealey, 2018.

Seppälä, Emma. *The Happiness Track: How to Apply the Science of Happiness to Accelerate Your Success*. Piatkus, 2017.

Siebert, Al. *The Survivor Personality: Why Some People Are Stronger, Smarter, and More Skillful at Handling Life's Difficulties*. TarcherPerigee, 2010.

Soojung-Kim Pang, Alex. *Rest: Why You Get More Done When You Work Less*. Basic Books, 2016.

Spicer, André. *Business Bullshit*. Routledge, 2017.

Stone, Biz. *Things a Little Bird Told Me: Confessions of the Creative Mind*. Macmillan, 2014.

Stone, Brad. *The Upstarts: Uber, Airbnb, and the Battle for the New Silicon Valley*. Corgi, 2018.

Sutherland, Jeff. *Scrum: The Art of Doing Twice the Work in Half the Time*. Random House Business, 2015.

Tokumitsu, Miya. *Do What You Love: And Other Lies About Success and Happiness*. Regan Arts, 2015.

Ton, Zeynep. *The Good Jobs Strategy: How the Smartest Companies Invest in Employees to Lower Costs and Boost Profits*. Amazon Publishing, 2014.

Voss, Chris. *Never Split the Difference: Negotiating as if Your Life Depended on It*. Random House Business, 2017.

Waber, Ben. *People Analytics: How Social Sensing Technology Will Transform Business and What It Tells Us About the Future of Work*. Financial Times/Prentice Hall, 2013.

Walker, Matthew. *Why We Sleep: The New Science of Sleep and Dreams*. Penguin, 2018.

Webb Young, James. *A Technique for Producing Ideas*, new ed. McGraw-Hill Education, 2003.

Wozniak, Steve. *iWoz: Computer Geek to Cult Icon*. Headline Review, 2007.

TED Talks and Videos

Sometimes a video can be a better conversation starter with your team than a book. Here are nine videos that can start a discussion about each of the themes shown.

How empty space is what leads to creative ideas

How Boredom Can Lead to Your Most Brilliant Ideas—Manoush Zomorodi
https://www.youtube.com/watch?v=c73Q8oQmwzo

Changing meetings

Want to Be More Creative? Go for a Walk—Marily Oppezzo
https://www.youtube.com/watch?v=j4LSwZ05laQ

Belonging and friendship at work

All You Need Is Love . . . at Work?—Sigal Barsade
https://www.youtube.com/watch?v=sKNTyGW3o7E

Reducing our dependency on our phones

Being Online All the Time—Leslie Perlow, author of *Sleeping with Your Smartphone*
https://www.youtube.com/watch?v=YVyEtSFW6UA

The power of chat in the office

Social Physics: How Good Ideas Spread—Alex "Sandy" Pentland
https://www.youtube.com/watch?v=HMBl0ttu-Ow

More about chat in the office

Using Analytics to Measure Interactions in the Workplace—Ben Waber
https://www.youtube.com/watch?v=XojhyhoRI7I&t=2s

Why you should ban phones in meetings

How to Build (and Rebuild) Trust—Frances Frei
https://www.ted.com/talks/frances_frei_how_to_build_and_rebuild_trust/

The Marshmallow Challenge (don't watch this one before you try it)

Build a Tower, Build a Team—Tom Wujec
https://www.ted.com/talks/tom_wujec_build_a_tower#t-45675

Changing the dynamics of safety in your team

Building a Psychologically Safe Workplace—Amy Edmondson
https://www.youtube.com/watch?v=LhoLuui9gX8

Notes

Author's Note

1. https://www.glassdoor.co.uk/blog/mission-culture-survey/

Introduction

1. https://www.forbes.com/sites/cherylsnappconner/2014/10/23/
the-job-stress-epidemic-is-making-us-sick/#6cab7c007e28
2. https://www.forbes.com/sites/kathryndill/2014/04/18/
survey-42-of-employees-have-changed-jobs-due-to-stress/#5e4aef273380
3. https://behavioralpolicy.org/wp-content/uploads/2017/02/BSP_vol1is1
_Goh.pdf
4. https://www.gallup.com/workplace/236495/worldwide-employee
-engagement-crisis.aspx
5. https://www.gallup.com/workplace/238085/state-american-workplace
-report-2017.aspx
6. https://www.buzzfeednews.com/article/annehelenpetersen/millennials
-burnout-generation-debt-work
7. https://twitter.com/elonmusk/status/1067173497909141504?lang=en
8. Zeynep Ton, *The Good Jobs Strategy*.
9. https://www.npr.org/sections/ed/2014/07/18/332343240/the-teacher-dropout
-crisis?utm_campaign=storyshare&utm_source=twitter.com&utm_medium=social
10. https://all4ed.org/reports-factsheets/path-to-equity/
11. https://americansongwriter.com/2006/01/the-strokes-hard-to-explain/3/
12. https://www.theguardian.com/music/2003/oct/17/popandrock.shopping4
13. http://ew.com/article/2003/10/31/room-fire/
14. These things obviously took their toll on Casablancas. He told *GQ* in 2014, "A
band is a great way to destroy a friendship, and a tour's a great way to destroy a band."
https://www.gq.com/story/the-strokes-retrospective
15. https://www.ccl.org/wp-content/uploads/2015/04/AlwaysOn.pdf
16. http://news.gallup.com/poll/168815/using-mobile-technology-work-linked
-higher-stress.aspx

17. https://www.researchgate.net/publication/6360061_The_moderating_role_of_employee_well_being_on_the_relationship_between_job_satisfaction_and_job_performance

18. http://news.gallup.com/poll/168815/using-mobile-technology-work-linked-higher-stress.aspx

19. https://medium.com/@kaifulee/10-jobs-that-are-safe-in-an-ai-world-ec4c45523f4f

20. https://www.theguardian.com/us-news/2017/jun/26/jobs-future-automation-robots-skills-creative-health

21. https://hbr.org/2018/01/the-future-of-human-work-is-imagination-creativity-and-strategy

22. https://eatsleepworkrepeat.com/are-the-robots-taking-over/

Part 1 *Recharge*

Introduction

1. https://news.efinancialcareers.com/uk-en/159654/salaries-and-bonuses-goldman-sachs-jpmorgan-citi-baml-morgan-stanley

2. http://alexandramichel.com/ASQ%2011-11.pdf

3. http://www.dailymail.co.uk/news/article-2397527/Bank-America-Merrill-Lynch-intern-Moritz-Erhardt-dead-working-long-hours.html

4. https://www.newyorker.com/magazine/2014/01/27/the-cult-of-overwork and https://news.efinancialcareers.com/uk-en/213166/what-goldman-sachs-j-p-morgan-cs-baml-and-barclays-have-done-to-cut-junior-bankers-working-hours

5. Yes, I've personally spent over a decade working for tech brands like YouTube, Twitter, and Google, but that doesn't mean I'm going to try to tell you that being on your phone *continuously* is a good thing, any more than someone who works at McDonald's would tell you to eat burgers 24/7.

6. A YouGov survey in 2015 said 51 percent of people reported feeling exhaustion or burnout in their current job. Another survey by Community Care said that 73 percent of social workers felt that way. https://www.theguardian.com/women-in-leadership/2016/jan/21/spot-the-signs-of-burnout-before-it-hits-you

7. US statistics suggest that exhaustion has increased by 32 percent in the past twenty years—to reach the current level of half the workforce. https://hbr.org/2017/06/burnout-at-work-isnt-just-about-exhaustion-its-also-about-loneliness

8. https://www.washingtonpost.com/brand-studio/wp/2018/07/19/cigna-addressing-loneliness-in-the-workplace-good-for-individuals-good-for-business/?utm_term=.99dfd3a55438

Recharge 1 Have a Monk Mode Morning

1. https://www.inc.com/business-insider/google-ceo-sundar-pichai-daily-routine.html

2. http://uk.businessinsider.com/netflix-ceo-reed-hastings-doesnt-have-an-office-2016-6?r=US&IR=T and http://uk.businessinsider.com/gap-ceo-doesnt-have-desk-office-2014-11?r=US&IR=T

3. https://www.ft.com/content/f400ae8c-9894-11e7-a652-cde3f882dd7b

4. http://fortune.com/2018/02/16/apple-headquarters-glass-employees-crash/

5. https://www.archdaily.com/884192/why-open-plan-offices-dont-work-and-some-alternatives-that-do

6. https://digest.bps.org.uk/2018/07/05/open-plan-offices-drive-down-face-to-face-interactions-and-increase-use-of-email/

7. https://www.sciencedirect.com/science/article/pii/S0003687016302514

8. https://www.bizjournals.com/sanjose/news/2017/08/08/apple-park-employees-floor-plan-hq-spaceship-aapl.html

9. https://daringfireball.net/thetalkshow/2017/08/06/ep-197

10. https://www.ncbi.nlm.nih.gov/pubmed/?term=21528171

11. https://www.telegraph.co.uk/science/2017/10/01/open-plan-offices-dont-work-will-replaced-coffice-says-bt-futurologist/

12. https://hbr.org/2014/07/the-cost-of-continuously-checking-email

13. From *Quality Software Management* by Gerald Weinberg, cited in Jeff Sutherland, *Scrum*.

14. https://ideas.repec.org/a/eee/jobhdp/v109y2009i2p168-181.html

15. http://edition.cnn.com/2005/WORLD/europe/04/22/text.iq/ and http://www.ics.uci.edu/~gmark/CHI2005.pdf

16. https://hbr.org/2011/05/the-power-of-small-wins

17. https://www.wired.com/1996/09/czik/

18. https://hbr.org/2002/08/creativity-under-the-gun

19. From Sutherland's conversation with the author. https://eatsleepworkrepeat.com/rory-sutherland-on-work-culture/

Recharge 2 Go for a Walking Meeting

1. Cited in Alex Soojung-Kim Pang, *Rest*, p. 95.

2. https://www.ted.com/talks/marily_oppezzo_want_to_be_more_creative_go_for_a_walk

3. https://www.apa.org/pubs/journals/releases/xlm-a0036577.pdf

4. https://web.stanford.edu/group/mood/cgi-bin/wordpress/wp-content/uploads/2012/08/Berman-JAD-2012.pdf

5. From a discussion on the *Eat Sleep Work Repeat* podcast. https://www.acast.com/eatsleepworkrepeat/thoughtleaders2-chrisbarezbrown?autoplay

6. https://www.nytimes.com/2011/04/13/nyregion/13mob.html?_r=1&hp

Recharge 3 Celebrate Headphones

1. Never, ever search HR forums.

2. https://hbr.org/2012/04/workers-take-off-your-headphones

3. His name is Douglas Conant, BTW. https://hbr.org/2014/03/turn-your-next-interruption-into-an-opportunity

4. From her truly wonderful groundbreaking book, *How Emotions Are Made*, p. 169.

5. https://www.npr.org/sections/krulwich/2012/03/30/149685880/neuroscientists-battle-furiously-over-jennifer-aniston

6. https://www.britannica.com/science/memory-psychology/Working-memory#ref985180

7. A brilliant exploration of the latest thinking on the neuroscience of creativity can be found here: https://www.frontiersin.org/articles/10.3389/fnhum.2013 .00330/full

8. From Sutherland's conversation with the author: https://eatsleepworkrepeat .com/rory-sutherland-on-work-culture/

9. https://www.tandfonline.com/doi/abs/10.1207/s15326934crj1004_2

10. https://hbr.org/2017/05/to-be-more-creative-schedule-your-breaks

11. https://www.researchgate.net/publication/277088848_Alternating _Incubation_Effects_in_the_Generation_of_Category_Exemplars

12. James Webb Young, *A Technique for Producing Ideas.*

13. https://www.fs.blog/2014/08/steve-jobs-on-creativity/

14. https://work.qz.com/1252156/do-open-offices-really-increase-collaboration/

15. http://journals.sagepub.com/doi/10.1177/0170840611410829

Recharge 4 Eliminate Hurry Sickness

1. The minimum time mandated by the Americans with Disabilities Act (1990) in the United States is three seconds. In the United Kingdom, the HM Government Building Regulations 2010 stipulate a legal minimum of five seconds.

2. https://www.nytimes.com/2004/02/27/nyregion/for-exercise-in-new-york -futility-push-button.html

3. https://www.radicati.com/wp/wp-content/uploads/2015/02/Email-Statistics -Report-2015-2019-Executive-Summary.pdf

4. Meeting stats: https://hbr.org/2017/07/stop-the-meeting-madness

5. Daniel Levitin, *The Organized Mind*, p. 6.

6. https://www.apa.org/images/state-nation_tcm7-225609.pdf

7. Jason Fried and David Heinemeier Hansson, *Rework*, p. 268.

8. Quoted in Manoush Zomorodi's TED Talk. https://www.ted.com/talks /manoush_zomorodi_how_boredom_can_lead_to_your_most_brilliant_ideas

9. https://www.ted.com/talks/manoush_zomorodi_how_boredom_can_lead _to_your_most_brilliant_ideas

Recharge 5 Shorten Your Workweek

1. https://en.wikipedia.org/wiki/Continuous_partial_attention

2. They were going to earn credits toward their qualification. http://assets.csom .umn.edu/assets/113144.pdf

3. https://twitter.com/DavidLawTennis/status/1011279272823189505

4. http://uk.businessinsider.com/yahoo-ceo-marissa-mayer-on-130-hour -work-weeks-2016-8

5. https://archive.nytimes.com/www.nytimes.com/learning/general/onthisday /big/0105.html#article

6. http://ftp.iza.org/dp8129.pdf

7. https://www.economist.com/blogs/freeexchange/2014/12/working-hours

8. Cited in Jeff Sutherland, *Scrum*, p. 101.

9. https://www.linkedin.com/pulse/why-best-bosses-ask-employees-work-less -scott-maxwell/

10. Jeff Sutherland, *Scrum*, p. 102.

11. Of course there's the inevitable chicken-and-egg debate here. It's interesting, though, that Pencavel's findings don't stand alone. https://www.economist.com /blogs/freeexchange/2013/09/working-hours

12. https://theenergyproject.com/

13. https://www.nytimes.com/2017/01/06/business/sweden-work-employment -productivity-happiness.html

Recharge 6 Overthrow the Evil Mill Owner Who Lives Inside You

1. http://www.businessinsider.com/best-buy-ceo-rowe-2013-3?IR=T

2. http://www.nj.com/politics/index.ssf/2016/01/christie_stupid_law_assuring _kids_recess_deserved.html

3. Thankfully, Christie's legacy has been reduced to a plane-captured photograph of him sunning himself on a New Jersey beach while the rest of the state was subject to beach closures. Modern life now requires an understanding that we're on this world only to become a meme one day. It's deeply satisfying when someone's meme so brilliantly exposes their inner hypocrisy. https://www.nytimes.com/2017/07/03 /nyregion/chris-christie-beach-new-jersey-budget.html

Recharge 7 Turn Off Your Notifications

1. Lisa Feldman Barrett is magnificent on anything to do with the brain and emotions and very clearly articulates this in *How Emotions Are Made*, p. 70.

2. https://www.sciencedirect.com/science/article/pii/002432059600118X

3. https://hbr.org/2002/08/creativity-under-the-gun

4. https://www.theguardian.com/sport/2008/feb/03/features.sportmonthly16. Note, though, that this isn't just a matter of the stress on the players; there's also significant evidence that match officials exhibit something scientists call "avoidance," in other words, trying to avert vocal criticism of themselves by giving calls against the home team.

5. http://believeperform.com/education/crowd-and-the-home-advantage/

6. https://www.nytimes.com/2017/10/25/books/jd-salinger-new-books.html

7. https://www.nytimes.com/2008/12/07/jobs/07pre.html

8. https://hbr.org/2002/08/creativity-under-the-gun

9. https://hbr.org/2002/08/creativity-under-the-gun

10. The photos of this are rather grim. Wires hanging out of rats' skulls. None of this gives me any pleasure, but let's at least bank the learning.

11. http://discovermagazine.com/2012/may/11-jaak-panksepp-rat-tickler -found-humans-7-primal-emotions

12. From the live episode of *Eat Sleep Work Repeat* recorded for Advertising Week 2018. https://eatsleepworkrepeat.com/bringing-laughter-back-to-work/

13. https://pdfs.semanticscholar.org/c140/533bfa3d841fc016e6f82ab9e5fbd 67f2d75.pdf

14. http://www.lboro.ac.uk/news-events/news/2013/june/098email-stress.html

15. http://news.gallup.com/poll/168815/using-mobile-technology-work-linked -higher-stress.aspx

16. https://www.theguardian.com/small-business-network/2014/oct/03 /have-emails-had-day-modern-office-business

17. In Android, go to Settings, Gmail (or other email app), App Notifications, Off. In iOS, go to Settings, Notifications, Mail (or other email app), Turn off all notifications.

18. https://www.academia.edu/20670805/_Silence_Your_Phones_Smartphone _Notifications_Increase_Inattention_and_Hyperactivity_Symptoms?ends_sutd _reg_path=true

19. https://pdfs.semanticscholar.org/8637/403e90d5a6451ad99b96827d00db 63ef3d88.pdf

20. http://journals.plos.org/plosone/article?id=10.1371/journal.pone.0054402

21. https://pielot.org/pubs/PielotRello2017-MHCI-DoNotDisturb.pdf

22. https://www.newscientist.com/article/2142807-one-day-without -notifications-changes-behaviour-for-two-years/

23. https://pielot.org/2017/07/productive-anxious-lonely-24-hours-without -push-notifications/

24. http://oro.open.ac.uk/47011/1/Design%20Frictions_CHI2016LBW_v18 .camera.ready.pdf

25. https://www.newscientist.com/article/2142807-one-day-without -notifications-changes-behaviour-for-two-years/

Recharge 8 Go to Lunch

1. Transcript of Laura Archer's discussion with the author on *Eat Sleep Work Repeat*. https://eatsleepworkrepeat.com/honey-i-hacked-my-job/

2. https://www.right.com/wps/wcm/connect/right-us-en/home/thoughtwire /categories/media-center/Just+OneinFive+Employees+Take+Actual+Lunch+Break

3. https://www.researchgate.net/publication/242337761_Momentary_work _recovery_The_role_of_within-day_work_breaks

4. https://www.ncbi.nlm.nih.gov/pubmed/26375961

5. Theo Meijman and Gijsbertus Mulder, "Psychological Aspects of Workload," in Pieter J. D. Drenth, Henk Thierry, and Charles J. de Wolff, eds., *Work Psychology*, p. 20.

6. Daniel Pink, *When*, p. 50.

7. https://hbr.org/2016/02/dont-make-important-decisions-late-in-the-day

8. https://www.theguardian.com/society/2018/may/23/the-friend-effect -why-the-secret-of-health-and-happiness-is-surprisingly-simple

9. https://eatsleepworkrepeat.com/work-culture-follow-the-data/

10. https://journals.aom.org/doi/abs/10.5465/amj.2011.1072?journalCode=amj

Recharge 9 Define Your Norms

1. http://www.bbc.co.uk/news/magazine-22447726

2. https://ppc.sas.upenn.edu/sites/default/files/learnedhelplessness.pdf

3. https://www.ted.com/talks/leslie_perlow_thriving_in_an_overconnected _world#t-232888

4. The original quote says "work," not "it," but WWFD?

5. https://hbr.org/2009/10/making-time-off-predictable-and-required

6. https://hbr.org/2009/10/making-time-off-predictable-and-required

Recharge 10 Have a Digital Sabbath

1. I totally stole this turn of phrase from Geoff Lloyd, but he said he in turn stole it from an old colleague. In itself it's spreading in a gently fungal way.
2. https://hbr.org/2018/01/if-you-multitask-during-meetings-your-team-will-too
3. https://eatsleepworkrepeat.com/is-deep-work-the-solution/
4. https://www.aeaweb.org/articles?id=10.1257/jep.14.4.23
5. https://hbr.org/1988/01/the-coming-of-the-new-organization

Recharge 11 Get a Good Night's Sleep

1. The most comprehensive guide to everything that sleep can do for us can be found in Matthew Walker's *Why We Sleep*.
2. https://onlinelibrary.wiley.com/doi/full/10.1002/brb3.576
3. It makes me wince to hear about these poor animals. I used to be an active member of Animal Aid and Greenpeace as a kid. But science is science. Matthew Walker, *Why We Sleep*, p. 81.
4. http://citeseerx.ist.psu.edu/viewdoc/download?doi=10.1.1.409.683&rep =rep1&type=pdf
5. http://citeseerx.ist.psu.edu/viewdoc/download?doi=10.1.1.409.683&rep =rep1&type=pdf
6. Matthew Walker, *Why We Sleep*, p. 3.
7. https://www.ncbi.nlm.nih.gov/pmc/articles/PMC4340449/

Recharge 12 Focus on One Thing at a Time

1. http://worldhappiness.report/
2. http://worldhappiness.report/
3. http://www.pnas.org/content/109/49/19953
4. https://www.aft.org//sites/default/files/periodicals/TheEarlyCatastrophe.pdf
5. https://warwick.ac.uk/fac/soc/economics/staff/dsgroi/impact/hp_briefing.pdf
6. http://www.danielgilbert.com/KILLINGSWORTH%20&%20GILBERT%20 (2010).pdf

Part 2 *Sync*

Introduction

1. https://www.historyanswers.co.uk/kings-queens/emperor-frankenstein-the -truth-behind-frederick-ii-of-sicilys-sadistic-science-experiments/
2. https://pdfs.semanticscholar.org/5744/8ececb4f70edd8b31ab1fc9625b398 afcd29.pdf
3. http://www.apa.org/news/press/releases/2017/08/lonely-die.aspx
4. This is backed up in the study of firefighters conducted by Olivia O'Neill and Nancy Rothbard. https://journals.aom.org/doi/pdf/10.5465/amj.2014.0952
5. https://www.afar.com/magazine/coolest-travel-jobs-what-its-like-to-be -a-wildland-firefighter

6. Sigal Barsade, *All You Need Is Love . . . at Work?* Freedom at Work Talk. www.youtube.com/watch?v=sKNTyGW3o7E and also https://hbr.org/2014/01/employees-who-feel-love-perform-better

7. Chris Voss, *Never Split the Difference*, p. 33.

8. https://onlinelibrary.wiley.com/doi/full/10.1111/j.1475-6811.2010.01285.x

9. https://news.gallup.com/poll/241649/employee-engagement-rise.aspx. Also, https://news.gallup.com/businessjournal/165947/solving-productivity-problem.aspx

10. https://hbr.org/2017/03/why-the-millions-we-spend-on-employee-engagement-buy-us-so-little

11. It's worth cautioning that there may be other unaccounted-for factors here: tech firms strongly index for running experience-focused environments and have (by the nature of societal change) performed very well at all growth, profit, and revenue metrics.

12. All the culture documents you could wish to read are housed here: https://tettra.co/culture-codes/culture-decks/

13. http://uk.businessinsider.com/leadership-styles-around-the-world-2013-12

14. Stephen Lundin, Harry Paul, and John Christensen, *Fish!*

15. These are largely the output of Ken Blanchard, who had a series of top-selling follow-ups to *The One Minute Manager*. Each seemed increasingly screaming in its titular tone.

16. https://www.recode.net/2018/6/30/17519694/adam-grant-psychology-management-culture-fit-kara-swisher-recode-decode-podcast

17. Robin Dunbar, *Grooming, Gossip, and the Evolution of Language*, p. 271.

18. https://www.nytimes.com/2016/02/28/magazine/the-post-cubicle-office-and-its-discontents.html

19. http://fortune.com/disrupted-excerpt-hubspot-startup-dan-lyons/

20. https://www.linkedin.com/pulse/long-slow-death-organisational-culture-dr-richard-claydon/

21. Daniel Pink, *Drive*, p. 29.

22. http://journals.sagepub.com/doi/pdf/10.1177/0146167282083027

23. https://pdfs.semanticscholar.org/abbc/acaa273b8fea38d142e795e968051fa368ea.pdf

24. More on this in Daniel Cable, *Alive at Work*.

25. https://eatsleepworkrepeat.com/dan-pink-on-the-secret-of-drive/

26. https://hbr.org/2014/11/cooks-make-tastier-food-when-they-can-see-their-customers

27. https://www.fastcompany.com/3069200/heres-what-facebook-discovered-from-its-internal-research-on-employee-happiness

28. Note that Allport achieved this learning in lab conditions, but it's also been observed in real-life cases. https://brocku.ca/MeadProject/Allport/Allport_1920a.html

29. https://www.theguardian.com/science/2009/sep/16/teams-do-better-research-proves

30. http://downloads.bbc.co.uk/6music/johnpeellecture/brian-eno-john-peel-lecture.pdf

31. https://www.ncbi.nlm.nih.gov/pmc/articles/PMC4856205/

32. https://www.tandfonline.com/doi/abs/10.1300/J002v05n02_05?journalCode
=wmfr20

33. https://www.researchgate.net/publication/19261005_Stress_Social
_Support_and_the_Buffering_Hypothesis

Sync 1 Move the Coffee Machine

1. The most effective way to understand more about how the sociometric badges work is to read Pentland's book *Social Physics*.

2. Alex Pentland, *Social Physics: How Good Ideas Spread*. https://www.youtube
.com/watch?v=HMBl0ttu-Ow

3. Alex Pentland, *Social Physics: From Ideas to Actions*. https://www.youtube.com
/watch?v=o6lyeMJPo6I

4. Alex Pentland, *Social Physics*, p. 103.

5. Alex Pentland, *Social Physics*, p. 104. See also https://hbr.org/2012/04/the
-new-science-of-building-great-teams

6. https://eatsleepworkrepeat.com/work-culture-follow-the-data/

Sync 2 Suggest a Coffee Break

1. Further details of Ben Waber's experiments can be found on my podcast discussion with him, https://eatsleepworkrepeat.com/work-culture-follow-the
-data/, or in his groundbreaking book *People Analytics*.

2. Ben Waber, *Human Capital*, p. 87.

Sync 3 Halve Your Meetings

1. http://www.businessinsider.com/david-sacks-paypal-exec-hates-meetings
-2014-3?IR=T. See also the Quora article that provoked that piece: https://www.quora
.com/PayPal-product/What-strong-beliefs-on-culture-for-entrepreneurialism
-did-Peter-Max-and-David-have-at-PayPal

2. https://www.quora.com/Why-did-David-Sacks-crack-down-on-meetings
-at-PayPal

3. https://eatsleepworkrepeat.com/rory-sutherland-on-work-culture/

4. https://www.youtube.com/watch?v=1p5sBzMtB3Q

5. https://www.ted.com/talks/tom_wujec_build_a_tower#t-45675

6. http://www.bbc.co.uk/news/world-us-canada-43821509

7. https://hbr.org/2017/07/stop-the-meeting-madness

8. https://hbr.org/2018/01/if-you-multitask-during-meetings-your-team-will-too

9. https://www.researchgate.net/publication/258187597_Meetings_Matter
_Effects_of_Team_Meetings_on_Team_and_Organizational_Success

10. Average scores (for comparison, from Tom Wujec's test): business school students, 11 inches; lawyers, 16 inches; CEOs, 22 inches; preschool children, 26 inches; architects and engineers, 39 inches (they were a late addition to the experiment; anyone familiar with aerial/antenna construction did exceptionally well).

Sync 4 **Create a Social Meeting**

1. https://eatsleepworkrepeat.com/work-culture-follow-the-data/
2. From Heffernan's interview with Shane Parrish. https://www.fs.blog/2018/03/margaret-heffernan/
3. https://eatsleepworkrepeat.com/rituals-emotions-and-food/
4. Steve Wozniak, *iWoz*.
5. https://eatsleepworkrepeat.com/rituals-emotions-and-food/
6. From Heffernan's interview with Shane Parrish. https://www.fs.blog/2018/03/margaret-heffernan/

Sync 5 **Laugh**

1. Laurence Gonzales, *Deep Survival*, chap. 1.
2. https://eatsleepworkrepeat.com/the-culture-of-teams/
3. https://eatsleepworkrepeat.com/the-culture-of-teams/
4. Al Siebert, *The Survivor Personality*.
5. Robert R. Provine, *Laughter*. I adored this book. The recounting of chimpanzee humor in animals that have been taught sign language (about the sophistication of preschool children, it turns out) is alone worth the cover price (pp. 92–97).
6. Provine, *Laughter*, p. 7.
7. Provine, *Laughter*, p. 6.
8. Professor Sophie Scott talking at a recording of *Eat Sleep Work Repeat*. https://www.acast.com/eatsleepworkrepeat/laughter-howtobringthelolsback totheoffice?autoplay
9. https://www.youtube.com/watch?v=YcSI7irpU4U
10. https://www.newyorker.com/books/page-turner/the-two-friends-who-changed-how-we-think-about-how-we-think
11. http://journals.sagepub.com/doi/abs/10.1111/j.1467-8721.2009.01638.x and https://www.ncbi.nlm.nih.gov/pubmed/18578603
12. https://link.springer.com/article/10.1007%2Fs12110-015-9225-8

Sync 6 **Energize Onboardings**

1. https://www.kronos.com/resources/new-hire-momentum-driving-onboarding-experience-research-report
2. Daniel Cable, *Alive at Work*, p. 55.
3. https://sloanreview.mit.edu/article/reinventing-employee-onboarding/
4. Daniel Cable, *Alive at Work*, p. 58.
5. Chip and Dan Heath, *The Power of Moments*, p. 20.

Sync 7 **Don't Be a Bad Boss**

1. Story related on *Vanity Fair*'s *Inside the Hive* podcast, August 11, 2017. https://art19.com/shows/inside-the-hive
2. http://usatoday30.usatoday.com/news/health/story/2012-08-05/apa-mean-bosses/56813062/1
3. http://gruberpeplab.com/teaching/psych231_fall2013/documents/231_Kahneman2004.pdf

4. https://warwick.ac.uk/fac/soc/economics/research/workingpapers/2015/twerp_1072_oswald.pdf

5. http://usatoday30.usatoday.com/news/health/story/2012-08-05/apa-mean-bosses/56813062/1

6. https://www.ncbi.nlm.nih.gov/pmc/articles/PMC2602855/

7. https://warwick.ac.uk/fac/soc/economics/research/workingpapers/2015/twerp_1072_oswald.pdf

8. https://hbr.org/2015/01/if-your-boss-thinks-youre-awesome-you-will-become-more-awesome

9. https://onlinelibrary.wiley.com/doi/abs/10.1111/j.1475-6811.2010.01285.x

10. https://academic.oup.com/jeea/article-abstract/5/6/1223/2295747

11. Richard Reeves, author of *Happy Mondays*, in conversation with the author. https://eatsleepworkrepeat.com/friends-and-flow/

12. https://eatsleepworkrepeat.com/bad-bosses/

13. https://hbr.org/ideacast/2018/04/why-technical-experts-make-great-leaders

14. From the author's discussion with Tom Leitch, August 2018.

15. https://eatsleepworkrepeat.com/bad-bosses/

16. http://eprints.whiterose.ac.uk/93685/1/WRRO_93685.pdf

Sync 8 Know When to Leave People Alone

1. https://www.nytimes.com/2012/01/15/opinion/sunday/the-rise-of-the-new-groupthink.html

2. https://www.linkedin.com/pulse/20141007161621-73685339-why-steve-jobs-obsessed-about-office-design-and-yes-bathroom-locations/?trk=tod-home-art-list-large_0&trk=tod-home-art-list-large_0&irgwc=1

3. https://www.newyorker.com/magazine/2012/01/30/groupthink

4. https://www.newyorker.com/magazine/2012/01/30/groupthink

5. http://www.musicweek.com/interviews/read/diamonds-are-forever-elton-john-bernie-taupin-on-their-50-year-songwriting-partnership/070518

6. https://www.hollywoodreporter.com/lists/inside-writers-rooms-how-14-hit-shows-get-created-1119139/item/inside-writers-room-handmaids-tale-1119116

7. https://www.hollywoodreporter.com/lists/inside-writers-rooms-how-14-hit-shows-get-created-1119139/item/inside-writers-room-will-grace-1119130

8. Tom DeMarco and Timothy Lister, *Peopleware*, p. 43.

9. https://www.gwern.net/docs/cs/2001-demarco-peopleware-whymeasure performance.pdf

10. https://dl.acm.org/citation.cfm?id=274711

11. https://eatsleepworkrepeat.com/work-culture-follow-the-data/

Part 3 *Buzz*

Introduction

1. Alice Isen and Margaret Clark, "Duration of the Effect of Good Mood on Helping: 'Footprints on the Sands of Time,'" 1976. https://clarkrelationshiplab.yale.edu/sites/default/files/Duration%20of%20the%20effect%20of%20good%20mood%20on%20helping_%20Footprints%20on%20the%20sands%20of%20time.pdf

2. https://www.psychologie.uni-heidelberg.de/ae/allg/mitarb/ms/Isen_2001.pdf

3. https://www.ncbi.nlm.nih.gov/pmc/articles/PMC3122271/

4. https://www.ncbi.nlm.nih.gov/pmc/articles/PMC3122271/

5. https://www.psychologie.uni-heidelberg.de/ae/allg/mitarb/ms/Isen_2001.pdf

6. https://onlinelibrary.wiley.com/doi/abs/10.1111/j.1559-1816.2002.tb00216.x

7. http://psycnet.apa.org/record/1980-22992-001

8. The answer, if you've been scratching your head, is "bath."

9. https://www.psychologie.uni-heidelberg.de/ae/allg/mitarb/ms/Isen_2001.pdf

10. Concept of the photo re-created using images from Unsplash; house photo by Luke Stackpoole; man photo by Tanja Heffner.

11. http://www.pnas.org/content/103/5/1599

12. https://greatergood.berkeley.edu/article/item/are_you_getting_enough_positivity_in_your_diet and http://www.jneurosci.org/content/32/33/11201

13. https://www.psychologie.uni-heidelberg.de/ae/allg/mitarb/ms/Isen_2001.pdf

14. http://www.acrwebsite.org/search/view-conference-proceedings.aspx?Id=6302

15. https://www.independent.co.uk/life-style/72-of-people-get-their-best-ideas-in-the-shower-heres-why-a6814776.html

16. https://www.youtube.com/watch?v=EOF-AB5c-ko and http://www.hollywood.com/general/aaron-sorkin-showers-up-to-eight-times-a-day-59438552/

17. https://www.ncbi.nlm.nih.gov/pmc/articles/PMC3132556/pdf/nihms90226.pdf and https://www.sciencedirect.com/science/article/pii/0749597889900320

18. https://www.ncbi.nlm.nih.gov/pubmed/11934003

19. https://www.ncbi.nlm.nih.gov/pmc/articles/PMC3132556/

20. https://www.ncbi.nlm.nih.gov/pmc/articles/PMC3122271/

21. https://www.ncbi.nlm.nih.gov/pmc/articles/PMC3122271/

22. http://www.scirp.org/(S(351jmbntvnsjt1aadkposzje))/reference/ReferencesPapers.aspx?ReferenceID=1389597 and http://www.psy.ohio-state.edu/petty/PDF%20Files/1995-JPSP-Wegener,Petty,Smith.pdf

23. https://www.youtube.com/watch?v=LhoLuui9gX8

24. From Adam Grant's *WorkLife* podcast, Season 1, Episode 10 (bonus discussion with Malcolm Gladwell). https://itunes.apple.com/gb/podcast/bonus-a-debate-with-malcolm-gladwell/id1346314086?i=1000411094716&mt=2

25. This is also observed in surgeons. A surgeon's results tend to be a reflection of the whole team she works with; if she goes to another hospital the results won't necessarily match and may more often reflect her familiarity with the team there. http://citeseerx.ist.psu.edu/viewdoc/download?doi=10.1.1.361.1611&rep=rep1&type=pdf

26. https://www.newstatesman.com/2014/05/how-mistakes-can-save-lives

27. http://qualitysafety.bmj.com/content/early/2015/05/13/bmjqs-2015-004129

28. http://www.hbs.edu/faculty/Publication%20Files/02-062_0b5726a8-443d-4629-9e75-736679b870fc.pdf and https://www.researchgate.net/publication/8902776_Social_Influence_Compliance_and_Conformity

29. https://eatsleepworkrepeat.com/rory-sutherland-on-work-culture/

30. https://pdfs.semanticscholar.org/1df3/b01b9a58f2d5d70b21935763e511af 28b866.pdf

31. https://eatsleepworkrepeat.com/rory-sutherland-on-work-culture/

32. https://www.fastcompany.com/3027135/inside-the-pixar-braintrust

33. https://variety.com/2016/film/features/disney-pixar-acquisition-bob-iger -john-lasseter-1201923719/

34. https://uk.ign.com/articles/2016/02/18/how-disneys-story-trust-helped -change-big-hero-6-frozen-wreck-it-ralph-and-more?page=1

35. https://www.slideshare.net/reed2001/culture-1798664/

Buzz 1 **Frame Work as a Problem You're Solving**

1. André Spicer, *Business Bullshit*, p. 138.

2. https://www.cnet.com/news/nokia-hangs-on-to-second-place-in-mobile -phone-market/

3. http://journals.sagepub.com/doi/10.2307/41166164

4. Laurence Gonzales, *Deep Survival*.

5. Minimally invasive heart surgery was first pioneered by Dr. Joseph T. McGinn Jr. in 2005, but it was five years before it started being more widely adopted. https://www.prnewswire.com/news-releases/new-study-confirms-minimally -invasive-heart-surgery-the-mcginn-technique-mics-cabg-as-a-safe-and-feasible -procedure-232558201.html

6. https://www.youtube.com/watch?v=LhoLuui9gX8

7. All of the above from https://www.hbs.edu/faculty/Publication%20Files/02 -062_0b5726a8-443d-4629-9e75-736679b870fc.pdf

Buzz 2 **Admit When You've Messed Up**

1. https://www.telegraph.co.uk/news/uknews/defence/8472610/SAS-the-chosen -few-who-are-a-force-like-no-other.html

2. http://phd.meghan-smith.com/wp-content/uploads/2015/09/katzsports.pdf

3. http://web.mit.edu/curhan/www/docs/Articles/15341_Readings/Group _Dynamics/Gersick_1988_Time_and_transition.pdf

Buzz 3 **Keep Teams Lean**

1. Story related in Jeff Sutherland, *Scrum*, p. 43.

2. Someone created a Google doc that includes many of the big firms using Scrum. https://docs.google.com/spreadsheets/d/1fm15YSM7yzHl6IKtWZOMJ5vHW96teHtC wTE_ZY7dP7w/edit#gid=5

3. Patrick Lencioni, *The Advantage*, p. 22.

4. https://www.hbs.edu/faculty/Publication%20Files/02-062_0b5726a8-443d -4629-9e75-736679b870fc.pdf

Buzz 4 **Focus on the Issue, Not the People**

1. The two hundred hours was estimated by CEB Inc., a workplace analytics firm, as an estimate of the amount of time per employee that the average US firm spends on the processes involved in stack ranking. https://www.washingtonpost.com/news

/on-leadership/wp/2015/07/21/in-big-move-accenture-will-get-rid-of-annual
-performance-reviews-and-rankings/?utm_term=.2ed33229088a

2. *Or Wernham Hogg in Ricky Gervais' original.*

3. http://www.nber.org/papers/w19277

4. http://citeseerx.ist.psu.edu/viewdoc/
download?doi=10.1.1.118.1943&rep=rep1&type=pdf

5. https://www.dezeen.com/dezeenhotlist/2016/architects-hot-list/

6. https://eatsleepworkrepeat.com/architecture-of-work/

Buzz 5 Introduce a Hack Week

1. https://abc.xyz/investor/founders-letters/2004/ipo-letter.html

2. http://uk.businessinsider.com/mayer-google-20-time-does-not-exist-2015
-1?r=US&IR=T

3. https://eatsleepworkrepeat.com/dan-pink-on-the-secret-of-drive/

4. https://www.independent.co.uk/news/science/the-graphene-story-how
-andrei-geim-and-kostya-novoselov-hit-on-a-scientific-breakthrough-that
-8539743.html

5. https://eatsleepworkrepeat.com/designing-great-culture/

6. Biz Stone, *Things a Little Bird Told Me*, chap. 4.

Buzz 6 Ban Phones from Meetings

1. https://www.nytimes.com/2017/10/21/style/susan-fowler-uber.html

2. https://www.susanjfowler.com/blog/2017/2/19/reflecting-on-one-very
-strange-year-at-uber

3. https://www.theguardian.com/technology/2016/dec/13/uber-employees
-spying-ex-partners-politicians-beyonce

4. https://www.ted.com/talks/frances_frei_how_to_build_and_rebuild
_trust?language=en

5. https://hbr.org/2018/03/having-your-smartphone-nearby-takes-a-toll
-on-your-thinking

6. http://journals.sagepub.com/doi/abs/10.1177/0956797614524581

7. https://www.ted.com/talks/frances_frei_how_to_build_and_rebuild_trust
/transcript?utm_source=tedcomshare&utm_medium=email&utm_campaign
=tedspread#t-544013

8. http://ilo.org/global/about-the-ilo/newsroom/news/WCMS_544108/lang--en
/index.htm and http://ilo.org/wcmsp5/groups/public/---dgreports/---dcomm
/---publ/documents/publication/wcms_544138.pdf

9. https://hbr.org/2017/11/a-study-of-1100-employees-found-that-remote
-workers-feel-shunned-and-left-out

Buzz 7 Champion Diversity

1. https://hbr.org/2016/09/diverse-teams-feel-less-comfortable-and
-thats-why-they-perform-better

2. https://www.apa.org/pubs/journals/releases/psp-904597.pdf

3. https://www.mckinsey.com/business-functions/organization/our-insights
/why-diversity-matters

4. J. S. Mill, *Principles of Political Economy*, first published 1848.

Buzz 8 Replace Presenting with Reading

1. https://www.sec.gov/Archives/edgar/data/1018724/000119312518121161/d456916dex991.htm

2. https://blog.aboutamazon.com/2017-letter-to-shareholders/

3. http://www.cs.cmu.edu/~ab/Salon/research/Woolley_et_al_Science_2010-2.pdf

4. Figure 1: happy (photo credit: Hian Oliveira/Unsplash). Figure 2: angry (photo credit: www.pexels.com). Anyone can take the test online; give yourself a full ten minutes to complete it. https://socialintelligence.labinthewild.org/mite/

5. https://eatsleepworkrepeat.com/the-collective-intelligence-of-teams/

6. https://www.nytimes.com/2015/01/18/opinion/sunday/why-some-teams-are-smarter-than-others.html

Buzz 9 Conduct a Pre-mortem

1. Atul Gawande, *The Checklist Manifesto*, p. 32.

2. https://hackernoon.com/happy-national-checklist-day-learn-the-history-and-importance-of-october-30-1935-17d556650b89

3. https://hbr.org/2007/09/performing-a-project-premortem

4. https://hbr.org/2018/09/curiosity

5. https://www.researchgate.net/profile/Blake_Ashforth/publication/49764184_Curiosity_Adapted_the_Cat_The_Role_of_Trait_Curiosity_in_Newcomer_Adaptation/links/53eb7e6f0cf202d087cceb59/Curiosity-Adapted-the-Cat-The-Role-of-Trait-Curiosity-in-Newcomer-Adaptation.pdf

6. https://hbr.org/2018/09/curiosity

Buzz 10 Relax

1. https://eatsleepworkrepeat.com/the-culture-of-teams/

2. https://www.telegraph.co.uk/news/uknews/1547597/Replacement-of-Cambridge-cox-creates-ripples-in-rowing-world.html

3. https://www.researchgate.net/publication/273467469_Laughter's_Influence_on_the_Intimacy_of_Self-Disclosure

4. http://www.hbs.edu/faculty/Publication%20Files/02-062_0b5726a8-443d-4629-9e75-736679b870fc.pdf

5. From Noah's interview with Adam Grant on the *WorkLife* podcast, April 2018. http://www.adamgrant.net/worklife

Index

accountability, 112
affect. *See* negative/neutral affect;
    positive affect
age factor, 145, 276
algorithmic tasks, 120–21
Alliance for Excellent Education, 4
Allport, Floyd, 126
Amabile, Teresa
    on bad management, 176
    on extrinsic motivation, 121–22
    mixed model of work, 27, 28
    pressure and achievement, 67–68,
      69, 71
    on singular task focus, 27
Amazon, 261–62
Angello, Genna, 42
anger, 199
anxiety, 11, 49, 92
Apollo 13 space mission, 67–68
apologies, 228
Apple, 24, 25, 175, 246
Archer, Laura, 75–76, 78
artificial intelligence, 10–12
ASAP, 50
attention
    continuous partial, 53
    multitasking, 25–26, 72, 147–48
    shifts in, 25–26, 41–42, 50–51,
      72, 254
    smartphone demands on, 72,
      253–54
autonomy, 123, 125, 243
avoidance, 293*n*4

Bain, Adam, 256
Bank of America, 135–36
Barez-Brown, Chris, 33
Baron-Cohen, Simon, 263–64
Barsade, Sigal, 111–12
Baumeister, Roy, 109–10
Beeman, Mark, 166
belonging, sense of. *See also* loneliness
    autonomy and, 125
    as essential human need, 108–11
    pride and, 124–25
    synchronization and, 127, 128
    at work, 111–13
Berns, Gregory, 69
Best Buy, 63
Bezos, Jeff, 261–62, 265
Bilton, Nick, 175
Blanchard, Ken, 296*n*15
Blogger, 246
body budgets, 18
Boeing, 267–68
bosses, 176, 177–78, 179, 180–83
Boston Consulting Group, 85–87
brain
    cortisol's effect on, 67
    creativity and, 70–71
    effect of sleep on, 98–99
    emotional command systems in, 70
    number of decisions per day, 54
    positive affect and, 197–99
    socializing and, 79
    System 1–System 2 model, 39–40
brainstorming, 186